To Nina and Roland —

With warm wishes and admiration —

Samuel Ford

BOUNDARIES, NOT BARRIERS

Some Uniquely Jewish Perspectives on Life

By Samuel M. Stahl

SUNBELT EAKIN ★ Austin, Texas

*To **Willard and Lois Cohodas**,*
parents of my beloved, Lynn, who have
enthusiastically supported and
encouraged me in my work
and whose lives have exemplified the
ideals expressed in these pages.

Contents

Introduction

Human beings historically have been uneasy about others who are different. People whose language, race, religion, or nationality is unlike their own are all too often viewed with suspicion. Such has been especially true of those who have encountered Jews over the centuries.

In the book of Esther, the villain Haman convinced King Ahasueres to eliminate the Jews of his kingdom by criticizing their differentness: "There is a certain people scattered and dispersed among the people in all the provinces of your kingdom; their laws are different from all other people's, and they do not keep the king's laws. Therefore it is not fitting for the king to let them remain." (Esther 3:8)

Centuries later, following the French Revolution of 1789, age-old civic restrictions against Jews were lifted. Yet the French government essentially told the Jews that, as individuals, they could have everything; as a people, nothing. Jews were expected to lose their distinctively Jewish traits and assimilate into French society.

Until the mid-1960s, American society had similar expectations of its Jewish population. The ideal was the Melting Pot. All nationality and religious communities were to abolish their specific customs and mores and adapt their lives to the White Anglo-Saxon Protestant model, which dominated American life.

Unfortunately, in response, many American Jews wanted to assimilate and shun those religious and ethnic practices that they regarded as "too Jewish." Even many Jewish religious and communal leaders encouraged American Jews to become more American. They tended to downplay the fundamental differences between Judaism and Christianity and stress the similarities.

In the last few decades, the mood of the American people has changed. The metaphor of the Symphony Orchestra has replaced that of the Melting Pot. In this model, each instrument, like the violin, the oboe, the trumpet, and the piano, retains its distinctive sounds but, when sounded together with the others, contributes to the beauty of the whole composition.

It is now fashionable to be different. American Jews have recaptured and reclaimed customs and ceremonies that they once feared would marginalize them. A growing number of them have realized that, as Jews, they can legitimately be a part of the larger community and, at the same time, retain those ideals, values, and observances that set them apart from that community.

Furthermore, differences need not be distancing. Jews can uphold their Jewish integrity, while reaching out and participating in the lives of those who are not Jewish. The boundaries between Jews and others need not be barriers.

In this volume are brief essays on a variety of subjects which are crafted from a distinctively Jewish perspective, yet hopefully contain universal messages. Martin Buber, the eminent Jewish philosopher of the 20th century, expressed my sentiments succinctly when he said: "Being Jewish is my way of being human."

Many of these essays are adapted from sermons, lectures, and articles I have previously prepared, especially since the publication of my first book, *Making the Timeless Timely*, in 1993.

I am profoundly grateful to Lynn, my beloved wife of almost four decades, for her careful reading of this manuscript and for her perceptive suggestions for its improvement. The final responsibility of errors, however, remains mine alone.

I also thank Virginia G. Messer and Melissa Roberts, of Eakin Press, for their valuable assistance in producing this book.

I am also deeply indebted to the marvelous men, women, and children of Temple Beth-El of San Antonio, Texas, where

I served as Senior Rabbi for twenty-six years. Over the years, they enthusiastically encouraged me to share the riches of Judaism with them through the written and spoken word. When I became Rabbi Emeritus in June 2002, this congregation, as a retirement gift, presented me with a substantial grant to support my future publications, for which I am infinitely grateful.

SAMUEL M. STAHL

I

Meeting Life's Challenges

Forgiving Is Not Condoning

It is possible that numerous people might have emotionally bruised us. Our business partner might have taken unfair advantage of us. Our employer might have unjustifiably fired us. Our spouse might have been unfaithful to us. Our children might have disappointed us with their life's choices. Our friends might not have been there for us in a crisis. They might have broken a trusted confidence we had shared with them or talked maliciously behind our backs.

We might have tried valiantly to overlook and forget this offense, but in our hearts, we still feel hurt and possibly anger. Some of us might even be obsessed by what happened. We might be so totally preoccupied with what the offender did to us, that the assault is now eating away at us, distracting us from important responsibilities, diminishing our energy, and possibly even causing us headaches, rashes, and a whole host of other medical maladies. In short, this attack against us has consumed us. Yet, for some reason, we do not want to let it go. We want to hold on to it. Why is that?

First of all, usually the people who offend us most cruelly are those who are close to us. As hurt and hostile as we are at them, we, nonetheless, try to hold on to them and not let them go. We fear breaking a connection with those offenders. At some unconscious level, we choose to cling to the anger or hurt, because it keeps us attached to them. We do not want to forgive them, because we sense that forgiveness may mean rejecting or permanently ending our relationship. The father of psychoanalysis, Sigmund Freud, captured the significance of this hesitation when he said: "When I have forgiven a fellow everything, I am through with him." Thus we do not want to cut ties prematurely, or disconnect too quickly, so we withhold forgiveness.

Another reason we fail to forgive is that we may want to nurse our grudges. Some of us find delight in recounting our hurts. Some of us get a perverse pleasure in being the wounded party. Often the situation can turn into a power issue. Being the victim can make us feel morally superior. It can give us an advantage over the offenders. We are right, and therefore they are wrong. In our minds, we can dominate them and they can remain beneath us!

Simon Wiesenthal, the famous Nazi hunter, illustrated this twisted logic in his autobiography. He wrote that, when he was interned in a Displaced Persons camp, following World War II, a man living near him borrowed ten dollars from him. The man claimed that he had a package that was arriving from a relative any day and he would repay Wiesenthal within a week. After a week, the man gave Wiesenthal some flimsy excuse for not repaying the loan. This went on, week after week, for a year.

Finally, at the end of the year, the man came to Wiesenthal with a ten-dollar bill in his hand and said: "My visa for Canada just went through. Here is the ten dollars that I owe you." Wiesenthal ungraciously waved him away and said: "No, keep your ten dollars. For ten dollars, it's not worth my changing my opinion of you."

I have profound respect and admiration for Wiesenthal, but, in this instance, I believe that his response was unwise. For him to rid himself of a grudge, in my judgment, could have brought him total personal relief and a restored healthy relationship.

In fact, the ancient Rabbis taught that it is wrong to harbor anger indefinitely. They explained that an offender is required to ask for forgiveness three times. If, on the third time, the victim refuses to grant forgiveness, that victim is considered cruel and the offender is freed from any further responsibility.

Furthermore, we fear that, by forgiving someone, we are

giving approval to the offensive behavior. We must assert repeatedly that forgiving does not mean condoning. It is not the same as whitewashing what had happened. Forgiving does not mean that we now declare that cheating, lying, gossiping, or whatever the offense the person committed against us was not wrong. What was unjust remains unjust. No act of forgiveness can change that fact.

Rather, forgiveness means that our negative feelings, resulting from that offense, have now been alleviated. By forgiving, we have not sanctioned the misdeed. Instead we have unloaded our hostilities. We have ridden ourselves of those corrosive elements that have brought us down. We have cleansed our souls of their spiritual bacteria.

A prominent theologian, Lewis B. Smedes, says that forgiving means looking at the offender with "magic eyes." Smedes tells a graphic fable about a self-righteous baker in a small village whose wife betrayed him. He was convinced that whatever he did was right and whatever she did was wrong. Each time he thought about his wife's indiscretion, an angel would come to him and drop a small pebble on his heart. When the pebble landed on his heart, he would feel a stab of pain. Eventually, the pebbles multiplied and his heart became laden with all that immense weight.

Soon his heart grew so heavy that the top half of his body stooped forward. He now had to strain his neck upward to see straight ahead. As his infirmities grew worse, he wished that his wife were dead. At that point the angel, seeing his mounting distress, told him that he would bring him relief from his agony.

What the baker needed, the angel said, was a pair of "magic eyes." He had to look back at the beginnings of his hurt and start to view his wife differently. He had to see her, not as a woman who had betrayed him, but as a weak and needy person who craved validation and approval. Only with this new way of viewing her would his hurt be resolved.

The baker objected. Being as sure of what is right and wrong as he was, he insisted that nothing could change the past. What his wife had done was wrong. The angel told him that he was correct. His wife did commit a grievous mistake. Nothing can change the past. His wife was guilty, a reality that even the angel could not alter.

But the angel told him that he could get rid of his bitterness, if he wanted. The angel advised him that each time that he saw his wife through new eyes, a pebble would be lifted from his heart. Initially, the baker resisted. He had grown to enjoy his distress. He loved the feeling of superiority over his wife. However, his pain grew so excruciating that he became desperate to find relief. He decided to follow the angel's advice.

From that moment on, each time he saw his wife through new eyes, she began to change mysteriously in his mind. She was no longer the untrusting, unfaithful, and undependable spouse. Rather, she was an excessively needy woman, with normal human frailties and foibles, who really loved him. The angel kept his promise. Each time the baker perceived his wife in this new way, the angel lifted the pebbles one by one. The baker's heart grew lighter. He began to walk straight. Eventually he invited his wife into his heart, and they began a new relationship of hope and joy together.

Not every saga of forgiveness ends with a clear resolution of resentment and hurt. Sometimes a new relationship is not possible to reestablish. But, when all is said and done, we do gain at least one major benefit. By granting forgiveness, we free ourselves of an enormous and weighty burden. Smedes makes the following observation:

> When you forgive someone for hurting you, you perform spiritual surgery inside your soul; you cut away the wrong that was done to you ... through the magic eyes that can heal your soul. Detach that offending person from the hurt and let the hurt go, the way a child opens his hands and lets a trapped butterfly go free. (Lewis B. Smedes, *Forgive and Forget*, p. 27)

Besides relieving ourselves, there is still an additional

gain from granting forgiveness. I mentioned that one reason we hold on to a grudge is to retain power over the offender. But this is a false advantage. It grows out of impotence and weakness, not strength. Genuine forgiveness gives us authentic power. The sense of superiority we feel against the offender in harboring a grudge does not really empower us. It actually robs us of our self-respect and our inner strength.

By contrast, forgiving is empowering. Forgiving helps us to restore our sense of self-worth and inner strength by not allowing us to wallow in yesterday's pain, by not permitting a past hurt to prevent us from moving on in our lives and in our relationships. Forgiving enables us to become masters of the way we manage our own personal lives. Through forgiveness, we can become full, genuine human beings again. We can emerge into men and women who are not overcome by resentments and grudges.

Such power is illustrated in a story about two friends, Nagib and Mussa. They were journeying with their servants from town to town. As they were attempting to ford a river, Mussa almost drowned, but Nagib leaped in and saved him. Mussa then asked his servant to carve these words into a nearby rock: "Traveler! In this place Nagib risked his life and saved the life of his friend, Mussa."

On their return trip, by that very same rock, Nagib and Mussa began to quarrel. The argument grew nasty and Nagib said some very hurtful words to Mussa, whose life he had saved. Mussa, in reply, took a stick and wrote in the sand: "Traveler! In this place Nagib, during a trivial argument, broke the heart of his friend, Mussa."

One of Mussa's servants asked Mussa why he had carved the reference to Nagib's heroism in stone, while he had engraved his cruel remarks in sand. Mussa responded, "I will always cherish the memory of how Nagib saved me. As for the insults, I hope that I will forgive him for them, even before the words fade from the sand."

Mussa had the kind of inner self-confidence that we should emulate. Even though Nagib had not asked him for forgiveness nor had Nagib retracted his nasty words, Mussa made an effort to shrug off the strife between the two of them. Mussa knew that he did not want to lose a friend. He did not want a few moments of arguing to overshadow the years of affection between the two of them. He was ready to offer forgiveness, even before Nagib had asked for it. Mussa understood that being free of anger was more important than being right and that preserving a relationship could outlast any storm.

Thus, we should try to rid ourselves of those grievances that rage within us and snatch away our happiness and our inner peace. We need to emancipate ourselves from those enslaving thoughts of past insults and injuries. In short, by forgiving those who hurt us, we will disinfect our minds of the bad that they did. Instead, we will treasure them for the good that they are.

Sheheheyanu:
Thanking God That We Made It

We can never take the happy highlights of our lives for granted. We are painfully aware that so many factors can intervene to prevent those special moments from occurring. Thus when we are fortunate enough to experience them, we Jews are enjoined to intone the blessing, known as the *Sheheheyanu*. In it we thank God for enabling us to "make it."

This benediction has three parts. In it, we praise God, first, for keeping us alive; second, for sustaining us; and third, for bringing us to this time. As I reflect on these three phrases, I realize that each one points to the varying degree of control we have over our lives and over our destiny as human beings.

In the first instance, we thank God for keeping us alive, for maintaining our physical existence. Here we have limited control. Ultimately, the length of time that we spend on earth is in God's province. We can, however, exert some mastery in shortening or lengthening our life span by the care that we give to our bodies. We know, for example, that eating unhealthy foods and smoking excessively can cut years off our lives. On the other hand, watching our diets, exercising regularly, and, in general, living more healthily may increase our earthly days—if we have good genes and good luck.

Here modern medicine has also helped significantly. Decades ago, when diseases like smallpox and diphtheria were rampant, one was considered fortunate to have lived to the age of forty or forty-five. Now that we have vanquished these medical maladies, a lifespan of 100 can be within the grasp of many of us.

Yet, merely existing is not enough. Endowed with lungs that breathe and a heart that beats is insufficient. I think of the plea in our prayer book, *Gates of Prayer*, in which we ask God to awaken those who have forgotten how to live. After all, some people go through life like selfish zombies. They let their minds atrophy. They neglect the needs of others. They commit themselves to nothing transcendent.

Paraphrasing the author of Psalm 90, we assert that it is important not just *limnot yameinu*, to count our days, but also to make our days count. We need not only to exist, but we also must invest our earthly life with significance. Such is what is meant by the second phrase, thanking God for sustaining us. God grants us unlimited spiritual resources to make our lives worthwhile, and here we have our greatest control. We can develop our minds by reading quality literature, by attending cultural events, and by participating in high-level study programs. We can also move beyond our egocentric preoccupations and pursue volunteer service and worthwhile causes.

But there is even another way that God sustains us with boundless spiritual gifts. With these, we can find true happiness in life. Happiness has nothing to do with our external circumstances. We know people who are affluent, professionally successful, and physically healthy, but who remain unsatisfied. Nothing is enough for them. They always crave more. Their needs are insatiable. As endowed as they are by outward standards, they feel a gnawing emptiness. Their souls are vacant.

Yet we know others whose bodies have been wracked by illness and pain, who have suffered financial reverses, and who have endured the deaths of numerous loved ones. Yet they remain content. They are grateful for their blessings. What is the difference? It is all how we view a situation.

Victor Frankl, the noted psychotherapist and Holocaust survivor, recalled a poignant scene in the death camps. There were inmates who went around sharing their last crumb of bread with others. He observed that there is one right that no one can take away from us: it is the ability to choose our attitude in any given set of circumstances. God, as our Sustainer, gives us the limitless ability to reframe any situation, to find the light concealed even in the shadows of life.

A perceptive observer of human nature once wrote: "Two men in prison looked through the bars: one saw the mud, one saw the stars."

Occasionally in popular music we find great wisdom. Peggy Lee was a blues singer with a passion for realism. She sang in a low, eerie, haunting, throaty style, which conveyed both pain and endurance. One profoundly touching song she wrote in 1969 was "Is That All There Is?...," a story in four segments, going from childhood to old age.

As a little girl, she watches a fire destroy her home at night. Helpless, she stands outside of her home, with tears flowing, as the flames consume every possession of her family. She sings: "Is That All There Is?"

Then, as a twelve-year-old, she goes to a circus. There she sees clowns, bears, elephants, and a swinging trapeze. But, even while being entertained, she realizes something is still missing inside of her and she sings: "Is That All There Is?"

Later, as a young woman, she meets a man and falls deeply in love. They enjoy a passionate, romantic relationship until, one night, he sneaks away and does not return. She then sings again: "Is That All There Is?"

But then, in the fourth and final segment, her perception changes. It is not that her circumstances improve. Rather she finally understands that life calls upon us not to deny its vicissitudes and disappointments but to focus on the positive.

She is now an elderly woman, on her death bed, and she keeps asking herself: "Is That All There Is?" Then she responds: "If that's all there is, my friends, let's keep dancing!..."

With that statement, "Let's keep dancing," she proves that she is a woman of indomitable spirit. She has learned to overcome disappointment with the anticipation of the next adventure. Not even death can threaten her invincibility.

Peggy Lee illustrates a basic truth of our Rabbis, who were once asked to define a wealthy person. They responded that a wealthy person is not one who has amassed great financial assets. Rather, it is the one who is *sameah behelko,* who is contented with one's lot in life. True happiness is that which God, as Sustainer, gives us the boundless power to achieve. God enables us to find happiness with our immediate circumstances, regardless of what they are. If we can truly be "in the moment" and not focus on what we haven't amassed, what we haven't done, what we need to do or where we should be going, then we can know happiness as deep spiritual satisfaction.

And finally we move to the third of the reasons we praise God: for bringing us to this time. Here we have no control. To arrive at the celebration of a joyous event is beyond our human power. It is no longer a matter of choice, as before. It has become a matter of chance. Here we recall the Yiddish proverb that *"Der mensch tracht un Got lacht*—Man proposes, but God disposes."

A joyous event is not something we can take for granted. We know that random circumstances could have prevented us from participating in this event—something as serious as a sudden illness or a death, or something less devastating, such as the cancellation of a plane flight. In the climax of this blessing, we completely surrender ourselves to God for whatever occurs in our lives. We place our total trust in God, with the understanding that, for whatever reason, "This was meant to be."

In fact, the specific word used to describe time in this phrase, which is *zeman,* has a technical meaning. We thank God for bringing us to this *zeman,* which we loosely translate as an "auspicious moment." It means that worldly conditions, over which only God has power, have been propitious so that this event can proceed.

A similar notion is expressed when we wish someone *mazal tov,* which means "congratulations" or "good luck." The word *mazal* refers to a planet or constellation in the zodiac. Jews once believed that these astrological forces had influence over our life's events. When we say *mazal tov* today, we not only wish good fortune in the future; we also thank God for arranging the stars and the other heavenly bodies in such an intricate way that this joyous occasion has taken place.

And so we say this prayer with ecstasy in our hearts not only for our physical existence, over which we have limited control; for our spiritual outlook, over which we have the greatest control; and for arriving at this auspicious moment, over which we have no mastery. How privileged we are that God has singled us out from all humanity so that we can savor this peak experience in our lives and say again:

"*Barukh Attah, Adonai Eloheinu, Melekh haolam, sheheheyanu vekiyemanu vehigianu lazeman hazeh.*—Blessed are You, O Lord, our God, Ruler of the universe, for maintaining us physically, for sustaining us spiritually, and for bringing us miraculously to this sacred hour."

The Anatomy of Gossip

One of the most saintly figures of modern Judaism was Rabbi Israel Meir Hacohen Kagan. He was better known as the Chofetz Chayim, which was also the title of his first book. He spent his entire life in Lithuania, where he died in 1933 at the age of ninety-five. Though an ordained rabbi, the Chofetz Chayim never wanted to make the rabbinate his profession. After he married, he and his wife operated a small grocery store. He spent all of his spare time learning Torah and spreading his knowledge to the simple folk of his community.

As a devoutly Orthodox Jew, he observed all the Torah commandments. Yet he strongly emphasized one set of Jewish laws: the regulations forbidding speaking maliciously about another person. In fact, this was the subject of his first book. He even composed a prayer to be said each morning, asking God to protect us against the sins of slander and gossip.

Over the centuries, Judaism has repeatedly condemned these verbal abuses and has established strict laws to deal with them. In Leviticus 19, we are instructed not to go about as a talebearer in the community. In fact, there are many categories of oral transgressions. When we engage in *rechilut*, we talk about the minutiae of another person's life. When we are guilty of *leshon hara*, we pass negative information about another person, even though it may be true. When we are *motzi shem ra*, we spread malicious mistruths about another.

Some rabbinic authorities have made the laws of gossip even more stringent. They say that we may not repeat defamatory information about another person, even if that information is now public knowledge and even if that person will not suffer any further harm with its repetition. They also mandate that when we hear gossip about someone, we must automatically believe that it is not true.

The effect of verbal sins can be devastating. It can cause emotional, financial, and physical harm and can engender animosity between family members and friends. It can split whole communities. The Rabbis of the Talmud believed that the Second Temple was destroyed and the Jewish people went into exile, which lasted for more than 1900 years, because one Jew slandered another. (b. *Gittin* 55b)

The Rabbis go as far as to regard the slanderer as a murderer. When one blemishes another person's reputation, it is as if he or she has destroyed that person. In fact, the Rabbis claim that slander kills three people: the one who tells it, the one who receives the tale, and the one about whom the tale is told.

The lethal effects of gossip are far-reaching. The Rabbis tell us: "*Emor b'roma uk'til b'suria*—A slanderer in Rome may kill someone in Syria." (*Gen. Rabbah* 98:23). The damage caused by gossip is often permanent and irrevocable. A Hasidic tale points out how impossible it is to correct the wrongs resulting from irresponsible slander.

A rich farmer once had a servant who was a good worker but a vicious gossip. The farmer repeatedly scolded his tale-bearing servant and tried to impress upon him the gravity of his sins. The servant eventually became very remorseful and asked the farmer what he could do to remedy the damage that he had caused with his loose tongue. The farmer told the servant to take a pillow into the village, cut open the pillow, and spread its feathers throughout the village. The servant returned to the farmer with his mission accomplished.

The farmer then said: "Now, return to the village, gather up all the feathers, and put them back into the pillow case." Of course, it was an impossible task. The wind had already blown the feathers all over the place. The farmer told the servant that, like the strewn feathers, slanderous words can never be called back or recaptured.

The best and the brightest of us at times enjoy juicy gossip and idle chatter about another person. We find this tendency hard to curb. Several solutions have been suggested to cope with it. One is to widen our cultural vistas and intellectual concerns beyond the trivial. We should broaden our knowledge of world and national news. We should read high-quality works of fiction and non-fiction. We should attend concerts and plays, visit museums, and, if we can afford it, travel widely. These experiences will greatly enrich our conversations and wean us away from gossip. This strategy bears out an insight articulated some years ago:

1. People with great minds talk about ideas.

2. People with average minds talk about events.

3. People with small minds talk about other people.

In Israel, another remedy is offered. Some synagogues annually hold what is known as a *ta'anit dibbur*, a speech fast. Those observing the speech fast must not speak about any mundane matters for an entire day. They must devote that day to praying and studying Torah. Such selective silence, when structured in this way, can be a marvelous boon to our spiritual development. It can enable us to live one full day without harmful words or hurtful gossip.

But these are external ways of dealing with our propensity for gossip. Something more profound is needed. We need to be aware that we gossip the most when we are feeling the most insecure. We talk ill of other people primarily when we are unhappy with ourselves. We view other people negatively and speak about them disparagingly when we feel bitter and unsatisfied about our own lives.

In Numbers 12, Miriam, who was Moses' older sister, spoke ill of Moses' wife, who was a Cushite, or an Ethiopian. Obviously Moses' wife was black. Miriam was swiftly punished for her verbal transgression. She was stricken with leprosy, a devastating affliction which caused her skin to turn white.

Our Rabbis, using a play on Hebrew words, have repeatedly argued that gossiping results in leprosy.

But if we read the narrative about Miriam carefully, we will discover the real reason for Miriam's despicable action. Miriam slandered her sister-in-law because Miriam, at that moment, was suffering from poor self-esteem. Miriam was intensely jealous of her younger brother, Moses. God had been speaking to her brother, Moses, and not to her. She believed that God favored Moses over her. Miriam's own insecurity led her to defaming Moses' wife.

Therefore, the real antidote to gossip is to achieve a sense of inner happiness, peacefulness, and self-acceptance. The ultimate cure for gossip is liking ourselves. Finding that sense of *shalom* results from appropriate self-love.

Secrets Parents Never Told You

When we adopted Heather, our older daughter, in 1971, friends asked Lynn and me, "What are you going to tell her?" Our answer was that, to Lynn and me, her adoption was a non-issue. Just as we would tell her that she is a Jew and an American, we would also inform her that she was adopted. We followed the same plan when we adopted our younger daughter, Alisa. We have always tried to raise our two daughters with candor and honesty.

Many in previous generations were not reared in that manner. Their parents kept a multitude of secrets from them. There were myriad skeletons in the family closet that remained hermetically sealed.

We were told that Uncle Albert died of a sudden heart attack. The truth is that, desperate over his failing law practice and his dire economic situation, he fatally shot himself in his office.

We were told that Cousin Mary loved being near the water and went on an extended vacation to Galveston. The truth is that Cousin Mary was profoundly depressed and spent eight months in Graves Hospital in Galveston, a psychiatric facility.

We were told that Grandpa Norman was married only once. The truth is that he had a brief marriage that ended in divorce before he married Grandma Belle.

We were told that Grandma Molly was eighty at her gala birthday celebration. The truth is that, because she married a younger man and did not want to appear older than he, she had lied about her age. She was really eighty-five.

We were told that Skipper, our favorite family dog, had died of internal bleeding after being struck by a car on the street in front of our house. The truth is that our parents asked the veterinarian to euthanize her.

We can multiply examples of such closely guarded secrets that our parents never wanted to disclose to us. Another striking one is the case of children who suddenly, one day, are informed that their parents, after twenty-five years of marriage, will be getting a divorce. The children are shocked. They were never told that there were any problems between their parents They had never heard their parents argue, or even respectfully disagree, in front of them.

Why do parents not want to reveal these secrets to their children? First of all, many parents hope to protect their offspring from confronting life's harsh realities. They try to shield them from pain and suffering. It is for this reason that some parents forbid their children to view exhibits or films about the horrors of the Holocaust. They fear that their children can't handle an exposure to such gruesome brutalities and bestialities.

Parents who keep secrets from their children often do not trust. Not only are they not confident that their children can handle the difficult reality; they also fear that that they cannot deal with their children's reaction. Many parents were especially tested with the horrific tragedy on September 11, 2001. They were at a loss in finding ways to explain to their children that the world, in general, and the United States, in particular, had been robbed of their assumed safety.

Similarly, when a loved one, like a grandparent, dies, they tell their children that the grandparent went away on a long trip. They underestimate the capacity of young people to deal with the more painful and seamier side of life. As a result, these children may become frightened when their parents announce they are leaving on a trip, for fear that they, like Grandpa, will never return.

Furthermore, many parents want their sons and daughters to remain children all their lives. I never before realized the profundity of the statement "Knowledge is power." Yes, secrets are a powerful tool. They enable parents to maintain the upper hand with their children, even when their children grow older. They help parents to preserve their children's naiveté and keep their children perpetually dependent on them. Parents have an intense fear of "letting go."

A woman of sixty once told me that she still felt like a child whenever she was around her aged mother. Her mother was incapable of seeing her daughter as an independent adult.

Unfortunately, keeping secrets from children will produce some dire consequences. First of all, if children learn from others the truth their parents have been concealing from them, they may become hostile to their parents. Furthermore, children generally model their own behavior after their parents. How profound is the Rabbinic observation: *"Ma'aseh avot siman levanim*—The deeds of the parents are replicated in their children."

By keeping secrets from their children, parents, by example, teach their children to keep secrets from them. The relationship between parents and children then becomes strained and dishonest. For example, gay children who observe parents behaving this way are fearful of revealing their sexual orientation to their parents. Some homosexuals suffer in such a private hell that they resort to desperate measures—even suicide. Daughters who become pregnant out of wedlock are afraid to disclose their condition to their parents. In desperation, they seek a life-threatening backalley abortion.

There is yet another negative result of parents' hiding reality from their children. Children learn not to trust their parents, even when their parents are telling the truth. Since, on many occasions, their parents have withheld information or distorted the truth, they approach their parents with skepticism.

An even more serious consequence is that children learn not to trust themselves. When children are raised thinking that their parents' marriage is ideal, and then suddenly these parents separate, they will suffer a crisis in self-confidence. They will be plagued by self-doubt. They will lose faith in their own judgments and perceptions in the future.

Fortunately, our whole culture is moving toward greater openness. We now have right-to-know laws. We can gain access to school records, IQ test results, doctors' files, and other documents, which earlier were classified and closed. Most physicians today believe that they should tell their terminal patients the grim prognosis rather than sugar coat the truth.

Traditionally, Judaism has always encouraged one to face reality, without masking or disguising it. At a *Brit Milah*, the foreskin of an eight-day-old male is surgically removed in a ceremony with hosts of family and friends as witnesses, even though some who are present may choose not to watch the proceedings.

It is true that, in recent centuries, some ultra-Orthodox Jews have become prudish and puritanical about sexual matters. In their communities women must wear long sleeves, thick stockings, and other items of clothing to cover all evidence of flesh. However, our Biblical teachers and ancient Rabbis, by contrast, were far more open. They discussed the details of sexual anatomy and functioning graphically, without any inhibitions or reservations.

Similarly, we Jews are urged to face death as the stark reality that it is. We are discouraged from viewing the cosmeticized remains of a loved one lying in state in a coffin. In addition, traditionally Jews do not leave the coffin above ground at the conclusion of a funeral. Instead, we lower the coffin into the grave and cover it with earth before leaving the cemetery to demonstrate the finality of death.

Thus, in raising children, honesty and candor are the best policy. First of all, they encourage children to trust parents' words and actions and to nurture confidence in themselves. Furthermore, they enhance the relationship between the generations. Parents and children can interact with each other without pretense and deception. And finally, honesty and candor enable parents to carry out their true role: to raise their children to become independent, self-sufficient adults. Secrets should not be used to keep the apron strings intact.

The poet Kahlil Gibran states this role of parenthood so eloquently when he urges us to remember:

> Your children are not your children.
> They are the sons and daughters of life's longing for itself.
> They come through you, but not from you,
> And though they are with you, yet they belong not to you.
> You may give them your love, but not your thoughts.
> For, they have their own thoughts.
> You may house their bodies but not their souls,
> For their souls dwell in the house of tomorrow, which you can not visit, not even in your dreams ...

The Genius of the Priestly Blessing

Both Jews and Christians invoke the famous Priestly Blessing at sacred occasions. Found in Numbers 6:24-26, it consists only of fifteen Hebrew words spread over three lines with an interesting progression. The first line has three words; the second line, five; and the third line, seven. In ancient days, the priests pronounced these fifteen words in the Jerusalem Temple.

Each of the three lines of the Priestly Blessing conveys a powerful and profound message. The first line is: "*Yevarekhekha Adonai veyishmerekha*—May the Lord bless and keep you." We need to ask: "Bless us with what? Keep us from what?" One commentator understands the meaning of that verse, in this way: "May God bless you with possessions and may God keep you from letting them possess you."

Judaism has never glorified poverty. Judaism has never insisted that we deprive ourselves of material goods. However, Judaism does instruct us not to let our acquisitions create an insatiable craving for more and more. Judaism also tells us how to spend what we have. We are to do good with our wealth and donate it generously.

Our Biblical and Rabbinic teachers maintain that our wealth ultimately belongs to God. It is not ours, even if we hold title to property. God has merely lent it to us for our earthly use. Such is the meaning of those magnificent words in the *Union Prayer Book*, reminding us that "all that we have and prize is but lent to us and we are but stewards of whatever we possess." We must share a portion of what God has lent us with those who have less.

Such is the reason for the obligation of *tzedakah*. "Charity" is a poor translation, because charity is something voluntary. *Tzedakah* is mandatory. It makes us outer-directed. It enjoins us to do good for others. Thus, when God blesses us with material abundance, God also mandates us to part with a portion of it to better the lives of those stricken with hunger and privation.

The second line of the three-fold Priestly Blessing is: "*Yaeir Adonai panav eilekha veehuneka*—May God cause the light of the Divine face to shine upon you and be gracious to you." Our commentators expand upon the meaning of this verse. They understand it to mean: "May God cause the light of Torah to shine on you and make you a person of grace." In this blessing, we ask God to enable us to fill our heads with learning, without letting it go to our heads. We have to be on guard not to become intellectual snobs nor insufferable exhibitionists of what we know.

Some of the most scholarly people can be the most obnoxious. Our tradition reminds us that we acquire learning not to show off our mental prowess but to lead a better life. We study in order to refine and purify our character. Knowledge is to make us nobler human beings.

The great Rabbi Meir understood the purpose of Torah study when he said:

> If you study Torah in order to learn and to do God's will, you will acquire many merits: it clothes you with humility and reverence. It enables you to become righteous and saintly, upright and faithful. It keeps you from sin and brings you near to virtue. You benefit humanity with counsel and knowledge, wisdom and strength. It keeps you far from sin and brings you near to virtue. You benefit humanity with counsel and knowledge, wisdom and strength.... You are modest, slow to anger, and forgiving of insults ... (M. *Avot* 6:1)

Rabbi Meir so poetically grasps the real objective of learning: to cultivate our humanity.

Now that God has given us both prosperity and learning, what else is there? The final line of the three-fold blessing is:

"*Yisa Adonai panav eilekha veyaseim lekha shalom*—May God lift up the Divine face upon you and give you peace." Our commentators understand that to mean: "May your acquisition of wealth and of learning win God's favor for you so that God will bring you peace." Some people are both affluent and brilliant. They are rich and learned. Yet they are tortured and miserable human beings.

In the 1940s a noted rabbi, Joshua Loth Liebman, wrote his magnum opus, *Peace of Mind*. In this work, Liebman related that, as a young man, he drew up a list of earthly desirables. He included such components as health, beauty, talent, power, riches, and fame. He then showed it to his teacher.

His teacher commented that the list was excellent. However, the most important element was missing. The teacher then crossed out all of the items on the list and wrote in their place, "Peace of Mind."

Liebman observed that this is the choicest gift that God can offer. God gives talent and beauty to many. Wealth is common. Fame is widespread. But peace of mind is rare. God gives it sparingly. Some never receive it. Others are advanced in years before they know it. But peace of mind can be acquired.

Peace of mind does not mean a life that is trouble-free. It is not a life without burdens. It means that, with a certain inner calm, we can manage the storms and handle the stresses of life, because our soul is attuned to God. Peace within is God's highest benediction.

George Granville beautifully captured the meaning of "Peace of Mind" in these words:

> Happiest of all mortals is he
> Whose quiet mind, from vain desires is free;
> Whom neither hopes deceive, nor fears torment,
> But lives at peace, within himself, content.

When one acquires peace of mind, one can ultimately promote world peace. Let me share with you a Jewish legend, illustrating this insight. A meeting of animals and birds took place in the forest. At the end of the meeting, someone asked the lion why he thought he deserved to be king.

He answered that he should be king because he could produce the loudest and most powerful noise of all. To prove his point, he made a terrible roar that frightened all the other animals and birds at the meeting.

Shortly thereafter, when it became quiet, the thrush spoke up. It said: "While it is true that you, O Lion, can produce the loudest roar, your voice is strong only at the beginning. It grows weaker and less audible as the distance increases. A mile or so from the place, no one can hear you.

"My voice, on the other hand, is weak compared to yours, but as I begin to sing, other birds and creatures join me in song. After a while, the entire forest is filled with melodious music."

This, then, is our goal: to be like the thrush, not the lion; to operate from quiet strength from within, and not from insecurity and inner torment that leads to bravado and domineering behavior.

Indeed, the fortunate person is not the one with a powerful roar that frightens others into submission. Rather, it is the one with inner calm and peace of mind—the one who, like the thrush, can bring about sweet harmony and cooperation among all people.

Liberation from Workaholism

Several decades ago, Rabbi Mordecai Kaplan, one of the towering Jewish religious leaders of the past century, issued a new Haggadah for Passover. In it he wrote a masterful selection on modern forms of slavery. He singled out three ways that people are held captive today.

First of all, they are enslaved to themselves, because of destructive emotions, like envy, jealousy, bitterness, and cowardice. Second, many are enslaved by poverty and inequality. In desperation, they resort to dishonesty and violence and to defending the guilty and accusing the innocent in order to get ahead. Others must perform work at starvation wages that fattens the coffers of their bosses but deprives them of life's necessities.

Finally, people are also enslaved to intolerance. Kaplan wrote this selection in the early 1940s, when bigotry and prejudice were far more severe than they are today. At that time, many Jews were denying their religious identity in order to advance, both socially and vocationally. Were Kaplan alive to revise this Haggadah selection today, he would probably add a fourth category, because we now are enslaved to work.

Workaholism is a modern addiction. I have been afflicted by it, as much as anyone else. How many of us today are guilty of simultaneously reading our mail, talking on the telephone, writing a letter, and watching the clock so that we won't be late for our next appointment?

The pace of life today has quickened. Many of us seem to be chained to our computers, typing madly, complaining that our keyboards can't keep up with our thoughts. We skip lunch, rush through dinner, and cheat ourselves out of hours of sleep. Modern technology has not alleviated the problem; it has exacerbated and complicated it.

Not long ago, in our places of work, the only communications to which we had to respond were phone messages and regular mail, today called "snail mail," and we could take our time in answering our regular mail. Today we have, in addition, e-mail and faxes. We are expected to respond to them instantly.

Not long ago, our telephones were confined to our offices and our homes. Now mobile phones are ubiquitous. People talk on them at restaurant tables, in public bathrooms, and in automobiles. When I visited Israel for the first time in 1963, one had to wait five or more years for the installation of a single telephone. Now everyone has a cell phone. A joke circulates in Israel that there is only one Israeli in the entire country without a cell phone and the Secret Service is still trying to find him.

A proliferation of airplane flights has shrunk our global community, but has also enervated and exhausted us. Some people have careers that require them to spend more than half of every week in the air, going across the country, and even to Europe and Asia and back. Eventually, such travel takes its toll on their bodies and their psyches.

There is no question today that the pressure is on to work longer hours, to produce more, to make more money, to become a dazzling success. This troubling phenomenon inspired the author Jonathan Lazear to write two self-help books: *Meditations for Men Who Do Too Much* and *Meditations for Women Who Do Too Much*. In each volume there are 365 pages of quotations and commentaries, one for each day of the annual calendar. They wisely advise us how to cope with our bondage to workaholism.

I believe the problem is particularly acute for Jews in America because we have been influenced by two cultural streams. One is the Puritan ethic, which places a supreme value on work. The other is the lingering heritage of the

Jewish immigrants, who came to these shores from Eastern Europe.

They believed that if one worked hard enough, one could pull oneself up by the bootstraps and become a "good provider." This need was so strong among them that, even though they were otherwise observant Orthodox Jews, they violated an important religious commandment and worked on the Sabbath.

Women's liberation has also spread this addiction, once confined to men. Many women today feel under the same pressure to produce and get ahead, but, at the same time, to create a sound and sturdy family life. The expectation to become a "Super Woman" is intense.

Though many Jews are workaholics, workaholism is not prized in Judaism. We can see this notion clearly in the way that traditional Jews write dates in letters and in sacred documents. In Hebrew, the days of the week have no names. They are identified only by ordinal numbers. Only the Shabbat has a name. The reason is that we are encouraged to do whatever work is necessary during the week, so that we can welcome and observe Shabbat properly. The Shabbat is the climax of the week.

For example, Monday is written *"Sheni b'Shabbat,"* the second day leading to the Shabbat. Tuesday is known as *"Shelishi b'Shabbat,"* the third day leading to the Shabbat.

Of course, our tradition does recognize that earning one's own money honestly can bring a measure of personal satisfaction. Our Psalmist tells us: "When you eat the work of your hands, you shall be happy and it shall be well with you." (Psalm 128:2). Also, making a living keeps a person off the charity rolls. No one should voluntarily become idle so as to depend on the largesse of others. In general, though, the workaholic is not a religious hero in Judaism. Work is regarded solely as a means to an end. Work, *per se*, is not glorified in Judaism.

I believe that the cause of workaholism is that our vocational achievements are tied up with our self-image. We believe that, by working longer hours and completing more projects, we will enhance our self-worth. We will eventually discover that this approach is a terribly misguided one.

Often a signal accomplishment in our career offers us only a temporary quick fix. The person who makes a million dollars annually finds it is not enough. He or she soon wants to go for the second million and then the third. An author, after finishing a book, feels a sense of exhilaration. But it is soon followed by emptiness and despair and a feeling of "Is that all there is?" Today, no one is satisfied to rest on his or her laurels any longer. We want more and more and never seem satisfied.

Also, our workaholism tends to distance us from our immediate families. At one time, men were expected to become superior breadwinners and nothing more. Today they need to be nurturers and communicators at home, as well. Workaholism impels us to labor longer and longer hours, and thus have no time to be physically and emotionally available to our loved ones. What happens in the process is that intimacy soon dies.

Perhaps the most serious result of workaholism is that it distances us from ourselves. Work can burn us out, leaving us to go "on empty." We are so busy that we have no time to reflect, to involve ourselves in deep and honest self-exploration, to engage in the kind of religious discipline required by the High Holy Days: to search our souls, to face our shortcomings, and to correct our errors.

Our busyness leads us to excessive denial and an estrangement from the core of our beings. It makes us less-than-full human beings who are unable to appreciate all the blessings that God has made available to us in this world. The author Alice Walker once observed that we make God angry if we walk by the color purple in a field and do not notice it. "Smelling the roses" is a religious requirement, which workaholism prevents us from fulfilling. Workaholism stunts our spiritual growth.

That is why Judaism favors Shabbat, the day of rest, over

the workaday week. On Shabbat, we are to be, not to do; to reflect and not to produce. It is on this day, more than on the weekdays, that we better realize that we are made in God's image, and, therefore, our self-worth is really inestimable.

Our value is not dependent upon the size of our income, the dimensions of our homes, the number of our publications, or the volume of our awards. Each of us is a child of God, even without these outer trappings that are the fruits of our work.

Therefore, as we ponder the various kinds of bondage that rob us of our personal freedom, we need to begin to liberate ourselves from workaholism. In this way, we will restore our souls and grow them properly.

Reviving Our Souls

There is an ancient Jewish legend that God opens a large ledger on Rosh Hashanah, the Jewish New Year. In it, God begins to inscribe the fate of those who are completely good. They will be rewarded with at least another year of life. God also records in that ledger the destiny of those who are completely wicked. They will be denied another year of life.

With very rare exceptions, no one fits into either of those two categories. The overwhelming majority of people are somewhere on a continuum between the extremes of being totally noble and totally wicked. According to this legend, God defers judgment for them. Their reward or punishment will be decided by their behavior during the next ten days between Rosh Hashanah and Yom Kippur, the Day of Atonement. If they make a sincere effort to change their ways, they will be granted at least one more year of life. If not, they will be denied it.

Unfortunately, many get "hung up" with the literalism of that tale. They think of life and death as physical states. They believe that if they improve their conduct, God will prolong their lives. If they don't, God will end their lives.

I prefer to think of life and death in this legend, not as physical states, but as spiritual conditions. All of one's medical vital signs can be strong; yet that person can be spiritually dead. Death means simply the numbness of the soul. In one service in *Gates of Prayer*, the dead are defined as "those who have forgotten how to live." They are dead when they have allowed their spirits to stagnate, when they have not enabled their souls to grow, when they have kept their souls on ice.

People anesthetize their souls in three areas of their relationships: to themselves, to God, and to other people. How do they do so in relationship to themselves? First of all, they allow their sense of wonderment to atrophy. In this same prayer book, we read about walking "sightless among miracles." People become so distracted by their deadlines and their debts that they fail to take time out to thrill at the sight of radiant flowers blooming in the springtime, of little children laughing and playing together, of the gorgeous hues of the sun as it sets in the West. They are just too preoccupied to notice.

The Yiddish poet Aaron Zeitlin writes that God will condemn those who look at the stars and yawn. God will conclude that God created them in vain.

Robert Louis Stevenson prayed that God would rudely jar individuals out of such mindlessness:

> If beams from happy human eyes
> Have moved me not; if morning skies
> Books, and my food, and summer rain
> Knocked on my sullen heart in vain;
> Lord, Thy most pointed pleasure take
> And stab my spirit broad awake.

Not only have men and women been unperceptive of the awesomeness around them; they have also allowed themselves to remain stuck in their cultural ruts. Take their current reading tastes, for example. Do they still favor junk novels over serious, high-quality fiction? Do they read more than just the sports page, the society news, or the stock market quotations in the newspaper? Are they challenging themselves with the kind of literature that will stretch their minds and nurture their souls?

And what about those who smugly say, "That's the way I am. Don't try to change me"? They become so self-satisfied with their homes, their few close friends, and their recreational hours on tennis courts and golf courses and at mah jongg tables that they refuse to budge from this rut. "Stay this way," God is telling them, "and you will suffer a spiritual death in the coming year." Someone once astutely observed that the difference between a rut and a grave is only six feet.

They also can remain spiritually dead in their relationship to other people. Look at what has happened to so many who were the idealists of the 1960s. They marched for justice. They demanded civil rights for African-Americans. They volunteered for the Peace Corps. They taught the illiterate poor how to read.

But where are they today, a few decades later? Their high ideals have rusted and corroded. They see homeless men, women, and children on the streets here and do nothing. They read and hear about the suffering in Third World countries and are blasé. They have lost their youthful idealism. These veterans of the battles to end discrimination, homelessness, and poverty now do not respond. Some of them even defend the status quo.

The late Rabbi Stephen Wise, one of the great spiritual leaders of the last century, used to tell a story of what happened when he first visited China in the years before World War II. In that country the only means of transportation was by rickshaw. The problem was that the rickshaws were pulled by old, weak, frail men, who would cough constantly as they transported their customers.

At first, Rabbi Wise was horrified. He felt uncomfortable that his transportation should cause so much suffering by these rickshaw pullers. He was unable to sleep at night in the hotel, as he would hear their rasping coughs outside his window. He told his hosts how agonized and troubled he was by the coughs of the rickshaw pullers, but they reassured him: "Don't worry, Rabbi Wise. In two more weeks, you will get used to it. In a month, you won't even hear it." And so it was. And that, he said afterwards, was the saddest day of his life.

They who once cared so deeply have allowed themselves to become so unresponsive to acts of cruelty and selfishness. They have grown accustomed to them. They have seen these social ills so often that they are no longer shocked or shamed. They no longer even think about them or notice them.

What has happened to them? Some claim burnout. They explain that they worked so hard years ago to alleviate the suffering of others that they have no energy left. They are suffering from what some have called "compassion fatigue." Others have become comfortable materialists. They have gone from doing good to doing well. They have become obsessed with the bottom line. To them, profits have become more important than people.

And what about their relationship to God? They have allowed themselves to become theologically underdeveloped. They carry around with them an idea of God that is appropriate for six- and seven-year-olds: a man-like image in the heavens, with a long white beard, who strikes them when they are bad and strokes them when they are good.

Rabbi David Wolpe laments that many people don't even think about God. They don't struggle, they don't wrestle, they don't grapple with problems of belief. The Jewish tradition does not mandate that we have to find God ultimately. Rather, we must continue to struggle to search for God. But many don't want to think about the big questions of what God is and how God operates.

They also delude themselves into thinking that they don't need God, because they have complete control over their lives. They are so full of themselves that they leave no room for God. Or possibly they may rationalize that scientific explanations are sufficient for the way the world operates and that a belief in God is irrelevant to their lives.

Then catastrophe strikes. A doctor discovers that they or their loved one is afflicted with an inoperable malignant tumor, or their business fails, leaving them with a mountain of bills, or their child becomes paraplegic after a tragic automobile accident. Suddenly, they turn to God and expect instant reassurance. The problem is that, in these circumstances, they have not established an ongoing relationship with God. Thus, they are often disappointed in the results.

Let me suggest an analogy. Suppose that a woman has an uncle who is extremely wealthy. For the past twenty-five years, she has had absolutely no contact with that uncle. When his children invited her to his sixtieth birthday celebration, she did not even bother to respond to the invitation. She has never picked up the phone to see how her uncle is doing.

Then one day, she suffers a tremendous financial reverse and she desperately needs money. At that point, she picks up the telephone and calls her uncle to ask him for a gift. How do you think this uncle will respond? Depending upon his mood and inclination, he may or may not grant her request.

Like this uncle, people have ignored God. Yet there is a difference between the uncle and God. God will always be willing to listen to them and to respond to them. However, they will not know what God is trying to tell them, because they have been out of touch with God. They have failed to maintain constant contact with God. They have been spiritually dead in their communication with God. They have been totally unresponsive to the signs that God has given them. Those who are in a relationship with God will be open and sensitive to God's subtle signs along the paths of their lives. Others, however, will be blind to these signs and remain spiritually adrift.

Yes, they have permitted their spiritual numbness to persist. They have allowed their spirits to atrophy. They have not thrilled to the bounties of nature, nor have they expanded their minds with fine literature. They have been unmoved by human suffering, as hunger, bloodshed, poverty, and illiteracy do not faze them. They have clung to their infantile notion of God and have not wrestled with the big issues of life. Their spiritual growth has been stunted. They have remained spiritual midgets. They need to be shaken out of their spiritual slumber. They need to be jolted out of their soulful indolence and apathy.

In the famous High Holy Day prayer, *Unetaneh Tokef,* we find that it is not really God who will inscribe our fate for the coming year. It is we ourselves. We read, "*V'hotam yad kol adam bo.*" Freely translated, this means that the entries are in our own handwriting. We ourselves write the stories of our lives.

God does not really author the script, nor does fate, nor does some higher power. We produce the script. Of course, some things we can't control. Whether we are born healthy or handicapped, talented or average; whether a tornado will strike our home or spare it; whether the mugger or the malignancy will choose us or settle on some other victim—we can't decide any of that.

But how we deal with the life we are given, how we expend the time at our disposal—that is what we record in the Book of Life. If we remain spiritually asleep, we will decree a spiritual death for ourselves. If we remain alert and aware, however, we will assure ourselves a spiritually fulfilling, rewarding, and satisfying life ahead.

How Do We Want
to Be Remembered?

In the summer of 1996, my congregation granted me a mini-sabbatical. During those three glorious summer months, my wife, Lynn, and I rented a lovely apartment in Jerusalem. Our mini-sabbatical gave us an opportunity not only to explore the historical and religious riches of Israel. It also enabled us to spend time in the Arab lands of Jordan and the Sinai Desert.

The highlight of our Jordan itinerary was Petra. Petra is an ancient, hidden Nabatean city. It was carved out of soaring rose-red rock walls. With its grand ancient temples, graced with Corinthian columns, its amphitheater, its cardo, and its array of immense tombs, Petra is an indescribable wonder.

Until Jordan signed the Peace Accord with Israel, no Jew was legally allowed in Jordan. In fact, until 1994, Petra was, for many Israelis, like forbidden fruit. It always held out a special mystical, romantic, and often fatal fascination.

Along the border between Jordan and Israel are memorial markers. They recall the daring feats of those Israelis who lost their lives in the pre-treaty days by sneaking across the border to catch a glimpse of Petra.

On the way to Petra, we stopped at Mt. Nebo. This is the spot where God showed Moses the length and breadth of the Promised Land. However, God decreed that Moses would die before arriving there. As we stood on Mt. Nebo, we tried to sense the intense pain and agony of Moses as he looked at the Holy Land across the valley. His life's dream was to enter that land, but now that opportunity would be denied him forever. His dreams were shattered. His hopes were dashed.

Moses must have felt grossly cheated. After all, he had led the children of Israel out of their bondage in Egypt. He had brought them to the foot of Mt. Sinai to teach them the Torah. He had endured their complaining, bickering, and rebelling in the wilderness for forty years. All of this was to accomplish one goal, and now it was frustrated.

At this point, our Rabbis tell us that Moses repeatedly begged God to rescind the decree so that he could accompany his people to their final destination. God, however, was adamant. God insisted that the edict be upheld. All of Moses' pleadings to reach the Promised Land before his death were in vain.

Over the centuries, I believe Biblical interpreters have failed to explain convincingly why Moses could not enter the Promised Land. Some say that Moses had become out-of-touch with his people. He was no longer aware of their desires nor sensitive to their needs. He also did not understand the harsh conditions of life that he would encounter in the Holy Land. Joshua, his successor, was better fit to be their leader at this point.

Most of the ancient Rabbis, however, locate Moses' failure to reach the Holy Land at a place we visited outside of Petra. It is called Wadi Musa, which means, in Arabic, the Valley of Moses. In Wadi Musa, we entered a small shelter housing the famous rock that supposedly sealed Moses' fate. From that rock there now flows a natural spring which supplies water to that entire area.

In the Bible, we read that the children of Israel were suffering from thirst. They were demanding that Moses find a way to quench it. God ordered Moses to speak to that rock in order to produce water. Instead of speaking to the rock, however, Moses struck it, not only once but twice. Moses disobeyed God publicly. Therefore, God punished Moses. God robbed Moses of a chance to realize his life-long, cherished aspiration of coming into the Promised Land.

I do not necessarily accept this explanation. Rather, I agree with those who claim that, for whatever reason known only to God, God wanted Moses to die and not go to the Holy Land. The story about Moses' striking the rock is just a pretext so that God might not appear too unjust.

Once I visited an elderly woman who mentioned that her husband, who died in his eighties, accomplished everything that he wanted in life. The majority of us, however, are not so fortunate. Instead, we, for whatever reason God decides, will die like Moses, with unfinished goals, with thwarted promises, and with unfulfilled dreams. We think of those very young people, filled with so much vigor and talent, whose lives are cut off before they have a chance to fulfill their vast potential.

I recall a colleague who, after several decades of rabbinic service, retired. He and his wife were planning to travel extensively over the next several years—something that they could not do while he was in the active rabbinate. A week after his retirement, his wife died suddenly. His plans turned to ashes.

Standing at Mt. Nebo, we realized that, like Moses, we set goals, we chart hopes, and we fashion dreams. Yet only God has dominion over the length of our life span. Most of us die with unfinished business. As the Yiddish expression goes, "Man proposes, but God disposes."

There was yet one other painful lesson that we gleaned at Mt. Nebo. We cannot determine the content of our immortality. We cannot control how others will remember us. How others will revise our legacy after our death is outside of our grasp. Even while we are alive, people will insist that we have said and done certain things that we are convinced we never said or did. I have often quipped that some day I will probably live on through misquotation.

At Mt. Nebo, I realized that even Moses, the preeminent leader of the Jewish people, also could not fully shape his immortality. Countless generations of Jews have called Moses, *Moshe Rabbenu,* Moses our Rabbi and teacher.

Yet, it was at Mt. Nebo, the very spot where Moses learned

the bitter news that he couldn't enter the Promised Land, that his legacy as a Jewish figure has been diminished. At Mt. Nebo, about 1,400 years ago, a group of Christians built a memorial church. They did so to honor Moses, whom they venerate as a saint. Much later, in 1933, the Franciscan Biblical Institute restored that church with its magnificent mosaic floor.

Yet, at the entrance of that church, Moses' significance as a religious figure is now reduced. We saw there a large sign engraved with a quotation from the Gospel of John. It reads: "For while the law was given through Moses, grace and truth come through Jesus Christ." (1:17)

The message is clear. At Mt. Nebo, church builders imply that Moses is not as important as Jesus. It is true that Moses is God's faithful servant, but Jesus is God's son. Moses gave the Torah, but people no longer need the Torah to be saved. Faith in Jesus is what is critical, in their view.

Thus, reflecting on our visit to Mt. Nebo, where Moses spent his last days, I am sobered by the reality that the length of our lives and the way others will recall our memory are beyond our control.

However, these thoughts should not depress us, because there are vast areas of our life which we can control. One is the way that we fill that interval of years, between our birth and our death, regardless of how long that span is. Whether we are kind or nasty, thoughtful or insensitive, thankful or ungrateful is something that we can determine.

Furthermore, it is true that we cannot compel others to think of us in a certain way. Yet we must do the best we can and be pleasing in our own sight and in God's. In other words, though we can not govern our reputation, we do have power over our character. Who we really are, and not how others perceive us, is what is significant.

Alexander Woollcott once wisely observed: "Reputation is what you fall for. But character is what you stand for." Therefore we should strive to stand for the best.

Overcoming Shame

Rabbi Harold Schulweis told his congregation in Encino, California, about a distraught member in her late fifties. She had attended Sabbath morning services faithfully every week and seemed familiar with the prayerbook and the Bible. One Saturday, she asked to see him at the end of services. She sat across from his desk, and, trembling, she told Rabbi Schulweis this story:

> You may remember my son, who attended Hebrew High School and was a student at the University of Judaism. He kept the secret of his orientation to himself. Whenever the issue of gays and lesbians came up, he felt threatened, ridiculed, humiliated, hurt. I knew his sexual orientation and he knew how unhappy I was with the state of affairs. One day he announced that he was going to San Francisco for "the cure." A friend had suggested the right therapist who would change him, would teach him to be straight and normal. I kept receiving a number of letters from him. He was ebullient. Things were fine now. He had changed. He was a "new man." Then I discovered much too late that he was lying to me and to himself. My son took his life.

This story is shocking, and I hope that I never hear any story like it again. What I have cited is an extreme example of the horrifying pain that many gays and lesbians and their parents are feeling. Parents of gays and lesbians often do not know how many others there are within their immediate circle of friends, acquaintances, and work associates. They are hiding and are miserable. They are overwhelmed by bewilderment and isolation. They need each other desperately for support, but they refuse to acknowledge to each other their children's sexual orientation, even after their own children have come out of the closet.

There are so many others whose fear of humiliation has caused them to drive their problems underground. Some have had terrible financial reverses. They can't make their mortgage payments. Their power company is threatening to cut off their electricity. Their phone service has already been disconnected. They feel like utter failures, but they have too much pride to ask for help.

Some have been alcoholics. Their drinking to excess cannot be curbed. They are about to lose their jobs because they frequently fail to appear for work and perform poorly while there. Yet, if they are Jewish, in the back of their minds is that old slogan that Jews don't drink, that a *shikker* is a *goy*. Thus they are inhibited from going to treatment centers or Alcoholics Anonymous because they fear admitting that they have a problem.

Some have children who have been in trouble with the law. They have been caught stealing, or dealing drugs, or falsifying tax forms. They may even be serving a prison term. Yet many, especially in the Jewish community, believe that delinquency is not a Jewish problem. Therefore, something must be wrong with them as parents. Some of these people won't even appear in public because of their embarrassment.

Some women live with physically abusive husbands. Yet they suffer in painful silence. They are ashamed to admit that they contracted a bad marriage. They fear leaving their husbands not only because they worry about financial support; they also don't believe they are strong enough to make it on their own emotionally. Therefore, they suffer physical and psychic pain in silence.

There are people with severe clinical or biochemical depression. They have lost their appetite. Favorite pastimes no longer provide any enjoyment for them. They avoid crowds and would prefer staying in bed all day. Carrying out even the smallest task, like tying their shoes, seems overwhelming to them. They live in a mental torture chamber.

Yet they refuse to go for help. They believe that seeking assistance for an emotional problem is a sign of weakness. Furthermore, they have the mistaken notion that psychiatrists are for crazy people. Because of these terrible misconceptions, their clinical depression drives them more and more into the pits of despair.

Periodically, I have undergone periods of biochemical depression. It probably has not been obvious to most people with whom I come into contact. However, I have had to make an inordinate effort to get through each day, because this particular depression leaves me feeling totally exhausted. After getting some superb help, I have shared my situation only with a handful of people. My own sense of embarrassment has prevented me from sharing it with more.

Whether we are concealing homosexuality, or financial reverses, or alcoholism, or socially deviant children, or physically abusive husbands, or depression, we are like the Marranos of Christian Spain. They practiced their Judaism in secret and feared going public with it. We are overcome by what the popular counselor John Bradshaw calls "toxic shame."

Toxic shame is a terrible affliction. Toxic shame is that all-pervasive sense that we are flawed and defective as human beings. It gives us a feeling of worthlessness, of failing, of falling short as a person. Toxic shame is one of the most vicious forms of inner torment. It is a sickness of the soul. It cuts us off from our true selves, because we have to hide out from our real selves. It condemns us to complete isolation and aloneness.

There is a difference, however, between toxic shame and genuine guilt. Guilt, unlike shame, can sometimes be healthy. Guilt results when we do something that violates our beliefs and values. Guilt is a painful feeling of regret. It means that we accept responsibility for an action we did that was wrong. A student who cheats on a test, an executive who embezzles company funds, a physician who files fraudulent medical insurance claims, or a clergyman who engages in sexual harassment should feel guilty. In religious terms, these people have committed sins. These sins should engender guilt. With guilt, however, we have the possibility of doing *teshuvah*, of asking for forgiveness, of repenting, of being absolved. Guilt is not all-pervasive.

However, toxic shame is not just a remorseful feeling about our actions. It is a devastating image of ourselves as persons. It invades our core identity. Toxic shame does not come merely from breaking a moral or religious code. It is not as easy to shed, because it poisons and infects the core of our being.

How then do we deal with this toxic shame? First of all, we must admit that we have the problem. No one is going to reject us for our honesty and our candor. In fact, I find that people will rally to support and embrace us.

Furthermore, if we hide or distort the truth, we will feel even worse because of the deception. We will also have used even more energy in our efforts to coverup.

When we admit our problems, we realize that we are not alone. This is the lesson that Yom Kippur, the Jewish Day of Atonement and its most solemn annual religious holiday, drives home forcefully. All of us are frail, fragile creatures, prone to error, and susceptible to problems. We need to seek out people with similar circumstances from whom we can gain greater empathy and fuller understanding. Our Rabbinic sages were wise when they observed: "*Tzarat harabim hatzi nehama*—Half of our consolation comes from realizing the troubles of others."

We will also discover how safe it is to allow ourselves to be vulnerable. Opening ourselves up to each other is not as big a risk as we dreaded. We may fear that we will be judged badly. However, the fact is that most people are more uncomfortable with the "perfect" person than with those who will reveal their problems and trials in life. Laying bare our deepest feelings, our most private thoughts, creates a climate for others to do the same with trust, cooperation, and confidence.

We must also realize that, even with our problems, we are all people of value. Those of us who were associated with the

Marriage Encounter Movement know the slogan: "God does not make junk." We all have limitations, but we are still worthy Godly creations.

One astute rabbi observed that Rosh Hashanah, the Jewish New Year, and Yom Kippur, the Day of Atonement, come in the wrong order. Yom Kippur really should occur first. Yom Kippur is the day when we examine our sins and errors in the past year. On the other hand, on Rosh Hashanah, we hardly speak of sin. Instead, we emphasize positive themes. We affirm the goodness of creation, the glories of God's kingdom, and the promise of the New Year. Would it not be more sensible to atone or repent for the sins of the past year first and then turn to the hopeful future?

Logically, the correct order should be Yom Kippur and then Rosh Hashanah. However, psychologically, the order we observe is healthy. Before we can go through the ordeal of considering all the things that are wrong with our lives, we must first begin to affirm how worthwhile our lives are.

As people of value, as children of God, we are special. Our personal problems which have caused us shame do not diminish our value one iota. Disclosing our burdens openly and frankly to others will ultimately enhance our stature in our own eyes and in theirs.

If we do so, we may eventually feel confident enough to open ourselves up and to affirm the words of Dinah Maria Craik:

> Oh, the comfort—the inexpressible
> comfort of feeling safe with a person,
> Having neither to weigh thoughts,
> Nor measure words— but pouring them
> All right out—just as they are
> Chaff and grain together—
> Certain that a faithful hand will
> Take and sift them
> Keep what is worth keeping
> And with the breath of kindness
> Blow the rest away.

Has Religion Done More Harm Than Good?

Religious leaders have sometimes brought shame to religion. David Koresh, the demonic head of the Branch Davidians, near Waco, Texas, cavalierly used sacred language and symbols to wield his power over scores of compliant men, women, and children. They gave up their freedom to Koresh, whom they believed God had appointed. They trusted him as their exalted leader, but he betrayed that trust. Their end, as we all know, was catastrophic. Fifteen years before, Jim Jones, another cult leader, also used religion to seduce over 800 of his followers to commit mass suicide in Guyana.

Some fanatical Muslim leaders inspire young men and women to kill innocent Jews inside and outside of Israel by suicide bombing in order to please Allah and to win a place in Paradise. The nineteen Muslim extremists who wreaked havoc and destroyed thousands of lives at the World Trade Center in New York on September 11, 2001, were driven by distorted religious zeal.

When we hear about these incidents, we usually ask ourselves: "Has religion not done more harm than good?" Even as a teacher of religion, I must admit that this question has merit. Throughout history, much cruelty has been inflicted in the name of religion. The Crusaders and the religious zealots of the Spanish Inquisition tortured and even murdered blameless victims in an effort to impose Christianity, the faith of love. We Jews were often the prime victims of this religious zeal.

Note all the wars and violence carried out to advance religious causes. Catholics and Protestants are locked in conflict in Ireland. Christians have slaughtered Muslims in Bosnia, and Muslims have maimed and murdered Christians in Lebanon and in other parts of the world. And what about the militant pro-lifers, who are religiously inspired to murder physicians willing to perform abortions?

Even we Jews are not exempt from religious zealotry. Dr. Baruch Goldstein, a religious Jewish physician, opened fire on Muslims at prayer at the Tomb of the Patriarchs in Hebron and killed twenty-four worshipers. Yigal Amir targeted Yitzhak Rabin, Israel's prime minister, as a sinner for his willingness to offer land for peace to the Palestinians and assassinated him at a rally in Tel Aviv.

In Jerusalem, Hebrew Union College, the Reform Jewish seminary, is located on King David Street, not far from Meah Shearim, the ultra-Orthodox quarter of Jerusalem. My late teacher, Dr. Jakob Petuchowski, once quipped that the Hebrew Union College is just a stone's throw from Meah Shearim. This, of course, is a play on words. Not only are these locations a short distance from each other, but also some Jews in Meah Shearim and other ultra-Orthodox neighborhoods throw stones and rocks at cars if they drive through those areas on Shabbat.

Religion even tends to spawn corruption and hypocrisy in all major faith communities. The revelations about the sexual escapades of Jim Swaggert and Jim Bakker disillusioned millions of their followers who had invested huge sums in these ministries. More than a dozen alumni of programs of the National Conference of Synagogue Youth recounted incidents of sexual abuse and harassment over three decades by Rabbi Baruch Lanner, its former executive director.

The purity of every religious community is stained by people like these. According to police reports, Farhad Qaumi was arrested in Parramatta, Australia, for raping a sixteen-year-old girl. Qaumi informed the police that he had removed his Islamic pendant before attacking the girl and told her: "I have to take it off, as it is disrespectful."

Indeed, religion does sometimes lead to misguided judg-

ments. There are some churches and synagogues that use il-
legal means to raise revenue and falsify reports to their national denominational headquarters to save money. Power
plays, political infighting, and jockeying for leadership positions in churches and synagogues often dominate these religious institutions. Some churches and synagogues even hold
testimonial dinners to honor people whose morals and ethics
are highly questionable.

Thus, after all that has been said, we can indeed build a
strong case against religion. Religion can rob people of their
God-given right to choose, as happened at Waco or Guyana.
Religion can become so fanatical that it will inflict pain, and
even death, on non-believers. Religion can also promote deception, dishonesty, and corruption.

But let us draw a fair and accurate conclusion from
these charges. It is not that religion is bad. It is rather that
some people who embrace religion do things that are ir-
religious. Therefore, let us not judge a noble religion by its
ignoble practitioners, just as we should not judge the quality of a great symphony by the inferior orchestra that plays it.

It is also possible to do many positive and wholesome
things in the name of religion. Religion can confer many
benefits. Religion can give us a sense of belonging. Some
may come to worship services, primarily to fulfill an individual spiritual need, to commune with God. But I would
venture to say that many more who attend public worship on
a regular basis do so because they want to see friends and
acquaintances they enjoy, people with whom they share similar visions and values, people who understand them when
they hurt and laugh with them when they are happy.

Indeed, religion also gives us a sense of connection to an
entire tradition. When we Jews, for example, practice
Judaism at synagogue or at home, we pray and sing the same
words, like the *Shema*, the historic affirmation of faith in one
God, which our ancestors spoke. Religion can help us not
only to strengthen our ties with our community but also to
deepen our roots in our heritage.

Secondly, religion can teach us that we must live a life of goodness, even when some of its adherents do not live up to that ideal. Religion, when left undistorted, does promote justice, fairness, kindness, and love. Note the large percentage of the hospitals, the institutions of healing, in San Antonio alone, which are religiously connected: Christus Santa Rosa, Downtown Baptist, St. Luke's Baptist, and Methodist. The SAMM Center for the Homeless is governed and supported by a coalition of approximately eighty local churches and synagogues.

Many houses of worship are centers of compassion for the needy. At Temple Beth-El in San Antonio, for example, we solicit large funds on Purim to benefit the hungry and the homeless. On Yom Kippur, we collect non-perishable foods for distribution to the San Antonio Food Bank. Years ago, we sponsored Health-O-Rama at the San Antonio Convention Center. This was a massive program offering health screening, education, and referral services to thousands of San Antonians who otherwise could not afford this medical care. Mitzvah Day, when scores of congregants gather to render humanitarian services to people in need throughout the city, has become a highlight of each year's programming. This kind of compassionate outreach is typical of myriad churches and synagogues throughout the nation.

In addition, many of the struggles for human dignity have been religiously inspired. The battle for integration in the South took root in African-American churches. Martin Luther King derived his prophetic zeal for equal rights from Scripture.

Indeed, religion can promote good works. It can also help us gain a spiritual grounding, especially when grief and tragedy invades our lives. It can enable us to grapple with the big questions of human existence: Who am I? Why am I here on earth? What is my purpose in life? Has my life been empty or significant? Why do I still suffer if I have done so much good? Will death mean the end of me?

Religion can also help us to sustain a positive outlook on

life. This is reinforced at certain peak moments. We feel the presence of God at the birth of a child, in standing at our child's side at a Bar or Bat Mitzvah, and in viewing a gorgeous sunset.

Healthy then are the uses of religion when it gives us a people and a tradition to which we can attach ourselves, when we obey its mandates to act lovingly, and when we are aided in our spiritual search for meaning in life and in our need to face life with hope.

Let us remember that religion is practiced by fallible human beings, not saints. I recall an ancient Rabbinic legend that when God was about to give the Torah, the angels, those perfectly behaved creatures in heaven, strenuously objected. They argued that, placed in the hands of men and women, the Torah would become corrupted. God overruled their objection. God told them that it is easy to observe the Torah in heaven. On earth, the Torah is so much harder to follow but it is much more needed. Our challenge then is to live as best as we can, even as imperfect human beings, by the ethical and moral mandates of our sacred literature. If we do so, religion will do more good than harm.

Does God Need Our Thanks?

Prior to partaking of our sumptuous dinners on Thanksgiving Day, some of us pause for a moment to express our prayerful appreciation to God. We thank God for our home, for our family, for our country, and for many other blessings that we enjoy.

In Judaism, however, our liturgical offerings of Thanksgiving are not to be limited to Thanksgiving Day. Traditional Jews must pray three times a day: morning, afternoon, and evening. Each of these three services features a prayer of *Hoda'ah*, voicing our gratitude.

At this juncture, we must ask the question: "Does God need all of these thanksgiving prayers?" Is God not really beyond all of our praises and exaltations? God actually has no ego. God performs in a certain way, whether we like it or not. God does not determine future actions by public opinion polls. God does not crave our endorsement, nor is God swayed by our disapproval.

Why then are we constantly called upon to be thankful to God? There are three reasons. First of all, we need to sensitize ourselves to our many gifts. The Jewish tradition demands that we pronounce blessings to God for 100 different seemingly trivial situations that we may encounter daily. For example, we are obliged to offer a blessing before eating bread or drinking wine, upon seeing a tree or an animal of a species unknown to us for the first time, and upon viewing an ocean or a rainbow. There is even a blessing prior to performing a necessary physiological function in which we praise God, "Who heals all flesh and does wonders."

We need to offer these expressions of thanks and praise to

God so that we will take nothing in life for granted. In our Reform Jewish prayerbook, we are accused of "walking sightless among miracles." We see children at play, the changes of seasons, the cycles of human development, and are unmoved. Our attention is distracted. Our minds are elsewhere. We don't pay attention.

Robert Louis Stevenson once observed that a person who "has forgotten to be thankful has fallen asleep in the midst of life." Offering prayers of thanksgiving, therefore, serves as an antidote to our tendency to become blasé and complacent about the small wonders that unfold before our eyes myriad times during the day. These expressions of thanksgiving will revive our sense of wonder. They will enable us to see life as a series of miracles rather than mundane happenings.

There is yet a second reason that we need to thank God. We must curb our arrogance and realize that God, and not we, is ultimately in control of our lives. For many decades in American life, an eminently successful multi-millionaire would call himself a "self-made man." Whatever wealth he accumulated, whatever power he achieved, he ascribed to his own abilities. He left no room for God in assessing his triumphs.

A prayer of thanksgiving and praise, if taken seriously, would force that financial wizard to view God as the ultimate source of his stunning abilities and his impressive gains. Our Rabbis remind us that "the one who enjoys anything of this world without a blessing is like one who robs the sanctuary." They go on to tell us that a blessing is the price that we pay for being permitted to enjoy this world.

There is a third and final reason that we need to thank God. Prayers of thanksgiving maintain us in a constant relationship with God. Often one who is out of contact with God for a long time suddenly develops a serious illness or experiences a tragedy in his/her family. That person tries to pray but does not gain any spiritual comfort.

When we call on God only in a crisis, when we practice what has been called "Fox Hole Religion," we may rudely learn, to our serious disappointment, that God is not there for us. In such painful moments, it is not that God has abandoned us or that God has rejected us. It is just that we have not developed the skills for tuning in to God. Prayer takes practice.

Prayers of thanksgiving keep us in constant touch with God. In many ways, prayers of thanksgiving are superior to prayers of petition, in which we ask God for something that we want or need. Prayers of petition tend to turn us inward. They can, if left unchecked, make us egocentric and selfish. By contrast, prayers of thanksgiving direct us outward and keep us alive spiritually. For example, even a blind person must offer the prayer: "Praised are You, O Lord, who opens the eyes of the blind." That individual must show gratitude, in spite of his or her severe handicap, because others are visually normal.

The late Rabbi Solomon B. Freehof reminded us that the habit of praising and thanking God rather than begging from God helped our forebears. It conditioned them to find joy even in minor blessings. It helped them to surmount the tragedies of their life when they faced poverty and persecution.

Dr. Freehof observed that a forlorn, poverty-stricken Jew, living in torment and exile, in raising his last crust of bread to his mouth, might feel justified to curse his lot and denounce God. Instead, it would not enter his mind to eat of this tiny morsel of bread without offering the *Hamotzi*, thanking God for bringing forth food from the earth. Freehof concluded that the prayer of thanksgiving teaches us to overcome bitterness and self-pity. It enables us to think, not of what the world owes us, but what we owe the world and God.

Thus, God does not personally depend on our prayers of gratitude. Yet we need to offer them. We must thank God in order to gain a sense of wonder and mystery that is revealed before our eyes many times daily. We must remind ourselves that it is not we, but God, who is to be credited with our human achievements and victories. We must also thank God to keep us in a relationship with God in order to reduce our self-centeredness and to make our souls great.

The Rabbis tell us that at the end of days, all the prayers will cease, except for prayers of thanksgiving. Therefore, we need to enable our prayers of gratitude to ascend to the throne of Heaven, not only on Thanksgiving Day, but every moment of our waking hours.

Defeating Depression

Holidays can be times of happy family reunions, good food, cheery conversation, and joyous sights, smells, and sounds. But for some, these holidays engender the "blues." They are occasions of tears and pain. A widow may be spending her first holiday without her newly deceased husband. A child of divorced parents must decide how to divide the festivities between his mother and his father. A man who has been out of work for several months can't afford to buy gifts for his family and friends as he once did. Indeed, depression can blemish this gaiety and glitter.

Depression affects all of us at one time or another. It can appear after the rejection of a friend or a lover, the loss of a job, the serious illness or death of a loved one, or numerous other traumas. Such depression is normal and begins to diminish as the crisis recedes.

That is not the kind of depression I wish to discuss here. Rather, I want to focus on another type of depression: one that is abnormal, lethal, and devastating. It robs its victim of hope. It plunges one into a long-term, indescribable hell. It is not necessarily connected with a specific trauma. However, a trauma can ignite it in those who are predisposed to it.

This kind of depression has plagued people for centuries, even in the days of the Bible. Psalm 42 is a classic example. The Psalmist confesses that his tears have been his food day and night, because crying spells often accompany this kind of depression. Out of his anguish, the Psalmist poses this question to himself: "Why are you cast down, O my soul, and why do you moan within me?" This pathetic complaint clearly illustrates to what horrible psychic depths this Biblical writer has sunk.

This kind of depression has afflicted some of the giants of the arts and of government. Among its victims have been Vincent Van Gogh, Ernest Hemingway, Winston Churchill, and Abraham Lincoln. One of the most articulate sufferers of abnormal depression has been William Styron, author of *The Confessions of Nat Turner* and *Sophie's Choice*.

Styron has written a moving and gripping account of his morbid descent into the pits of depression. He has entitled his work: *Darkness Visible—A Memoir of Madness*. This memoir began as a lecture at a symposium sponsored by the Department of Psychiatry at Johns Hopkins University. It developed into a full-length essay published in *Vanity Fair*. Styron expanded it further into this slim volume.

He describes, in great detail, a monumentally significant day in his life in Paris in October of 1985. Styron was there to receive the coveted prize given annually in memory of Cimo del Duca. It is awarded to an artist or scientist whose work reflects a certain "humanism." Greatly esteemed in France, the prize carries a cash value of $25,000. Del Duca was an Italian immigrant, who became the proprietor of a leading Paris newspaper, a renowned philanthropist, and the head of a high quality publishing house.

Being chosen for this award should have significantly boosted Styron's ego and lifted his spirits. Yet on the day of the presentation, he felt totally joyless and worthless. In fact, loss of self-esteem is one of the most common symptoms of abnormal depression.

The awards ceremony was to take place at noon at an ornate palace on the Right Bank in Paris. A formal luncheon was to follow. Styron woke up at mid-morning. He had managed to overcome his insomnia, which is another bold sign of depression, and had gotten a few hours of sleep.

Styron observed that he was different from most victims of depression. The majority are laid low in the morning and can't get out of bed. They feel better, however, as the day goes on. The opposite was the case with Styron. He felt fairly normal at the early part of the day, but as the day progressed, gloom, dread, and acute anxiety overtook him.

After the presentation, Styron insulted Simone del Duca, widow of the man in whose memory the prize was endowed. He told Madame del Duca that he could not remain for the luncheon with the twelve who had selected him for this prize. What a terrible social offense he had committed! He had mindlessly arranged, the night before, to have lunch with his French publisher, instead.

Madame del Duca considered his decision thoughtlessly outrageous. The fact is that Styron had known for several months that the luncheon following the presentation was part of the pageantry of the day. Styron observed that his strange irresponsible behavior resulted from his depression. Confusion, lack of mental focus, and lapse of memory are clear signs of this mental disequilibrium.

Embarrassed and ashamed, he asked the aide of Madame del Duca to be restored to the guest list. In so doing, he blurted out words in French that one does not usually speak to a stranger: "I am sick—a psychiatric problem!" She was magnanimous in accepting his apology.

After the luncheon, a television crew was waiting to take him to the newly built Picasso Museum. There he was to be filmed looking at exhibits and exchanging comments with his wife, Rose. He arrived at the museum in a state of emotional shambles. This should have been a time of enormous pleasure; yet it had become one of excruciating mental pain.

Within the next few hours in the museum, his agony reached such a crescendo that he had to leave for his hotel. Upon arriving at his hotel, he lay on his bed and gazed at the ceiling, immobilized in a trance of supreme discomfort.

He managed to pull himself together enough to go to dinner with his French publisher, her son, and a friend. Halfway through the dinner, he lost his $25,000 prize check. He had put it inside his breast pocket, but, when he reached for it, he realized that it was gone. He asked himself: "Was it

intentional?" Because of his feelings of abject self-worthless-
ness, he might possibly have believed he did not deserve the
prize in the first place.

The rest of the dinner was a disaster. He had no appetite.
He could barely force laughter. Toward the end of the
evening he was almost speechless. He could utter only mono-
syllables. Fortunately, just as it was time to leave the restaurant, the son of the publisher found his check. He discovered
it had slipped out of Styron's pocket and flown under an ad-
joining table.

Styron vividly and graphically describes the torment that
the victim of abnormal depression experiences. However, he
acknowledges that even the greatest literary geniuses cannot
fully convey in words the total intensity of its hell. Styron does
make this impressive attempt:

> ...The great drizzle of horror induced by depression takes
> on the quality of physical pain. But it is not an immediately
> identifiable pain, like that of a broken limb. It may be more
> accurate to say that despair, owing to some evil trick played
> upon the sick brain by the inhabiting psyche, comes to re-
> semble the diabolical discomfort of being imprisoned in a
> fiercely overheated room. Because no breeze stirs this cal-
> dron, because there is no escape from the smothering con-
> finement, it is entirely natural that the victim begins to
> think ceaselessly of oblivion.

About one in every ten Americans becomes abnormally
depressed. Depression attacks people of all ages, races,
creeds, and socio-economic classes. Women are more susceptible to it than men. Artistic types are particularly vulnerable.
Cases of elderly people, who are prone to depression, are
often misdiagnosed as dementia.

The causes of abnormal depression are mysterious. It can
come from biochemical disturbances in the brain. It also has
genetic roots. Styron remembers that his father was hospitalized by a malady similar to his. The death or disappearance
of a parent, especially a mother, before or during puberty can

be a factor in depression. Such an incident can wreak horror, particularly if the mourning for the parent is incomplete. Styron had lost his mother at the age of thirteen.

Abraham Lincoln's melancholia was often linked with the untimely death of his mother, when he was nine. It was exacerbated by his sister's death when he was nineteen. Often a precipitating factor brings on the first symptoms. Styron believes that his withdrawal from alcohol, to which he had become habituated for forty years, was significant.

People afflicted by depression are grossly misunderstood. Loved ones grow impatient with them. They admonish them to "snap out of it," which is an impossible feat. Many depressives also feel a sense of shame or stigma. Such is unfortunate, because depression is an illness just like any other sickness.

But abnormal depression won't go away by itself. Styron himself was hospitalized for seven weeks, with a treatment plan which proved effective. There are three medical ways to combat depression: psychotherapy, medication, and electroconvulsive therapy, or shock treatments. But there is something that we, outside the medical community, can do to be helpful and supportive to victims of depression.

One of the important adjuncts to the medical treatment is for the victim to rediscover hope. In fact, the writer of Psalm 42 found enormous emotional release in crying out: "Hope in God." Hope is a central Jewish value. Therefore, close friends and family members of the victim need to encourage the sufferer to be hopeful. They should persuade him or her that life is basically worthwhile, that it is good to be alive.

Styron was fortunate. He conquered his depression and regained his capacity for serenity and joy. He concludes by saying that this blessing alone may be reward enough for having endured this despair beyond despair.

The Need to Change within Marriage

Philosopher and longshoreman Eric Hoffer once observed that, with every change, we die a little. In life, we need certain places and institutions to remain the same, because we have learned to negotiate and deal with them. We have mastered a certain vocabulary to do so. We have acquired the tools to respond to the various stimuli that are present. When these are altered, we feel out of control and unable to cope.

Perhaps this is the appeal of fundamentalist religions, which keep sacred doctrines and rituals the same for centuries. These religions enable their followers to know exactly what is expected of them, to gain a feeling of assurance and security, and to remain in control of their lives.

Sometimes change involves a loss of ego, as well. For many years, we might have championed a particular idea or cause. When the idea becomes dated or even discredited, we feel a loss of face. I remember visiting a moshav on my first trip to Israel in the early 1960s, when I was a rabbinical student. The founders of the moshav were driven by the pioneering spirit of working the land and living simply and frugally.

One elder moshavnik told me how distressed he was that members of the moshav were now buying refrigerators, which to him were unnecessary luxuries. For years, he had advocated the use of old-fashioned iceboxes and other trappings of a simpler lifestyle which had become out-of-date. I am sure he felt diminished by this development.

Yet, change, even with its risks and challenges, is necessary for our personal spiritual and emotional growth. If we do not change, we stagnate. We become irrelevant. Once we do change, however, others need to accept what we have become and not try to force us to retreat to our former selves. In fact, the ancient Rabbis warn us against reminding a *Ba'al Teshuvah*, a person who has improved himself or herself, about the less worthy character traits in his or her past.

The institution in our lives that illustrates the phenomenon of change most vividly is marriage. Marriage ideally passes through three stages. In Stage 1, passion dominates. When couples first meet, begin to date, and then later, become an "item," they are head-over-heels in love. Romance and rhapsody charge their lives with passion. Physical desire is intense. The couple is euphoric. There may be glaring, irreconcilable differences between the couple. Yet they tend to gloss over them at this first stage.

There is an insightful Yiddish admonition that instructs us to keep our eyes wide open before marriage and our eyes half closed after marriage. Unfortunately, most couples do the very opposite. They keep their eyes half closed before marriage and wide open after marriage. They ignore any troubling issues before marriage. However, once the wedding and honeymoon period end, they focus intently on those irritants and impediments in their relationship they previously overlooked.

This is Stage 2, when sobriety and reality take over. Differences in personalities, habits, values, and perspectives assume center stage, when previously they were hiding in the wings. Now we hear the complaint: "This isn't the same person I married." Husbands and wives discover that the life's partner each has chosen is sorely lacking in certain ways. Conflicts and disagreements sometimes erupt at this stage. Physical passion begins to wane.

In this second stage, husbands and wives begin to try to change each other. Each attempts to win the other to his or her way of doing things, whether it is practicing religion, spending money, dressing, or raising children.

If the couple can eventually forego trying to alter the

other in their relationship, they can finally enter Stage 3. Here the challenge is not to change the other, but rather accept the other as he or she has changed.

How this stage is negotiated is critical to the ultimate success of the marriage. We know that all husbands and wives change in the course of a marriage. In fact, there is an ancient rabbinic legend that tells us that, since no other officiant was available at the marriage of Adam and Eve, God alone conducted their wedding ceremony.

However, instead of using only one *huppah*, one marriage canopy, God erected ten *huppot*, ten marriage canopies. Why ten? Because if a couple is fortunate, the bride and groom will be married at least ten different times, but always to the same person. The Rabbis emphasize in this legend that a marriage is a work in progress.

The goals and aspirations of a husband and wife can never remain static because their life's circumstances keep changing. The addition of children, the search for different jobs, the building or purchasing of new homes, the reality of the empty nest, the time of retirement all impact the evolution of marriages.

Here the husband and wife have accepted the fact that they are not married to the same person they met when they first began to date. Each one has evolved into someone else. At the same time, each has at last grasped the fact that he or she cannot change or mold the other, according to his or her design. To do so would mean stepping over necessary, appropriate boundaries.

In this stage, they can finally harvest the ripe fruits of their marital partnership. Here they can appreciate and rejoice in each other's changes and not feel threatened or diminished by them. Here they can feel an inner glow in their stunning accomplishment that they have grown together, healthily and positively, without coercion on either side. The humorist Sam Levenson put it well when he said: "Happy marriages begin when we marry the one we love. Marriages blossom when we love the one we married."

By looking at the dynamics of marriage, we can derive several lessons about change. First, change is a necessary part of human growth and development. Second, we cannot, nor should not, mold or shape a person according to our own blueprint. Third, we need to allow a person to change according to his or her own inner needs, drives and values, and accept that person as he or she has become.

The American poet Carl Sandburg eloquently describes this positive strategy of confronting change. Here he envisions an individual speaking to his beloved and saying:

> I love you for what you are, but I love you yet more for what you are going to be ... Not always shall you be what you are now. You are going forward toward something great. I am on the way with you and therefore I love you.

Being Fully Present

Shortly after 6:00 one evening, I left my office to drive to dinner at a nearby restaurant. I knew that I didn't have much time, because I had to return by 7:00 for the first rehearsal of our Temple's Confirmation class for its annual festival service. I stopped my car momentarily at a busy intersection.

However, my mind was focused on scores of Confirmation details and not on my driving. Without looking carefully in both directions, I mindlessly pulled out of the intersection. Suddenly, I felt a pickup truck crashing into the left side of my car.

Fortunately, no one was injured in this collision. Yet my car was beyond repair, and it was declared a total loss. Because this was not my first episode of mindless driving, my insurance company decided not to renew my policy. Consequently, I had to find other coverage with a premium that cost me three times as much.

As a result of my decades-old habit of mental wool gathering at the wheel, I resolved to be a more alert and careful driver and hope that I am succeeding. I admit that it is not easy to break old, well-established unhealthy habits. Now I try to keep both hands on the wheel at all times, to be extra cautious at intersections, and to focus my mind solely on driving and not every other imaginable distraction!

My inattentive driving is just one illustration of the myriad times I have not been focused on the task at hand, that I have been daydreaming and not fully present. I assume I am not alone in this tendency.

The *New York Times* featured an article about Dr. Ellen Langer, Professor of Psychology at Harvard. She is called the

"Scholar of the Absent Mind." Though very mindful herself, she studies the psychic and physiological dynamics of mindlessness.

Sometimes, mindlessness leads to even more serious consequences than my own collision. A story is told about Dr. Martin Buber, the famed Jewish philosopher. After leaving Germany, Buber had become a faculty member at the Hebrew University in Jerusalem. One day, while Buber was deeply immersed in mystical ruminations, a despondent friend came to him to pour out his heartache and anguish. Buber, however, was not fully present. He was listening only half-heartedly, as he was eager to return to his esoteric speculations that he deemed to be more important. Unfortunately, his friend left the conversation with his troubles intact, and the next day he committed suicide.

Some claim that this tragedy led Buber to develop his famous I-Thou philosophy of dialogue. In the I-Thou relationship, I bring everything that I am and everything that I have into my relationship with you. In our meeting, you confront all of me and I do the same. We are fully present to each other.

However, often we relate to others in an I-It fashion. Here the other person becomes an object, whom I can manipulate. In this situation, I do not relate fully to that person and am not completely present in that encounter.

In fact, the watchword of the Jewish faith begins with the call to pay attention: "*Shema Yisrael*—Hear, listen, O people Israel!" In anticipation of the Jewish High Holy Days, Rabbis Harold Kushner and Jack Riemer, some years ago, penned an insightful commentary on this injunction to listen:

> Judaism begins with the commandment: Hear, O Israel, but what does it really mean to hear?
> The persons who attend a concert with their minds on business, hear—but do not really hear.
> The persons who listen to the words of their friends or their spouse or their children and do not catch the note of

urgency: "Notice me, help me, care about me," hear—but do not really hear.

The persons who listen to the news and think only of how it will affect the stock market, hear—but do not really hear.

The persons who stifle the sound of their conscience and tell themselves they have done enough already, hear—but do not really hear.

The persons who listen to the rabbi's sermon and think that someone else is being addressed, hear—but do not really hear.

The persons who hear the Shofar sound and do not feel the need to change their ways, hear—but do not really hear.

As the New Year begins, O Lord, strengthen our ability to hear.

May we hear the music of the world, and the infant's cry, and the lover's sigh.

May we hear the call for help of the lonely soul, and the sound of the breaking heart.

May we hear the words of our friends, and also their unspoken pleas and dreams.

May we hear within ourselves the yearnings, that are struggling for expression.

May we hear You, O God, for only if we hear You do we have the right to hope that You will hear us.

Hear the promises we make to You this day, O God—and may we hear them, too.

The ancient Rabbis spoke about *kavvanah*. *Kavvanah* means focused attention and concentration. Rabbi Rami Shapiro offers a charming, modern approach to *kavvanah*. Rabbi Shapiro writes that he prefers to wash dishes by hand, rather than use a dishwasher. He loves the warmth of the water on his hands. He enjoys the sensation of the soap film guiding the brush over the dishes and the squeaky clean feel of a just-rinsed glass or plate.

Rabbi Shapiro does not hurry when washing dishes. He does not worry that someone will soon dirty the dishes that he just washed. He feels no past or future in washing. It is just the art of washing itself that dominates his mind and heart. He tries to push aside all extraneous thoughts and distractions and sense the wonder of an everyday activity through staying focused. He realizes that, at that moment, neither the past nor the future can make any real difference.

Another writer similarly admonishes: "Quit rehashing the past. Do not worry about the future. Instead, be in the present where aliveness lives." Indeed, mundane acts like washing dishes can help to train us to be present in the more consequential and significant tasks of life.

My wife, Lynn, and I once visited the Santa Katerina Monastery near Mt. Sinai, where the Torah, according to Jewish tradition, was given to the Jewish people. On the grounds of the monastery we saw a remnant of the Burning Bush. In the Book of Exodus, the Bush represents a miracle. The Bush contained a flame which, in that intensely hot desert climate, did not consume the Bush. The fact the fire did not destroy the Bush defied all scientific laws.

Many of Moses' contemporaries probably passed by the Bush and paid no attention to this miracle. The Rabbis tell us that, by contrast, Moses alone turned around and looked at it carefully. Because he was not otherwise mentally preoccupied at that moment and because he stayed focused on the Bush, God rewarded him. God made him the liberator of the Jewish people from Egyptian slavery.

Several years ago, the famed classical guitarist Andres Segovia was asked about the secret of his performance technique. Segovia answered: "I must be present for every note." What a stunning strategy to apply to all areas of life!

II

Moral and Ethical Issues

Old and New Controversies over the Ten Commandments

The Kerrville, Texas School Board, in 2002, in a vote of 4-3, refused the gift of a display case, housing historical documents. The reason is that one of those documents was the Ten Commandments. The trustees feared a lawsuit over the possible violation of the separation of church and state. They also were suspicious about the source of the gift. It came from Rev. Joseph Fegenbush, of Faith Christian Church. Fegenbush, a fundamentalist preacher, had tried unsuccessfully, during the previous month, to restore organized prayer on school campuses.

One would think that the Ten Commandments would not create all that much controversy. After all, it is a moral code that almost all civilized people can embrace. It offers wise and sound guidance for good behavior. It seems to be as benign and inoffensive as "Motherhood and Apple Pie." However, though its rules for conduct seem safe and reasonable, the Ten Commandments is essentially a religious document. As such, it has no place in public buildings. In fact, if exhibiting the Ten Commandments were allowed, it would ignite a whole debate over which text to display.

The Ten Commandments is found twice in the Bible, once in Exodus and then again in Deuteronomy, in a slightly altered form. In fact, religious people who endorse the Ten Commandments cannot even agree on how to number them. The verse, "You shall have no other gods before me," is the second Commandment in the Jewish version, but the first Commandment in the Christian version. Furthermore, in some editions, the commandment, "You shall not murder" is translated incorrectly as "You shall not kill." Should we who are purists tolerate showing a text of the Ten Commandments with that mistake?

Disputes over the Ten Commandments are not new. Today, the problem with posting them in public schools and other government facilities centers on the church-state issue. However, our Jewish forebears had their own challenges with the Ten Commandments hundreds of years ago. Their concern was whether or not to recite them during a worship service. In the ancient Temple in Jerusalem, the Ten Commandments was always proclaimed before the *Shema*. Strangely enough, however, outside the Temple, the practice was banned. What was the problem?

It is revealed in a charming story about an astronomer and a theologian who were flying next to each other on an airplane. The astronomer smugly turned to his seatmate and said: "You know, there is no need for all those millions of volumes of religious literature. The whole essence of religion can be summed up in one simple phrase: 'Love thy neighbor, as thyself,'" whereupon the theologian retorted, "And the whole science of astronomy can be summed up in the simple phrase, 'Twinkle, twinkle, little star.'" In this charming dialogue, we see clearly the human tendency to reduce very complex ideas to simple, pithy slogans. Such is the reason for the popularity of bumper stickers.

When the Temple was still in operation in Jerusalem, some heretics were demonstrating that same phenomenon. They were claiming that the only part of the Torah that God revealed was the Ten Commandments. It alone constitutes the essence of religion. Nothing else is important. The laws and traditions in the rest of the Torah are all superfluous. The Jewish religious authorities feared that allowing the Ten Commandments to be recited throughout the Holy Land might reinforce the perception that Judaism consists of nothing more than the Ten Commandments.

When the Temple was destroyed 2,000 years ago, the synagogue replaced the Temple as the dominant public institution of Jewish prayer. However, the Ten Commandments never became part of the synagogue service, except on three occasions: when the Exodus version is part of the assigned Torah reading; when the Deuteronomy version is part of the assigned Torah reading; and when the holiday of Shavuot occurs. Shavuot recalls the moment when God gave the Torah to the Jewish people on Mt. Sinai.

Some Reform congregations in North America and Great Britain, at one time, did include the recitation of the Ten Commandments in every Shabbat service. Some Reform rabbis even revived the claim that only the Ten Commandments were given at Mt. Sinai and need to be followed in every generation. The rest of the Torah, including the laws about holiday observance, was given only for a particular time and place and is not essential or binding.

Some Reform Jews, even today, will argue that to be a religious Jew means to follow the Ten Commandments and nothing else. They will further insist that attending services, offering the Shabbat Kiddush and fasting on Yom Kippur are of little consequence. In other words, ethics, not ritual, is what Judaism is really about. However, as important as leading the good life is, ethics is only one component of Jewish responsibilities. There is so much more. Another Jewish duty is study. Still another is prayer. Still another is support of the State of Israel. Judaism is a multi-dimensional enterprise.

On the festival of Shavuot, recalling the time of the giving of the Torah, Temple Beth-El in San Antonio and numerous other Reform congregations hold their Confirmation ceremonies. This scheduling is done to illustrate that just as our forebears on Mt. Sinai accepted the Torah 4,000 years ago, so, too, do these young people receive the Torah and repeat the same pledge, "*Na'aseh v'nishma*—We will do and we will obey." At a key moment in the Confirmation ritual, two or three members of the class unroll the Torah scroll and read each of the Ten Commandments in Hebrew. After each, the rest of the class, now standing, responds with the English translation.

Toward the end of the service, the Confirmands offer a group prayer. In it, they outline a broad comprehensive program for living a full Jewish life. It includes the ethics of the Ten Commandments but also goes well beyond those ethics. They say:

> Our mission is nurturing our families and serving our congregations.
> Visiting the sick and comforting the bereaved.
> Feeding the hungry and helping the needy.
> Welcoming the stranger and becoming the friend.
> Lighting Shabbat candles and brightening the world.
> Practicing our faith and sharing our faith.
> Learning Torah and living Torah.

How succinctly our Confirmands tell us, in this prayerful utterance, that our goal is not merely to be a good Jew; it is rather to be a total Jew.

Separating Conjoined Twins:
An Ethical Dilemma

When visiting circuses as a child, I vividly remember the side shows. Often they were insensitively called "Freak Shows." Siamese or conjoined twins and others with gross physical abnormalities would perform at these shows for the sick amusement of the spectators. Many would cruelly refer to these twins as "monstrous births." In the past, the most that Siamese twins could hope to achieve in life was to become stars in a circus side show, or in a vaudeville theatre.

The name "Siamese" emerged after the birth of Chang and Eng. These were conjoined twins born in Siam, now called Thailand, in 1811. A small band of flesh connected them at their lower chest. Through this band, their livers were bound together.

Chang and Eng came to the United States for a short time when they were eighteen. Then they left for England to go on exhibition as "Siamese Double Boys." Here, they performed acrobatics and showed the audiences the connecting band of flesh. They were a tremendous hit.

However, immigration authorities denied them entrance into France. They irrationally feared that pregnant women who saw them would bear children with similar deformities. Superstitions about these Siamese twins abounded. Some claimed that their birth resulted from God's anger or from the Devil's influence.

When they were twenty-one, they returned to the United States and settled in a small town in North Carolina, where they became farmers. Eventually, they married two sisters and together they fathered twenty-one children. Throughout their lives, different medical experts toyed with the idea of separating them surgically, but none ever attempted such a daring operation.

In their fifties, for a short time, they returned to the entertainment field, where they worked for the famed circus showman P. T. Barnum. Eventually they resumed their life in North Carolina. Eng, at age sixty-three, awakened in the middle of the night and realized that Chang was dead. Eng died a few hours later.

In the twentieth century, the most famous conjoined twins were Violet and Daisy Hilton. They were born to an unmarried mother, who quickly sold them to a local midwife. Their guardian, Mary Hilton, held them captive for nearly twenty years and forced them into show business. They dramatically escaped from this confining life and went to court to gain their freedom. Violet and Daisy at last became independent.

Now, free to be on their own, they flourished in their career. They performed in the film "Freaks" in 1932. Some years later, they starred in a movie titled "Chained for Life." This is a gruesome tale in which one of the sisters was accused of murder. The debate raged around whether or not it was fair to send her to jail if her innocent sister had to go, as well.

Both sisters married unsuccessfully. By 1960 their careers were over. Like Chang and Eng a century before, they spent their last years in North Carolina, where they worked as checkout clerks in a local grocery store. Both died in 1969 from complications of influenza.

Since the Hiltons, we heard very little about the phenomenon of conjoined twins, until the summer of 2000. Jodie and Mary, which are not their actual names, were born on August 8, as conjoined twins in Manchester, England. Their parents are devout Roman Catholics. They had come to England for treatment from a remote Mediterranean island.

The twins were fused at the abdomen. Their arms and legs were at 90-degree angles to their upper bodies. Only

Jodie had lungs. They shared one heart, which was forced to bring oxygen to both.

The doctors concluded that if they were not separated, they could live a maximum of six months. However, if they were separated, only Jodie would live and Mary would die. They shared a common aorta. With it, Jodie's heart pumped oxygenated blood through Mary's body, since Mary's organs were not able to sustain life.

The fact is that Jodie was keeping Mary alive. Mary was exerting a huge strain on Jodie. If this state of affairs would continue, it would cause Jodie's death and Mary would die soon thereafter. The question before the medical, legal and theological experts of England was: "Can surgery be performed to sustain and save Jodie's life, while allowing Mary to die?"

Their parents would not consent to the operation. Both twins were equal in their eyes and both were deserving of love. They insisted that God willed them to be born the way they were and God would determine the span of their lives. However, the authorities of St. Mary's Hospital wanted to act in the best interests of the viable child. Therefore, they took the case to court to override the parents' decision. The parents did not contest the ruling. But, the moral dilemma still haunts us: "Can one accelerate the death of one person to save another?"

The judges produced 130 single-spaced pages of judgments in this case. They first dealt with the matter of whether Jodie and Mary constituted one human being or two, since they had only one heart. They concluded that they were two individuals, both of whom were of inestimable value and worth.

Secondly, they decided that Jodie was acting as a life support system for Mary, since Mary was incapable of an independent existence. Therefore, separating the twins was equivalent to pulling the plug. It was letting the person die naturally, without administering any heroic means.

They also believed that Jodie's doing the work of two

posed a severe burden on her. If she continued, she would eventually suffer cardiac arrest. Jodie had a chance to live a normal productive life, though with some slight possible disabilities. It was actually Jodie's welfare that was the determining factor in the judicial decision to separate them.

In early November, a team of surgeons, in a twenty-hour operation, operated on the conjoined twins. As expected, Mary died, but Jodie survived. Doctors reported that Jodie would probably need further surgery to reconstruct some organs that were damaged in the surgery, as well as some skin grafts.

To my knowledge, Jewish legal authorities have never confronted the question of conjoined twins. Though the Jewish legal literature does not contain any information about conjoined twins, it has dealt with similar cases, with two conflicting opinions. On the one hand, Jewish tradition maintains that all life is equal. In the Talmud, the Rabbis do so by asking the bold question: "Whose blood is redder than whose?" Therefore, we can do nothing.

On the other hand, it has become an established principle of Jewish medical ethics that one may allocate limited life-saving resources where it will bring the greatest medical benefit. We are commanded to save life. Therefore, we should apportion those resources first to the twin who has the better chance of being saved. Thus, if one twin is more likely to survive the operation in good health than the other, then that is the twin we must favor.

In addition, Jewish tradition does permit what we call "passive euthanasia." We need not perform any extraordinary measures to keep alive a patient destined to die. Thus, since Jodie's body was acting as Mary's life support system, that system could be removed.

Furthermore, Mary's continued existence was draining the life out of Jodie, the healthier twin. In Jewish law, Mary could be considered a *rodef*, one who pursues another person in order to take that person's life. In self-defense, one can kill a *rodef*. On this basis, Mary's death could be justified.

As we ponder this case, let us never for a moment forget the pain and suffering that the parents of these twins have had to endure from the moment that they were born. Yet, the purpose of the operation was not to kill Mary intentionally. Rather, the reality was that her own body could not sustain life on its own. Furthermore, this operation gave Jodie a reasonable chance of a long and normal life. It is hoped that the parents will now be granted the joy of seeing Jodie grow and mature, into early adulthood and possibly beyond.

Boy Scouts and Homosexuality

In 1998, two roofers left a bar in Laramie, Wyoming, with Matthew Sheppard, a twenty-one-year-old gay college student. Physically small, Sheppard was a personable, well-groomed young man. The two roofers took him to the edge of town, where they robbed and pistol-whipped him and left him tethered to a fence. Tragically, Sheppard died five days later.

The national response to this vicious hate crime was swift and horrified. Yet it revealed the bitter reality that too many people still hold a deep-seated revulsion against homosexuals, especially gay men. The causes of this abhorrence are complex. I believe that one reason for this pathological animosity to gays is that people erroneously assume that a homosexual is a perverted child molester. The truth is that a homosexual is no more likely to abuse children sexually than a heterosexual.

Numerous national religious bodies are now struggling with whether or not to include gays as ecclesiastical leaders. This issue is tearing mainline Protestant denominations asunder. Presbyterian, Episcopal, and Methodist church bodies, in particular, are locked in controversy about whether or not to permit ordaining homosexual clergy and officiating at same-sex unions.

By contrast, the institutions of American Reform Judaism have unabashedly supported gays in every arena of religious life. As far back as 1977, the Union of American Hebrew Congregations opposed all forms of discrimination against gay and lesbian persons. Ten years later, the Union adopted a strong resolution affirming that one's sexual orientation should not be a consideration for membership or participation in the activities of any affiliated Reform congregation.

Then three years later, in 1990, the Central Conference of American Rabbis, the official international association of Reform rabbis, with almost 1,700 members, approved the ordination of openly gay rabbis. In 2002, this same rabbinical body went on record endorsing the prerogative of rabbis who choose to solemnize unions between two Jews of the same sex, who are in a committed relationship.

Reform leaders adopted these revolutionary decisions after grappling with the age-old prohibitions of the Torah against sexual relations between two males. Lesbian relationships are generally not discussed in Jewish sacred texts, incidentally. Those who cite the Bible to object to gay unions ignore the fact that these same texts also prescribe stoning people who kindle fire on Shabbat. They also condone slavery and treat women as domestic property.

We do look to our Torah as our chief source of moral guidance and inspiration. Yet we recognize that its authors lived in a pre-scientific age in which males and females were not considered equal. Those who crafted these texts never conceived of the possibility of two men or two women who live together in a loving, monogamous relationship.

Even the American Psychiatric Association has roundly rejected its previously negative stance towards homosexuality. At one time, the APA regarded it as a behavioral aberration practiced by deviant individuals. Now these mental health professionals understand that homosexuality is not a behavioral choice. They emphasize that such is the way people are born and that homosexuals are just as emotionally normal as heterosexuals are.

Yet, many people still feel threatened by homosexuality and would like to banish gays and lesbians from their midst. Perhaps this mentality led to the decision of the Boy Scouts of America to forbid a gay man from becoming a scoutmaster. The case of James Dale, in New Jersey, has become a cause célèbre. At the age of eight, Dale joined the Boy Scouts and eventually attained the rank of Eagle Scout. When he became eighteen, he assumed an assistant scoutmaster position.

Upon entering Rutgers University, he got in touch with his gay sexual orientation and joined the university's Lesbian Gay Alliance. When leaders of his local Boy Scout council learned of his "coming out," they instantly revoked his membership. They advised him that the Boy Scouts "specifically forbids membership to homosexuals."

Dale soon brought a lawsuit against the Scouts. The New Jersey Supreme Court heard the case and ruled that the Boy Scouts was a public accommodation. Therefore, it could not legally deny membership to gays under the state's non-discrimination statute.

However, on June 28, 2001, in a 5-4 decision, our United States Supreme Court reversed the New Jersey Supreme Court's ruling. The majority argued that this is a matter of our constitutionally guaranteed freedom of association. We have the right to form private clubs to promote our own points of view and to exclude people who don't conform to those views.

After all, even a synagogue can legally deny the presidency to one who is not Jewish. It can also forbid women, if it so chooses, to be called to the Torah or to be counted in the *minyan*, the required quorum of ten for public worship.

Furthermore, organizations like the Boy Scouts receive no public funds. Thus they can set rules for leadership that reflect their own particular belief system. Boy Scout officials argue that an avowed homosexual is not a proper role model for the values expressed in the Scout Oath.

However, I embrace an opposing point of view. I agree that any club or organization can establish its own criteria for leadership and membership. However, the real question is: Can we support an organization that blatantly excludes people on the basis of their religion, race, ethnicity, or sexual orientation? The obvious answer is no.

But this response becomes particularly painful when we apply it to the Boy Scouts. We all recognize that the Boy

Scouts has, for decades, exerted a most positive favorable influence on the character and citizenship of young men. It imparts to adolescents important lessons for wholesome human development.

Yet, the Boy Scout policy is discriminatory. It has set off a firestorm of protests among previously passionate champions of the Boy Scouts. It boils down to an issue of human rights. Many former Eagle Scouts, including Rabbi Paul Menitoff, the Executive Vice-President of the Central Conference of American Rabbis, have returned their badges to Boy Scout headquarters in Texas.

Some Reform Temples have evicted the troops that they have sponsored for decades from their premises. Rabbi Steven Foster, senior rabbi of Temple Emanuel in Denver, the largest Jewish congregation in that city, with almost 2,000 families, is a former Eagle Scout. Not only did he return his badges, but, with the support of his Temple Board of Trustees, told the leaders of Troop 37, which Temple Emanuel had hosted for forty years, that they could no longer meet in the Temple. He stressed that the membership policies of the Boy Scouts of America are contrary "to all that he holds dear and true."

Opposition has spread to the wider community, as well. United Way agencies give millions of dollars nationally to the Boy Scouts of America. Now, a growing number of United Way Chapters have greatly reduced or eliminated their financial support of Boy Scouts. Paradoxically, one of these is the United Way in Evanston, Illinois, the city which was the national headquarters of the Woman's Christian Temperance Union.

How, then, should we react to this Boy Scout ban against homosexual leaders? Scout parents and leaders should direct messages of protest to Boy Scout officials to have this policy overturned. I would not suggest that congregations which sponsor Boy Scout troops evict them. Rather, I would suggest that they notify the Boy Scouts of America that they would permit a homosexual to become a Boy Scout troop leader, even though it contravenes national policy. Then, if the Boy Scouts of America forbids them to continue sponsorship under these conditions, so be it.

In this connection, rabbis face two sensitive situations. Often rabbis are asked to write references for those who aspire to the rank of Eagle Scout. In my own case, I will continue to do so, but will now include a paragraph strongly objecting to Boy Scout policies against homosexuals. Today we would consider them contrary to the will of God.

A more delicate situation arises when rabbis are asked to offer an invocation or benediction at a ceremony when one of the young men of their congregation becomes an Eagle Scout. This is far from a black-and-white situation. On the one hand, they want to share their pride with this young man and his family over this monumental achievement in his young life and not mar the joy of the occasion. On the other hand, many will feel impelled to register their strenuous objection to this policy of exclusion.

In short, I believe that all of us need to articulate our own fierce opposition to this national Boy Scout policy. We must convince its leaders that this policy is not, in the words of the Scout Oath, "morally straight."

Ethical Uses of Money

Someone once observed that if we want to know about a person's values and ideals, we should examine the stubs in his or her checkbook. What a profound observation! Indeed, the way we spend our money is proof of what we believe and hold dear. Some narcissistic people who are affluent squander their money in self-indulgent pursuits—lavish entertainment, luxury cars, expensive restaurants, and deluxe travel. Yet these same people often give paltry sums to philanthropic causes. Their money is used solely to heighten their own pleasure and enjoyment. Others, who are less wealthy, often deprive themselves of luxuries in order to contribute, well beyond their means, to charitable purposes.

Judaism does not condemn the accumulation of money. It does not consider poverty a virtue. Unlike some other religions, Judaism does not ask its adherents to take vows to impair their financial well-being. In fact, Maimonides reminds us that if a once wealthy person becomes impoverished, others must help that person to attain the high status that he or she enjoyed before the financial reverses struck.

However, one should never convert money into a god nor allow it to become the chief object of one's adoration. Comedian Jack Benny used to perform a humorous, but revealing, routine. A robber would seize Benny and put a pistol to his back. The gunman would then say, "Your money or your life!" Benny would slowly respond, "I'm thinking, I'm thinking."

Jewish tradition sees money in a radically different way. It is a loan from God. We are just stewards, and not masters, of whatever we possess. God allows us to use money primarily as a way to do good and to avoid evil. We believe that God actually owns all of our money. We borrow it from God in order to spend it responsibly and caringly.

The Hebrew term *tzedakah* does not mean charity. Charity is voluntary. *Tzedakah* means justice. We Jews are *required* to give. *Tzedakah* is not a choice but a mandate. Jewish tradition requires one to give a minimum of 10% and a maximum of 20% for *tzedakah*. Judaism is realistic in setting the cap at 20%. No one should become excessively philanthropic. If we deny ourselves the necessities in life, we may eventually become dependent on others to help us.

Besides giving *tzedakah*, many investors are beginning to build their portfolios with ethical values. They refuse to hold stocks in corporations that are not socially responsible. Many Jews, for example, will not invest in companies that participate in Arab boycotts of Israel, pollute the environment, or torture animals.

These conscientious Jews, on the other hand, want to support those companies that advance human welfare. Arnold Hiatt, former CEO of the Stride Rite Corp., is chairman of Business for Social Responsibility. He asserted that one cannot separate the company's well being from the community's. Hiatt said, "If we're not providing the community with access to day care and elder care, if we're not providing proper funding for education, then we're not investing properly in our business."

Some ethically conscious Jewish investors, however, do have legitimate differences of opinion about other businesses. Some, for example, avoid buying stock in nuclear power companies. Yet, in the early 1990s, the National Jewish Community Relations Advisory Council (now called Jewish Council for Public Affairs), representing the broadest coalition of national, secular and religious organizations within the Jewish community, disagreed.

It endorsed companies that develop nuclear energy. It did so because of the fear of our country's becoming dependent on oil-producing Arab nations. Only the organizations of the

Reform movement and the National Council of Jewish Women dissented from this position of the National Jewish Community Relations Advisory Council. Obviously, this is one of those complex issues on which conscientious, ethically motivated people can reach opposite conclusions.

Yes, the amount we spend on ourselves, the sums that we give for *tzedakah*, and the ways we invest our money provide the evidence about who we are as people. According to Jewish tradition, an individual should view money as a means to serve God. In Deuteronomy, we read that we should love God "with all your heart, with all your soul, and with all your might." Tradition interprets the words "with all your might" to mean "with all your money." Our real challenge is to love God with our money, so that we spend our money in ways which we believe that God would wholeheartedly endorse.

Is a White Lie Ever Justified?

There was a rabbi, famed for his learning and his wit. Once his students asked him why he so often illustrated a concept by telling a story. He said: "I can best explain that through a story, a parable about Parable itself.

"There was a time when Truth went among people unadorned, as naked as his name. And whoever saw Truth turned away, in fear or in shame, and refused to welcome Truth. So Truth wandered through the lands of the earth rebuffed and unwanted.

"One day, very sad, Truth met Parable. Parable was strolling along happily in a handsome many-colored garb. Parable asked him cheerfully: 'Truth, why do you seem so sad?'

"Truth replied: 'Because I am so old and ugly that all people avoid me.'

"'Nonsense,' laughed Parable. 'That is not why people avoid you. Here, borrow some of my clothes, and see what happens.'

"So Truth dons some of Parable's lovely garments and, lo, everywhere he went, he was welcomed."

The rabbi smiled and said: "For the fact is that people cannot face Truth naked; they much prefer Truth disguised."

We know that people do not like the unembellished and unvarnished truth. Harry Truman once said: "I never give them hell. I tell them the truth and they think it's hell." Because people find truth difficult and painful, they often resort to telling a "white lie." A white lie is an untruth or partial truth which has no evil intent.

There are several reasons for telling a white lie. One is to spare the feelings and sensibilities of one to whom it is told. In this sense, the white lie is a charitable act. For many generations, numerous parents tended to shield and protect their children from harsh realities. Thus they would tell their children white lies, especially about matters of sex, illness, and death.

Then, too, we tell white lies to avoid revealing something highly personal and confidential. Furthermore, we resort to a white lie to promote harmony and good will between people. If we would tell them the truth, a rupture could occur in our human relationships.

Normative Judaism seems to condone the white lie. There is a *baraita* which says that lies are forbidden, unless they are spoken to make peace.

In our Bible is a striking example of a white lie. It is told by God, Himself, in the Genesis account of Abraham and Sarah. After Sarah had become ninety years old, an angel visited her. The angel predicted that Sarah would become pregnant for the first time and give birth to a son.

Sarah laughed within herself and said: "After I am withered, can I have pleasure, my husband being old also?" (Gen. 18:12). When God reported Sarah's reaction to Abraham, God edited Sarah's words. Here is what God quoted in Sarah's name: "Shall I surely bear a child, seeing that I am old?" Note that there is no reference to Sarah's mentioning Abraham's advanced years. God omitted the last part in which she called her husband old in order to preserve their domestic tranquility and happiness.

The Rabbis tell us that scholars should always tell the truth. Yet they can tell white lies in three situations: regarding their learning, their marital relations, and their hospitality. A modest scholar who knows the Mishnah thoroughly can say that he is unfamiliar with a particular Mishnaic tractate in order not to flaunt his knowledge. In addition, if any scholar is asked intimate and personal details about his married life, he need not answer truthfully.

Furthermore, a man who has been treated well by his host

may decide not to tell the truth about the gracious hospitality he received. He may fear that, as a result of his praise, his host would be deluged by hordes of unwelcome guests.

There are two instances in Jewish law, when the white lie is not only allowed but is actually mandated. Jewish tradition enjoins us not to tell a seriously ill patient about his or her critical medical condition. Instead, we should minimize the actual danger. We should stress the positive aspects of his or her health. We should encourage that stricken individual to become optimistic and to fight for recovery.

In addition, in a funeral eulogy, the preacher is not ordered to cite merits that the deceased never had. However, the preacher is expected to exaggerate and magnify the virtues the deceased person did have in order to give maximum comfort and solace to the mourners.

One group of rabbis, however, was strenuously opposed to the white lie. This was the School of Shammai. The School of Shammai was constantly in dispute with the School of Hillel about the white lie and a host of other legal issues.

The Schools of Hillel and Shammai debated the proper words that one should sing at a wedding while dancing around the bride. The School of Hillel maintained that, regardless of how unattractive the bride may be, one should say that she is "beautiful and gracious." The School of Shammai disagreed and argued that "one must describe her as she is. To say otherwise would be to lie, which is forbidden in the Torah."

The School of Hillel responded to the School of Shammai. They asked that if, in the opinion of Shammai, someone made an unwise purchase in the marketplace, would they try to make that person feel good about it or would they stress the mistake? The School of Hillel insisted that we must sympathize with a person's condition and feelings, especially when something is a *fait accompli*. How much the more so at a wedding, when the marriage is already official and when the love of the groom for the bride is at stake, should people offer every encouragement, even by distorting the truth.

The School of Hillel, in this Talmudic account, seemed to have the last word on the subject of the white lie at a wedding. However, I tend to be inclined to Shammai's position on truth telling. White lies, it is true, do spare feelings. They do promote harmony. They do protect one's secrets, but *only* for a short while. The long-term effects of the white lie are not beneficial, however.

The person who tells a white lie loses credibility when the real truth is revealed. Eventually, people will come to lack faith and trust in the white liar. Furthermore, in the case of children, the white lie does not prepare them for the real world. Children will grow up with some fantasies which will prove harmful. I know of cases of parents who told their children that they never disagreed with each other about anything. They managed to argue behind closed doors and never in front of their children. When their children grew up and got married, they were unprepared for any unpleasantness in the marriage relationship. They were ready to walk out of their own marriages, after their first argument with their spouses. I am pleased to see that mental health professionals are now advising their clients to avoid the white lie.

Parents no longer tell their children that a stork brought them into the world. Many are candid and frank in relating the reproductive details which lead to childbirth. They also do not tell their sons and daughters that grandpa, who recently died, just went away. They realize that when the child later discovers that the deceased grandpa will never return, the child will become shaken.

Most physicians now insist on divulging to the terminal patient his or her actual grim prognosis rather than camouflaging and disguising the discouraging facts, as was the case in former years.

White lies are ultimately destructive. One can tell the truth without being brutal, callous, and insensitive. The goal, in my judgment, is to tell the truth as it is, directly, but kindly. We can dress up the truth. However, we should not amend or misrepresent the truth.

What the O. J. Simpson Case Taught Us about Ourselves

The handsome and charismatic O. J. Simpson had been not only a famous football player. He was also a television promoter of Hertz car rentals, an occasional movie star, and a sportscaster on NFL telecasts. In 1994, he stood trial for the brutal murder of his ex-wife, Nicole Brown Simpson, and her friend, Ronald Goldman, in front of her condo in Brentwood, California. However, not enough evidence could be marshaled to convict him.

The case of O. J. Simpson became the sensational media circus of the year. Even people who rarely followed the news knew the names of the judge, the defense attorney, and many of the other principals in this trial. We need to ask ourselves why this trial became such a fascination for us. What deeper chords did this crime touch within us?

First of all, we worried that this trial would be fair and just. A famous and popular black man was accused of killing a white woman and a white man. To many Americans, the stereotyped criminal is the black man. Too often, the African-American male is unfairly regarded as the drive-by shooter, the dope dealer, the sex fiend, and the rapist. In fact, *Time* magazine, when featuring O. J. on its cover, shortly after the murder, portrayed him with much darker skin than he has. This touch-up photography reinforced this stereotype.

We also know that the death penalty is meted out more liberally to black men than to white men. A black man attacking white women seems to be the detestable exemplar of all crime. Many Americans who are prejudiced look on black men as savages who defile pure innocent white women.

Yet this case of O. J. Simpson was more complex. He is not the ordinary black man, but a celebrity and a folk hero. Thus we feared that some jurors might judge him more harshly because of his skin color, while others might judge him more leniently because of his popularity. The Torah warns us that in the courtroom, we cannot show favoritism to the mighty, on the one hand, nor to the disadvantaged, on the other. The Torah mandates: "*B'tzedek tishpot amitekha*—With equity, you shall judge your fellow."

More significantly, the O. J. Simpson trial represented a case of domestic violence. O. J. always appeared so suave and charming. Yet there was a long, sordid history of his physically abusing Nicole during and after their stormy marriage.

Down deep, we know that all of us, even the most gentle and sweet, are capable of such cruelties. Often we are shocked to learn, after a murder, that the killer appeared to his neighbors as an upright, responsible, and caring citizen.

Judaism has always recognized our propensity to violence. A century ago, two eminent philosophers reached entirely different conclusions about whether we are essentially bad or good. On the one hand, Thomas Hobbes argued that violence is our natural state. Hobbes maintained that basically we are nasty, raw, and brutish creatures. Therefore we need a strong authoritarian government to hold these impulses in check.

Jean-Jacques Rousseau strenuously disagreed. He claimed that human beings are fundamentally good and loving creatures. The changes of civilization have transformed the human being into the ferocious animal that some human beings have become.

Our Rabbis have not fully agreed either with Hobbes or with Rousseau. They identified a *yetzer tov,* a good inclination, and a *yetzer hara*, an evil inclination. They maintained that we human beings are composites of noble impulses and destructive impulses. None of us is actually good or bad. We are potentially good or potentially bad. It is up to us to choose which path to follow.

We are capable of both tenderness and caring, but also of barbarism and savagery.

Even the most laid-back among us, when we bottle up anger against employers, colleagues, spouses, or children, can explode into a fit of rage and destruction. Self-control has its limits in the best of us. A tough fact of life is that we and the inmates on death row in the state penitentiary in Huntsville, Texas, are not that different in our basic natures. William Blake described this phenomenon in his poem from "The Poison Tree":

> I was angry with my friend.
> I told my wrath, my wrath did end.
> I was angry with my foe:
> I told it not, my wrath did grow.
> And I watered it in fears,
> Night and morning with my tears:
> And I sunned it with smiles
> And with soft deceitful wiles.
> And it grew both day and night,
> Till it bore an apple bright.
> And my foe beheld it shine,
> And he knew that it was mine.
> And into my garden stole,
> When the night had veiled the pole;
> In the morning glad I see
> My foe outstretched beneath the tree.

We, as Jews, have a hard time accepting this reality. We have been conditioned to believe that aggression is un-Jewish. More than a generation ago, young Jewish men were raised with the adage: "Nice Jewish boys don't fight. They don't beat their wives."

In actuality, battering occurs in 20 to 30% of American Jewish homes, the same percentage as in non-Jewish homes today. Even in Israel, battered wives represent one out of six women. No group of Jews is free of this evil. Spousal abuse occurs in Reform, Reconstructionist, Conservative, Orthodox, secular, Ashkenazic, Sephardic, and Hasidic homes. No Jewish household is immune to domestic violence.

Our major Jewish problem today is denial. A Jewish woman will remain in an abusive house far longer than a non-Jewish woman. Noted Orthodox Jewish author Blu Greenberg recalls her first visit to a woman's shelter in 1985. She looked closely at the arms and legs of Yardena, a Jewish woman, who had just arrived to take refuge. Greenberg was shocked that anyone would beat such a tiny woman, kicking her a dozen times. Yardena had gone back to her husband after he knocked out her front teeth two years earlier.

Yet her mother told Yardena, "I survived it. You'll get through it." Her father was no better when he said, "There'll be no divorce dishonoring our family!" She had enough self-esteem to see her rabbi about getting a divorce. The rabbi said, "He promised he'll never lift a hand to you. Go home for the sake of *shelom bayit*, household harmony." Obviously her husband did not keep his promise. Thus she ran to the shelter with her three small, wide-eyed children, who seemed to see and know everything.

Many Jewish women stay in these marriages because they believe they deserve such treatment. They get no significant support from family and friends who rationalize the problem or suggest that she suppress it. She also believes that she has no chance to survive financially in the world. She is terrified that, if she would leave her husband, she would be left jobless and unable to provide for herself and her children.

As we reflect on Yardena's plight and the O. J. Simpson case, we realize that every human being is capable of inflicting cruelty and even committing murder. The tendency toward violence is present in the most pious and gentle of men and women. The propensity to harm others is a basic element of the human condition. It is unleashed when unexpressed hostility becomes so intense that we can no longer contain it.

Therefore we constantly need to be on guard when we feel anger welling up from within us and learn to manage it before it explodes and we do irreparable damage. We can do so by writing in a journal, pounding a pillow, exercising, and even exploring our hostilities with a trained counselor. Such healthy coping skills will help us to avoid inflicting harm on ourselves and on others.

How Jewish Is Privacy?

A friend of mine, whose ancestors were from Scotland, and I were discussing the issue of privacy. In the course of our conversation, he shared with me his encounters with the people of Scotland, where he has visited and studied frequently.

The Scots are a very private people. They reveal very little about their own personal lives. They consider it highly improper for someone to ask any personal questions. They would not even think of addressing a new acquaintance by his or her first name. They refrain from commenting on the affairs of others and generally adopt a "live and let live" philosophy. They guard their feelings zealously and put a lid on their emotions. One Scotsman is even quoted as saying: "Sometimes I love my wife so much I can hardly keep from telling her."

Those who grew up in intensely Jewish neighborhoods, especially in the Northeast, experienced the very opposite kind of behavior. Here, emotions were openly vented. Anger was expressed, but so was love. Privacy was not an ideal. In fact, the need for privacy was basically ignored. Everyone felt close to and familiar with each other. No one in those communities seemed to recognize any personal boundaries. The notion of "minding your own business" was generally overlooked.

Neighbors would openly criticize others if they did not attend synagogue services on the High Holy Days or failed to send their sons to Hebrew school. They would also chatter among themselves if someone bought a new home, a new car, or a new fur coat. Friends would walk uninvited into each other's homes without knocking, comment on their taste in furniture, open their refrigerators, and help themselves to food.

Parents would not hesitate to instruct their adult sons and daughters and their spouses where to live, which careers to pursue, and how to raise their own children. An alternate life style in those days meant not keeping a kosher kitchen. Both Philip Roth and the now infamous Woody Allen have satirized these Jewish families of previous generations.

They were generally headed by immigrants from Eastern Europe or their first-generation American-born children. They came from an environment where they lived in poverty and oppression. They never knew when a pogrom would strike. They had to band closely together for mutual support and protection. The relationships that they developed with each other under these conditions of duress led to this kind of intensely intimate conduct.

In Israel today, we see some of the same behavioral patterns, often for the same reasons. Noah J. Efron describes the total disregard for privacy among many Israelis: "Strangers give advice—insistently, infuriatingly—about every imaginable thing: Your child isn't dressed warmly, your hair is mussed, the book you're reading isn't worth the effort, anything. (A popular joke: Why won't Israelis have sex in public? Because a crowd would gather to tell them what they're doing wrong.)"

As I present these sharply different patterns between Scots and Jews, both American and Israeli, I realize that these generalizations are not true in every case. Many who come from Italian, Greek, or other backgrounds originating in the Mediterranean area have had experiences similar to those Jews who were raised in the Northeastern United States or in Israel. On the other hand, I know many Jews who grew up in homes, especially in Texas, where the Scottish or Anglo-Saxon ideal of restraint was stressed. I am not that familiar with many Scottish households, but I am certain that there must be some where privacy is spurned.

Here, then, we have two contrasting approaches to the

way that people live: the Anglo-Saxon, which puts a premium on privacy, and the traditional Jewish one, which has little patience with privacy.

Some people who are not members of these two communities do not find them appealing. To outsiders, the Anglo-Saxon lifestyle seems overly reserved, cold, and unwelcoming. On the other hand, the typically Northeastern Jewish or Israeli pattern seems intrusive and emotionally suffocating. Other outsiders, however, find them appealing. Some observers note that these two contrasting lifestyles may be a major factor in the galloping increase in the rate of intermarriage between Jews and non-Jews. Here opposites do tend to attract.

Those who were raised in highly concentrated Jewish neighborhoods sometimes feel overpowered by the barrage of emotions and look for an escape. A spouse from an Anglo-Saxon home would provide such an escape.

Conversely, those who grew up in Anglo-Saxon homes sometimes feel emotionally starved by the aloofness and detachment of their families and friends. They are drawn to traditional Jewish families, which they find warm, embracing, and loving.

At this juncture we need to ask ourselves: How authentically Jewish is this seemingly blatant disregard of privacy? Not all behaviors of Jews accurately reflect what Jewish tradition teaches. Such is true with regard to the absence of privacy in many Jewish households.

Privacy is an important value in Judaism, regardless of the way some have historically disregarded it. Privacy is a sacred right granted to us as children of God. It assures us of selfhood and prevents our dehumanization. *Leshon hara*, or gossiping about another, is expressly forbidden throughout Jewish religious literature.

In Deuteronomy 24:10-11, we learn that we are not to enter another's home uninvited, even when we hold the rights to an article within it: "When you lend your fellow any thing, you shall not go into his house to fetch the pledge. You shall stand outside, and the one to whom you lend shall bring the pledge outside to you."

Furthermore, the Talmud informs us that when Balaam, the heathen prophet, was about to curse the children of Israel, he observed that the entrances to their tents were not directly opposite each other, so that one family could not violate the privacy of the other. (Cf. b. *Bava Batra* 60a) In the eleventh century, Rabbenu Gershom expressly forbade opening another's mail.

In short, minding another person's business is antithetical to Jewish tradition. Louis Brandeis, the eminent Supreme Court justice, who was Jewish himself, so aptly captured the proper Jewish attitude toward privacy when he wrote: "Privacy is the most comprehensive of rights and the right most valued by civilized men."

Privacy, however, is not the same as withholding expressions of genuine affection and love, as is prized in some Anglo-Saxon cultures. These positive feelings need to be shared, freely and without reservations. Rather, privacy refers to our prerogative to maintain healthy boundaries to protect our personhood and that of others.

III

The Jewish People

Dreyfus Trial and French Anti-Semitism

On January 5, 1895, in the bitterly cold courtyard of the Ecole Militaire of Paris, French Army Captain Alfred Dreyfus was publicly humiliated. In a secret court-martial that took place a few weeks earlier, Dreyfus was accused, tried, and convicted of selling secrets to the Germans. In this humiliating ordeal, Dreyfus was forced to stand at attention as the general of the army shouted: "Alfred Dreyfus, you are unworthy to bear arms. In the name of the French people, we degrade you!"

A senior non-commissioned officer then approached Dreyfus and cut off his badges and medals. He removed Dreyfus's sword and broke it across his knee. Dreyfus was then marched around the courtyard, while he shouted that he was innocent and remained a loyal Frenchman.

Outside the courtyard stood an immense and agitated crowd. Their whispers and chants soon grew to a scream as they yelled: "Death to Dreyfus. Death to the Jews." Dreyfus was then sent to Devil's Island to serve a life sentence without parole.

It was clear that Dreyfus was innocent and the charges against him were trumped up. In the fall of 1894, a French officer had sent a classified army document to the German Embassy in Paris. A cleaning lady at the Embassy salvaged this unsigned paper from the wastepaper basket and delivered it to the French Intelligence Service. Based on the similarity of handwriting and other flimsy evidence, the court convicted Dreyfus of treason.

It was clear that Dreyfus's military associates were out to get him. They personally disliked him. Dreyfus was cold, rich, snobbish, arrogant, and aristocratic. Hating the Germans, these French officers were also suspicious of Dreyfus. Dreyfus's family had come from Alsace, which was then a German territory. More significant was the fact that Dreyfus was a Jew, the only Jew on the French army general's staff.

The inner circle of the military establishment did not want to disgrace the army with the revelation of this spying incident at the German Embassy. They needed a scapegoat to save the French army's honor, and Dreyfus was their target. Even after the real spy, French Major Ferdinand Esterhazy, was discovered, many continued to hold Dreyfus guilty.

The country was soon divided between anti-Dreyfus and pro-Dreyfus forces. Supporters of the army refused to believe that Dreyfus was innocent. To them, it was better to let one Jew rot on Devil's Island than to ruin the reputation of France by reversing a court-martial.

Eventually, supporters of Dreyfus demanded a second court-martial five years later. At this time, his sentence was reduced to ten years. Dreyfus was then offered a presidential pardon on one condition: that he would promise not to appeal the case. He agreed to that condition.

However, in 1906, his supporters insisted on calling the Court of Appeals into session. This court canceled the original judgment against Dreyfus. He was free and restored to the French army. However, it was a pyrrhic victory. Those who had opposed Dreyfus and their successors became the founders of the pro-Nazi Vichy government in France in 1940.

The Dreyfus case shocked the Jews of France. After the French Revolution one hundred years earlier, France became the first country in Europe to grant equal rights to Jews. Most French Jews believed that anti-Semitism was rapidly diminishing. They assumed that if they would behave like loyal, cultured, and patriotic citizens of France, anti-Semitism would soon disappear completely. The Dreyfus case proved them to be grossly in error. Alfred Dreyfus was the epitome of the assimilated French gentleman. Yet when the French army wanted to preserve its honor, Dreyfus, the Jew, became its victim.

The Dreyfus case is instructive for us today. It can teach us how to deal with the awful presence of anti-Semitism. Anti-Semitism is a persistent, irrational virus that lies dormant in every society, regardless of how civilized and cultured it is. However, social unrest and an economic downturn can activate it from time to time.

The French Revolution of 1789 promised liberty, equality, and fraternity for all the people of France. French Jews were also given their freedom, but they were told: "To Jews as human beings, we give everything. To Jews as Jews, we give nothing." In other words, in order to gain full rights and privileges in France, a Jew was expected eventually to give up his or her Jewishness.

Paradoxically, many of the thinkers who inspired the French Revolution and passionately voiced their belief in human equality were rabidly anti-Semitic. The best example is Voltaire, the French writer, philosopher and champion of human rights, who died shortly before the Revolution. Voltaire was an avowed atheist. He fought religious intolerance and helped those who were victims of religious persecution.

But Voltaire had a quirk. He passionately despised Jews. In his *Philosophical Dictionary*, Voltaire claimed that Jews are well-trained in the art of usury. He accused them of being a totally ignorant nation. For many years, he claimed that they have combined contemptible miserliness and superstition with a violent hatred of all those nations that have tolerated them. Then he charitably added that, in spite of their gross shortcomings, Jews should not be burned at the stake.

By the 1890s, shortly before the Dreyfus trial, conditions in France were ripe for the revival of anti-Semitism. The French leaders were experiencing financial unrest. France had committed large sums to build the Panama Canal. These plans soon went bankrupt. Jews were allegedly involved in bribing several members of government to support the project.

In addition, France at this time was led by a liberal secular government. The army did not like being under the control of civilians. Furthermore, the French Catholic Church, which had always been anti-Semitic, resented the rule of nonbelievers. The conservative religious and military leaders needed to vent their frustration on someone or some group. The Jews were their most accessible target.

Another lesson that we glean from the Dreyfus case is that modifying one's Jewish character to "fit in" will not reduce nor alleviate anti-Semitism one iota. Any changes Jews make to alter themselves will be totally ineffective. In fact, one anti-Semite suggested that when you baptize a Jew, you should hold his head under water for ten minutes.

At the time of the Dreyfus trial, the Jews of France were highly assimilated. They thought that if they would be nice and very French, no one would bother them. They then represented less than one-quarter of a percent of France's total population of 40 million. French Jews considered themselves super patriots. In fact, the Grand Rabbi of Paris in 1891 called the French "the elect people of modern times."

Nevertheless, the French people resented their Jewish citizens. Unfortunately, Dreyfus never caught on. Even after he was restored to the army and became a major and then a lieutenant colonel, he remained an unrepentant assimilationist.

The Jews of Germany, throughout the 1930s, also never learned that lesson. They also believed that blending in would stop anti-Semitism. How tragically they learned otherwise! Some of the most un-Jewish Jews in Germany became Hitler's first victims.

We can never eradicate anti-Semitism. All we can do is to hold it in check. One way is to make *aliyah*, to take up residence in Israel. In fact, the Dreyfus trial inspired Theodore Herzl to become the father of political Zionism. Herzl, a native of Budapest, lived in Paris as permanent correspondent of a liberal daily newspaper from Vienna.

Herzl himself was a thoroughgoing assimilationist with little connection with Judaism. Herzl was one of the only correspondents permitted to report both at the court-martial in 1894 and the degrading of Dreyfus in the military school courtyard a few weeks later.

Herzl became suddenly transformed. He concluded that Jews, as one united nation, will always be subject to abuse if they live among other people. There was only one solution for coping with anti-Semitism: Jews need a state of their own. This new revelation inspired Herzl to take the beginning steps that culminated in the establishment of the independent Jewish State of Israel in 1948.

The other way to cope with anti-Semitism is to work to change our environment. Decades ago, we taught that America should become a melting pot. Just as a good Frenchman was to be a white Catholic, a good American was to become a white Anglo-Saxon Protestant. The closer Jews approximated this ideal of becoming like the white Protestant American, the more Jews thought that they would become accepted. It was an illusory goal.

Now, we speak of cultural pluralism. No one has to give up his or her distinctive religious or national identity in order to be accepted. America is not like a melting pot, but a symphony orchestra. Here every instrument plays its own distinctive part, but contributes to the musical beauty of the whole. The more Jewish Jews are, the better Americans they will become.

Rabbi Arthur Hertzberg is a recognized authority on the Jewish significance of the French Revolution and the Enlightenment. He summed up the legacy of the Dreyfus case in these words:

> Herzl knew Jews would not be secure by becoming model members of the majority wherever in the world they lived ... they would have to persuade the world to help Jews become again a nation among nations. Even those who did not follow Herzl's Zionism knew, as he did, that

Jews could not live in the world on approval and, therefore, as candidates for victimhood ...

At the Ecole Militaire that day, the Jewish people learned an upsetting lesson. Even in a liberal republic, in France, their freedom is not secure. They could not always depend on the good will of others. In the next century, Jews would have to continue to fight for a more inclusive society ...

The Rescue of Danish Jewry

There is a famous legend about King Christian X of Denmark. When the Nazis invaded Denmark in April 1940, Christian X supposedly wore a yellow armband to show his solidarity with his Jewish subjects. The truth is that the king never wore a yellow armband, nor, for that matter, did any Jews ever wear them in Denmark. What is true is that King Christian X was a consistently steadfast friend and a staunch defender of the Jewish people. He was a defiant symbol of resistance to the Nazis.

As early as April 1933, he demonstrated his fierce loyalty to the Jewish people. The Great Synagogue in Copenhagen was about to celebrate its 100th anniversary. Across the border, Germany had just declared a boycott against Jews. The Jewish community of Denmark had invited Christian X to take part in its festive centennial service. At that time, other European leaders were trying to appease Hitler. Some thought that the king would cancel his appearance at the synagogue, lest he do something to offend the Nazis. Instead, King Christian X ignored the Nazis and proudly participated in the synagogue service.

After seizing control of Denmark in 1940, the Nazis painted swastikas on the Great Synagogue of Copenhagen and tried to burn it. Appalled by this sacrilege, Christian X sent a hand-written letter to Chief Rabbi Marcus Melchior, stating that he shared the pain of the Jewish people. The king even agreed to pay to repair the damages.

The Nazis kept pressing King Christian X about the Jewish Question. He would consistently answer: "There is no Jewish Question in this country. They are only my people." In fact, at the time of the Nazi occupation, the 8,000 Jews of Denmark were unique. The Jews of many other European countries were considered second-class. Danish Jews, by contrast, were full-fledged Danes, entitled to all the privileges and rights of citizenship.

Because of their equal status, Danish Jews were left basically unharmed for about three and one-half years after the Nazis came to Denmark. The Danes handled the Nazis very cleverly. They collaborated with Nazis, and, at the same time, extended full protection to the Danish Jews and their property.

Hitler had regarded Denmark as a model protectorate. As long as the Danes lived by the Danish-German agreement, the Nazis were not interested in molesting Danish Jews. In fact, the Nazi officials in Denmark went out of their way to avoid a conflict with the Danes over the Jews. Eventually, all this ended.

After over three years of cooperating with the Nazis, more and more Danes began to rebel. The Danish resistance movement was mounting. As a result, shortly before the High Holy Days in 1943, Germany canceled its agreement with the Danes, and life for Danish Jews became precarious.

As Jews assembled in the Great Synagogue in Copenhagen that Rosh Hashanah, Rabbi Melchior made a frightening announcement. He informed his congregation that the Germans had decided to arrest all Danish Jews and to deport them to concentration camps. The operation was to begin that night. Rabbi Melchior assured them that this was not a mere rumor. He had received word from reliable sources in the German High Command. Indeed, Hitler was now determined to rid Denmark of its Jews.

Rabbi Melchior warned his people in these words:

> What will be, I can not say. We have no plan. I only know that when you leave this synagogue, you can not go home. Do not go home! Go anywhere, see friends, find hiding places, but do not go home! When we shall see each other

again I do not know. The pastor down the street has promised to hide our Torahs, our prayerbooks, and our sacred objects in the cellar of his church. Pastor Hans Kildeby from the church in Orslev has asked me to bring my family to him for safekeeping.... We will go into hiding, like animals. This the Nazis have done to us. But first, like men, like Jews, we shall remain here a little while, and we shall worship God.

Rabbi Melchior's announcement began a series of events of unparalleled humanitarianism and courage, leading to the saving of Jews from deportation and death. Overnight, myriads of ordinary Danish citizens rushed to rescue their Jewish citizens. During the following three weeks, they transferred and hid the majority of Denmark's 8,000 Jews in fishing villages along a thirty-mile coastline between Copenhagen and Elsinore. These villages faced neutral Sweden, only a few miles away.

It was an extremely dangerous operation. Nazi soldiers had fortified and patrolled the coastline, which was ridden with minefields. At great risk to their lives, Danish resistance fighters discovered ingenious methods to hide Jews. Some drove them in ambulances to hospitals. Others used hearses to transport them to churches.

Left Donde, who is a Jew, served as Denmark's Consul General in New York. In 1943, he was a six-year-old boy living in Copenhagen. One late afternoon, his father came home and told him and his family that they had to leave immediately, as the Germans could come at any moment. His father said that there was no time to pack and told Leif to wear as much clothing as possible. They spent the night in the apartment of some non-Jewish friends.

The next day, they went by train to the southern part of Denmark. Two days later, they and twelve other Jews sailed for eleven hours on a small fishing boat to Sweden. The seas were rough. The engine broke down several times. German patrol boats, equipped with search lights, pursued and fired at them. Two hours after finally arriving in Sweden, the dilapidated boat sank to the bottom of the harbor. Stories about the rescue operation like this abound.

The Danes managed to send ninety percent of Denmark's 8,000 Jews to Sweden. Sweden was the only country in the world to offer asylum to a whole nation of Jews who were under Nazi occupation. The Germans seized those Jews who chose to remain in Denmark and moved them to concentration camps. Fortunately, in early 1945, most of them, through the Swedish Red Cross, were also brought to Sweden. Only two percent of Denmark's Jews died in the Holocaust. After the war, the Danish Jews left Sweden to return to Denmark, and found their home and property intact.

Why did the people of Denmark, unlike those of other Nazi-occupied countries, take such risks to save their Jewish population? The Danes have always been committed to human rights and individual liberty. They were determined not to let the Nazis destroy the democratic traditions which they, over the centuries, had tenaciously upheld.

In many countries, Jews have been on the margins of society. In Denmark, however, Jews have always been a central part of Danish life. Danish Christians have always enjoyed close professional and social connections with Danish Jews. What is amazing is that the Danes, like almost all Holocaust rescuers, never regarded their actions as heroic or extraordinary. They did not clamor for praise. According to them, they did what is normal and expected of any human being. By defending Denmark's Jews, they were defending their own freedom.

We salute the people of Denmark for their extraordinary acts of humanitarian bravery. As we ponder the Nazi atrocities of the Holocaust, we often become cynical about human nature. We can easily conclude that human beings are, in essence, untamed and heartless beasts. They are corrupt and evil to the core.

Such an idea, however, goes counter to Jewish teachings. We Jews hold a more optimistic view of human nature. We believe that people can, indeed, do great evil, but they can also do much good. We are given a choice. Most Nazi-occupied countries chose the way of cruelty and inhumanity. Denmark, however, pursued the path of justice, kindness, and love. The people of Denmark seek no special recognition for their noble choice. Yet they still deserve our boundless gratitude and commendations.

As Leni Yahil stated so eloquently in her magisterial work on Danish Jewry: "... the rescue of the Jews of Denmark shines with greatest luster, for it was here that humane democracy stood its test."

Secular Jews: Then and Now

Many of us were shocked when we first visited Israel to discover that most Jews in Israel are not formally religious. In fact, many of the *halutzim*, the pioneers who came to build the land of Israel at the turn of the last century, were downright hostile to religion. The majority had fled the ghettos of Eastern Europe which they despised. To them, the ghetto was a place where they suffered degradation and humiliation. Anything connected with the ghetto was to be spurned. The central feature of the ghetto was religion. They were repelled by the overly strict rabbis that ruled the ghetto. Therefore they directed their anti-ghetto feelings against religion.

This antipathy to religion was evident in the *kibbutzim* founded by the *Hashomer Ha-tzair*, the leftist socialist movement. At one time, in these *kibbutzim*, on Friday afternoon, an argument would rage: Should they use a white tablecloth in the dining room that night? To adorn the table with a white tablecloth was tantamount to marking Shabbat in a religious sense, which would be unacceptable.

There was a time that anti-religious Israelis would flout their disdain for the rules of tradition in the presence of observant Jews. They would drive their motorcycles and cars through Orthodox neighborhoods in Israel on Shabbat. They would sit opposite synagogues on Yom Kippur, the holiest day of the Jewish calendar when fasting is mandated, and eat.

Yet these same rebels against traditional Jewish ritual were men and women of profound social idealism. They passionately wanted to develop a model Jewish state, founded on the principles of justice, equity, and compassion. They were also deeply knowledgable about the Bible, Talmud, and other texts of the tradition they rejected. Fortunately, today much of this animosity to religion has diminished in Israel. Yet, most Israelis still classify themselves as either *dati*, or religious, meaning Orthodox, or *hiloni*, meaning secular.

Some of the Eastern European Jews who came to the United States at the turn of the last century emerged from the same background and bent as these *halutzim*. They were ardent secularists. Revolting against the life of the ghetto, they became Yiddish socialists. They founded organizations like the Workmen's Circle. To them, Yiddish was a surrogate religion. It was a way to be both modern and rational. They established Yiddish schools for children. For half a day students would study Jewish subjects, like Bible, from a secular point of view, and for the other half, regular school subjects. Everything was taught in Yiddish. To them, religion was superstition. They were famous for holding balls on Yom Kippur eve and picnics on Yom Kippur day.

Like the pioneers who came to Palestine, these Yiddishists considered themselves the heirs of the Biblical prophets. They fought for social justice. They demanded the rights of workers everywhere. They were the leaders of the labor union movement. The secular Jews of decades ago, whether kibbutzniks in Palestine or Yiddish socialists in America, had a mastery of Bible and Talmud. Though they did not observe the traditions, they knew what the traditions were. They were proud ethnic and cultural Jews with a strong allegiance to the Jewish people.

Secular Jews today, in the United States, are far different. In former times, they were *apikorsim*, learned, but angry, nonbelieving Jews. Today they are *am haaratzim*, Jewishly ignorant Jews. Few have much background in Judaism. Many of them have little or no feeling of Jewish connection. Most are not hostile to Jewish religion. They are just apathetic about it. Their view of Judaism is dominated by "don't's." They don't join synagogues. They don't belong to Jewish community organizations. They don't contribute financially to any Jewish causes, here or in Israel.

But what about those who are connected religiously to the Jewish community today, those who do belong to synagogues? Many of them do have this formal religious connection. Still they view themselves essentially as secular Jews. Many have joined a Temple or synagogue to find a community and to obtain three basic services: a rabbi for their life-cycle ceremonies, a religious school for their children, and a seat for the High Holy Days.

If they are Jewishly involved at all, they are drawn to the non-religious features of Jewish community life. They may serve on synagogue boards and finance committees, while rarely, if ever, attending weekly worship or adult education courses. They may be leaders in the wider Jewish community and involve themselves in organizations like the Jewish Federation, the Jewish Community Center, and the American Jewish Committee.

Yet even though they may be affiliated and may even be prominent Jewish community leaders, they are secular Jews in most respects. They tend to restrict their religion to the brief time they spend in the confines of the sanctuary. Most of their daily decisions in life are not governed by religious values. Their faith has little impact on their everyday life.

Some time ago, the Center for Ethics and Corporate Policy carried out a study of members of various Jewish and Christian congregations in the Chicago area. It posed the question, "How separate or integrated do you view your faith and work?" The connection was the strongest for members of the Evangelical Covenant Church and weakest for Jews. Almost all the members of the Evangelical Covenant Church said that religion and its teachings are very important in their work lives. Under half the Jews made that assertion.

Yet in recent years there have been stirrings for spirituality among some secular Jews. The problem is that they seek to meet these spiritual needs outside of the framework of Judaism. Judaism is rich in spiritual resources, and it is hoped that these Jews will some day discover them.

Hebron and Jewish Nationalism

Before the holiday of Purim in March 1994, Dr. Baruch Goldstein, a Brooklyn-born Jewish physician living in Hebron, rushed into the compound of the tomb of our Biblical ancestors. There he opened fire on a crowd of Muslim worshipers. His shooting spree resulted in the deaths of twenty-nine people at prayer and the wounding of twenty-five others. It also cost him his own life.

Hebron has always been one of the hotbeds of Arab-Jewish hostilities over the years. The Goldstein massacre is one of the very few that have originated from the Jewish side. Most have been perpetrated by the Arab population.

Hebron is located south of Jerusalem in the West Bank. It is a city of 120,000 Arabs, a handful of Christians, and just 500 Jews. However, in the nearby community of Kiryat Arba, 6,000 Jews reside. They form the hard core of the ultra-nationalist religious settlers.

Hebron is steeped in Jewish history. It is considered the oldest Jewish community in the world. It was once the capital of the Holy Land, under King David. Hebron is also one of the four sacred cities of the Holy Land, together with Jerusalem, Tiberias, and Safed.

It was in Hebron that Abraham purchased a burial plot for his wife, Sarah. Later, Abraham himself, as well as Isaac, Jacob, Rebekah, and Leah, were interred in that same tomb, called in the Bible, "the *Makhpelah*." Only Rachel, who died in childbirth, was buried elsewhere, in a spot along the road to Bethlehem.

Jews have lived in Hebron continuously from the beginning of its establishment thousands of years ago until 1929.

The tomb itself represents the many changes of government over the centuries. Inside the huge walls surrounding the compound, the Christian rulers built a church. Later the Muslims converted the church into a mosque when they took control of Hebron. The Muslim rulers then forbade both Christians and Jews to pray inside the area. Jews could approach the cave by climbing the first five of its seven steps, but could go no higher during those years.

In 1929, a catastrophe struck. That year, the Mufti, the Palestinian Muslim religious leader, incited several riots against the Jews of Hebron. One day, his forces waged a devastating pogrom. They rampaged throughout the Jewish quarter and invaded the city's yeshiva. As a result, sixty-seven Jews lost their lives and sixty others were severely injured. To their credit, some Arab neighbors befriended the besieged Jews and offered them refuge from these vicious attacks.

For the next two years, from 1929 until 1931, no Jews remained in the city. Then thirty-five Jewish families resettled in Hebron. However, repeated Arab assaults against them forced the British authorities to evacuate the Jews. Thus no Jews were living there in 1948, when Israel became an independent Jewish state. That year Hebron went under the control of Jordan.

In 1967, however, a dramatic change occurred. Israel won the Six Day War and captured the entire West Bank, including Hebron. Jews from around the world came in droves to visit the ancient tomb of our patriarchs and matriarchs. However, for the first year, the Israel government did not want any Jews to settle in this all-Arab hostile community.

In the following year, 1968, however, a militant Israeli Rabbi, Moshe Levinger, dressed as a Swiss tourist. He reserved rooms for himself and nine other Jewish families in an Arab hotel in Hebron during Passover. Before the holiday was over, they barricaded themselves inside the hotel. They refused to leave it until the Israeli government permitted them to settle in Hebron. Finally the government gave in, and Hebron eventually became one of the biggest settlements of

Jews on the West Bank. Yet, the settlement has never been peaceful.

One tragedy after another has scarred the years in Hebron from Rabbi Levinger's settlement in 1968 until the present. In October 1968, a seventeen-year-old Arab youth hurled a grenade at Jews praying on the steps of the tomb's main gate. The assailant injured forty-seven Jews, including an eight-month-old baby.

In October 1976, on the Eve of Yom Kippur, a mob of Arab youths burst into the tomb and desecrated several Torah scrolls.

In July 1983, three Arabs attacked and stabbed Aharon Gross, a Beit Romano yeshiva student, in the market area. Gross later died of his wounds.

Then, in September 1986, a young Arab woman, whose father was the local mukhtar, knifed an Israeli soldier at the entrance of the tomb. Then she herself was shot and killed.

I already mentioned Dr. Baruch Goldstein's mowing down the Muslim worshipers inside the tomb in March 1994. Later that year, Arab terrorists opened fire from a passing car near the entrance of Kiryat Arba and shot a seventeen-year-old girl to death.

This bloodshed that has stained the saga of Arab-Jewish relations in Hebron leads me to two observations. First, since the Six Day War, Orthodox Judaism has radically revised its stance toward Zionism. Originally, most Orthodox Jews opposed Zionism. They believed that, only when the Messiah arrives, in the End of Days, could Jews have a state that they could call their own land. Until that time, the land must remain under foreign domination. In fact, the Jewish victims of the pogrom in Hebron in 1929, even though they resided in the Holy Land, were ultra-Orthodox and were either anti-Zionist or non-Zionist.

However, almost from the beginning of the Zionist movement, some Orthodox Jews embraced it. They argued that, by working for the Zionist cause, they were beginning the first phase of the final Messianic redemption. These Zionist

Orthodox Jews increased in numbers. Many became leaders of the government's religious parties when Israel was established in 1948.

From 1948 until 1967, Israel's National Religious Party (MAFDAL) and other Orthodox government groups demonstrated absolutely no interest in territorial issues. They left those concerns to the ruling Labor Party, consisting mostly of secular Jews. They focused on ensuring that Shabbat and kosher laws would be observed in all of Israel's public institutions and that all matters of personal status, like conversion, marriage, and divorce, would come under the sole jurisdiction of Israel's Orthodox rabbinical authorities.

Their lack of concern about land changed markedly in 1967, with the Six Day War. That year, Israel, in a dramatic, lightning-like victory, recovered the West Bank. Many of the Orthodox political leaders viewed this new acquisition as a Divine intervention. It was a sign from God that Israel must maintain permanent control over the entire Holy Land, whose borders are defined in the Torah. Now land has become an obsession with them.

To give up one inch of the land would mean delaying the advent of the Messiah. Therefore, large groups of passionately nationalistic Jews have settled in Hebron, Efrat, and other cities of the West Bank. They are determined that Israel will never surrender even an inch of land. To do so, in their view, would be a sin against God.

Thus they vehemently oppose the peace process. Of course, the Arabs who live in the West Bank also believe that the same land is theirs, by Divine right. These conflicting views of the Jews and Arabs are irreconcilable, and thus hostilities are inevitable.

But in Genesis 23, we read that such strife did not always blemish life in Hebron. Once relations were peaceful. When Abraham went there to find a burial spot for Sarah, his wife, he could have demanded that that burial plot was rightfully his. After all, God had promised the entire Holy Land to Abraham and his people.

Yet Abraham insisted on purchasing the land from the native population. Not only that, but he also demanded that he pay the full price. So harmonious were these relations in those days that the Gentile leader of the negotiations called Abraham a "*Nesi Elohim*, a prince of God," in their midst.

Would that such respect between Jews and non-Jews would return to Hebron today! Then harmony could be restored to that turbulent and troubled area, and Arabs and Jews, both children of Abraham, could live together in peace.

Those Who Deny the Holocaust

In our nation's capital, the United States Holocaust Memorial Museum opened its doors in 1993. Chartered by Congress in 1980, the museum stands on land donated by the federal government in the same area where many of our national monuments and shrines are located. When one visits the museum, one confronts the most dastardly deeds and the noblest actions of which human beings are capable.

It is possible to tour the three floors of the museum, each graphically exhibiting a different period of the Holocaust. The exhibit spans the years 1933, when the German government began its racial policies, through the horrors of the Holocaust and the liberation of the death camps, to the present day with its inspiring stories of Holocaust survivors. The museum challenges all Americans to remember what happens when government and science forfeit their moral responsibility.

Even as the Holocaust Memorial Museum prepared to welcome its first visitors on April 25, a number of self-proclaimed experts continued to insist that the Holocaust never happened. In fact, the Anti-Defamation League published a complete study of these Holocaust revisionists called *Hitler's Apologists*. Prominently featured in this volume is Bradley Smith.

Over the years, Smith has purchased full-page ads in more than a dozen college newspapers, including the *Daily Texan* of the University of Texas. Here he announces his spurious claims. Smith represents the Committee on the Open Debate on the Holocaust. His ads do acknowledge that Nazis singled out the Jews for special cruel treatment, but not to eliminate a whole people.

Rather, the Nazis were punishing Jews because Jews were the enemies of the state, in Smith's view. They were aiding and abetting international Communism. Smith also claims that Jews died in concentration camps because of typhus infections. According to him, the gas chambers were used not to exterminate Jews but as fumigation devices to delouse clothing. Smith asserts that 6,000,000 Jewish deaths in the Holocaust is an irresponsible exaggeration.

What Smith claims is dangerous nonsense. Reputable historians the world over have proven that the Nazis killed Jews just because they were Jews, irrespective of their behavior; that gas chambers were, indeed, part of the Final Solution; and that, if anything, 6,000,000 murders of Jews in Nazi Europe may be an underestimate. As a historian, Bradley Smith is a charlatan. In his autobiography, he writes that all the historians are wrong; that all the scientists, intellectuals, and academicians are wrong; and that he is right. Yet he has frankly confessed in that same autobiography that he has "never been interested in intellectual work. It takes too long."

College newspaper editorial boards who have run his ad defend their action on the basis of free speech. To do otherwise, they say, is to impose censorship. I believe these editorial boards are misguided. Maintaining editorial standards does not compromise the principle of free speech. As an editor of the *Journal of Reform Judaism* for six years, I rejected hundreds of pieces that did not meet our criteria for publication. In no way was I censoring.

Furthermore, publishing such an ad sets a dangerous precedent. If one group can place an ad asserting that the Holocaust never happened, another can do the same to argue that American Blacks were never slaves. Certain historical events are acknowledged facts. To regard them otherwise is to distort the truth.

Bradley Smith is closely tied to the Institute for Historical Review. This organization also operates under the facade of scholarship. Its Liberty Lobby is one of the best-funded anti-Semitic propaganda groups in America. It leads the drive to deny the Nazi genocide. The founder of the Liberty Lobby is Willis A. Carto, a rabid anti-Semite, who is the role model for all Holocaust revisionists. Carto once wrote:

> If Satan himself, with all of his superhuman genius and diabolical ingenuity at his command, had tried to create a permanent . . . force for the destruction of the nations, he could have done no better than to invent the Jews.

Each year, the Institute for Historical Review holds a conference. At this gathering, revisionists present papers rejecting the veracity of the Holocaust. One of the most notorious presenters has been Dr. Arthur Butz. Butz is professor of electrical engineering and computer science at the prestigious Northwestern University. Some years ago, he wrote *The Hoax of the Holocaust*, one of the first revisionist works ever published.

Another bizarre revisionist is Fred Leuchter. He describes himself as the chief engineer of the Fred Leuchter Associates in Boston. This is a firm specializing in selling gas chambers and hardware for executions to prisons throughout the United States. Leuchter insists that the Auschwitz, Birkenau, and Majdenek concentration camps did not house any execution gas chambers.

One of his publications announced that there has never been any question about Leuchter's expertise. Soon thereafter he was brought to trial on criminal charges of practicing engineering without a license. In fact, he has misrepresented himself as an engineer when selling products to correctional facilities. Investigators discovered that Leuchter has only a bachelor's degree in history from Boston University. He never even took an engineering license test in Massachusetts. In spite of this discrediting, Leuchter continues to spread his poisons. In fact, he blames Jews for his setbacks and threatens to take revenge on them.

Probably the most repulsive revisionist is David Irving, who accused Deborah Lipstadt, the eminent scholar of the Holocaust, of damaging his reputation. In her book, *Denying the Holocaust*, Lipstadt described Irving as "one of the most dangerous spokespersons for Holocaust denial." Because of this charge, Irving claimed that she caused him difficulty in finding a publisher for his books and earning a living as a writer.

The case of *Irving v. Lipstadt and Penguin Books* went to trial in London. The judge, Charles Gray, alone heard the case, without a jury. Irving represented himself without any legal counsel. By contrast, Lipstadt's defense team assembled a mass of 6,000 pages of witness testimony, costing 5,000,000 British pounds. Lipstadt herself refused to speak at the trial, on the principle that she does not debate with Holocaust deniers.

The trial lasted three months. Judge Gray found Lipstadt not guilty of libel and roundly excoriated Irving in these sharp words:

> The charges which I have found to be substantially true included the charges that Irving has for his own ideological reasons persistently and deliberately misrepresented and manipulated historical evidence, that for the same reasons, he portrayed Hitler in an unwarrantedly favorable light, principally in relation to his attitude towards and responsibilty for the treatment of Jews; that he is an active Holocaust denier; that he is anti-Semitic and racist; and that he associates with right wing extremists who promote neo-Nazism . . .

We are, indeed, repelled by the obscene claims of Smith, Carto, Leuchter, Irving, and other revisionists. We are outraged that they deny that Hitler's henchmen murdered 6,000,000 Jews in World War II.

Their activities and words represent today's most lethal manifestation of anti-Semitism. Listen to their twisted, sick logic: "If the Holocaust never occurred, Jews who insist on commemorating the Holocaust are liars. Americans continue to believe these falsehoods because Jews have become so influential. They have successfully gained control of history, the media, academia, and the world. Jews control the world, in order to fatten their pocketbooks." According to them, the

Jews have invented the notion of the Holocaust to earn huge profits, to gain world sympathy, to create the State of Israel, and to maintain their fraudulent status as the world's victims.

It is imperative for us not to let these revisionists succeed. Our persistent duty in Judaism is to remember: Remember that we were slaves in Egypt. Remember that we were inmates in Auschwitz. The noted Holocaust writer, Elie Wiesel, received his Nobel Prize in Oslo in 1986. In his acceptance speech, he powerfully reaffirmed the obligation to remember when he said:

> A young Jewish boy discovered the kingdom of night. I remember his bewilderment, I remember his anguish. It all happened so fast. The ghetto. The deportation. The sealed cattle car.... And now the boy is turning to me: "What have you done with my future? What have you done with my life?"
>
> And I tell him that I have tried. That I have tried to keep memory alive, that I have tried to fight those who would forget. Because if we forget, we are guilty; we are accomplices.

Why Support Israel?

In most American synagogue sanctuaries today stands an Israeli flag, in addition to the flag of the United States. Since synagogue members are American citizens, why would we want to display the emblem of a foreign nation? Exhibiting the Israeli flag raises the question of the relationship of the American Jew to the State of Israel.

Let me emphasize that we American Jews believe that the United States is our country. We vote in its elections, we serve in its military, and we express our political allegiance to it. However, we also have a non-political tie to the State of Israel. It is a bond that is primarily historical, cultural, and religious.

We see no contradiction between these two national attachments. Let me suggest an analogy. We can love both our spouse and our children. We love each differently, but we nonetheless love all of them just as intensely. Loving one does not diminish our love for the other.

Why then do American Jews love Israel? First of all, in our Bible, which we share with Christians, God promised that land to Abraham, Isaac, and Jacob, the original Hebrew patriarchs. God assured our descendants that the land would be theirs, as well. So cherished is that land that some Jews outside of Israel face Israel when they pray. Very pious Jews even want to be taken there for burial. In fact, Jews base much of their religious calendar on life in Israel. Some holidays, like Passover, are rooted in Israel's agricultural year. When we pray in our synagogues in the fall season for rain, we are not asking for rain in our local communities, but rather in Israel.

Furthermore, we Jews have traditionally believed that being in Israel brings us closer to God. Israel is the place where God mandated the Jewish people to carry God's message of ethical and moral living to the rest of the world.

We Jews are immensely proud of Israel. Its accomplishments since it was established in 1948 have been colossal. For hundreds of years, Jews could not own land or become farmers. Yet, in this relatively brief span of time that Israel has been a sovereign state, it has become one of the world's towering leaders in agriculture. In fact, many agronomists at Texas A&M have benefited immeasurably from their contacts with Israeli colleagues.

Israel is also a giant in medical technology. In the laboratories of the Hebrew University-Hadassah Hospital in Jerusalem, researchers are developing new procedures and medications to prevent, treat, or combat dreaded diseases.

But beyond all the reasons I have cited for the American Jewish bond with Israel is the central rationale. Israel is a security symbol for the American Jew. During the Hitler years, the Nazis annihilated 6,000,000 Jewish men, women, and children. He also exterminated 5,000,000 non-Jews, making a total of 11,000,000 victims. There is a major difference between the two groups, however. The Jews were destroyed because of who they were. If they had just one Jewish grandparent, they made Hitler's hit list. Genealogy was the sole criterion. Most of the 5,000,000 others were executed because the Nazis considered them political criminals, i.e., they lost their lives for something that they allegedly did, not for who they were.

During the Holocaust, no country wanted to admit European Jews, fleeing for their lives. The United States government was not much more accepting than the rest. In fact, someone asked an immigration official in Canada: "How many refugee Jews can we take into our country?" His answer was startling: "None is too many." His reply became the title of a book detailing Canada's draconian immigration policies.

During those war years, Palestine, as Israel was then called, was under the mandate of Great Britain. In 1939, Britain issued a White Paper, severely limiting the intake of

Jews from Nazi Europe. Had there been an independent Jewish state, many of the 6,000,000 could have been saved from their cruel and callous deaths.

Thus, to American Jews, Israel is a safety net, a haven of refuge. If, God forbid, anti-Semitism should erupt in our country, we would be assured of a place to go. Regardless of what we American Jews may think of certain government leaders or policies in Israel, we all are united in wanting Israel to be a safe, secure, and independent Jewish nation.

We also believe that it is in the best interests of our United States government to support Israel. It is the only democracy in the Middle East. Most Arab nations are repressive regimes. Arab rulers tolerate no dissent, and those who dare to protest will most likely face a firing squad. Israel, on the other hand, allows freedom of speech and freedom of the press. Unlike their counterparts in Arab countries, newspapers in Israel are not controlled by the government. If any group in Israel wants to rally against Israel's government policies or actions, they can freely do so without any fear of reprisal.

Furthermore, as a Jew, I cannot visit any Arab country, except Jordan and Egypt. By contrast, Arabs are not only citizens of Israel, but they can also serve in the Knesset, which is Israel's parliament. Most Arab leaders don't care a whit about the daily lives of their people. However, Israel constantly strives to better the condition of its citizens, by providing a sophisticated system of education, welfare, and health care.

Several years ago, Dr. Howard Mumford Jones, eminent professor of English Literature at Harvard, who was not Jewish, powerfully articulated why Americans of all persuasions should support Israel:

> I am sometimes asked why I, a non-Jew, take an interest in Israel that my questioner feels to be ... out of line. Sometimes he makes me feel he suspects me of some dark or hidden motive. . . .
> The State of Israel is a democratic outpost in the Near East. Despite some threat of theocratic control, it maintains a popular government, as we understand popular govern-

ment. Voting is fair, taxes are equitable, the status of women excellent, the care of the aged unexcelled. It goes in for art, music, literature, and scientific research in our terms. It welcomes industry and labor. With every temptation to yield to a military dictatorship, it has not done so.

Blot out Israel and, with a couple of shaky exceptions, there is no other example of democracy in the whole of the Near East. What surprises me is not that I am for the State of Israel. What surprises me is that there should be any question.

IV

Christian-Jewish Relations

Three Questions
Christians Ask of Jews

One morning, I received a call from a staff member of one of the student religious groups of a local junior college. He wanted to verify something that he had heard about Jewish wedding practices. He asked: "Is it true that when a Jewish couple gets engaged, the prospective groom washes the feet of his prospective bride?" In all of my years in answering questions about Jewish belief and practice, this one is the most outrageous.

So much ignorance about Judaism prevails in the wider community. Last month, I heard another glaring illustration of such misunderstanding. Years ago, Shearith Israel, the large Conservative congregation in Dallas, wanted to build its new synagogue on Douglas Avenue. A neighborhood group then started a petition drive to prevent this from happening. Why? The signers of the petition feared that the odors from the synagogue when the worshipers sacrificed their sheep and cows would be intolerable.

One of the main reasons why some hold such distorted ideas about Judaism is that they identify today's Judaism with the Judaism of the Bible. The neighbors of the Shearith Israel Synagogue worried about the noxious smells of animal sacrifices because in the Bible there were animal sacrifices. Jews haven't engaged in that practice for almost 2,000 years, ever since the Jerusalem Temple was destroyed.

The reality is that 95% of the Judaism Jews embrace and practice today developed after the time of the Bible. For example, the blessings over Sabbath candles and wine cannot be found in the Bible. Neither can we find any reference to Bar and Bat Mitzvah, the popular Jewish coming-of-age ceremonies there.

I spend a significant portion of my time in interfaith activities, which I find extremely gratifying. Over the years, I have spoken in numerous churches and Christian-based colleges. Following my presentation, of course, is a question-and-answer period. If I have failed to cover these three points, I can be assured that someone in the audience will ask about some or all of them: (1) "Why don't Jews believe in an afterlife?" (2) "Why don't Jews believe in Jesus?" and (3) "Are Jews a race?"

Let's take the first of these: "Why don't Jews believe in an afterlife?" The truth is that Jews do believe in an afterlife. However, the Hebrew Bible, which many mistakenly think describes the beliefs of Judaism today, hardly refers to any life after death. To the Biblical writer, the dead are gathered to a place called Sheol, the netherworld. This is merely a repository of corpses. Once the person dies, his or her life is permanently over. That is the end.

However, after the Bible was completed and canonized, Jews began to develop three different ideas of what happens to us after we die. First, to this day, Orthodox Jews believe in the actual resurrection of the dead. At the end of time, when the Messiah comes, the dead will be assembled from the entire world and they will be raised from the dead near the Temple Mount in Jerusalem. Because Orthodoxy clings to a belief in resurrection, cremation is prohibited. To cremate is to deny the resurrection, according to Orthodox Jews.

Those in the non-Orthodox community generally hold two other views of life after death. Few believe in resurrection. Rather, these Jews maintain that, after we die, the soul, the imperishable God-like part of us, will return to God. The body, on the other hand, will go back to the dust from which it originally came into life.

In addition, Jews maintain that our beloved dead live on in the hearts and minds of their survivors. *Gates of Prayer*, the

Reform Jewish prayerbook, expresses this belief in these felicitous words: "By love are they remembered and in memory do they live."

Thus, contrary to popular misconceptions, Jews do cling to a notion that life does not end at the grave. Some Jews embrace a belief in the resurrection at the end of time. Others, especially in the Reform community, maintain that we live on perpetually through the immortality of our souls. We also remain alive as long as our influence will continue to be felt after our demise.

Let's now address the second question, about Jesus. Here we enter an emotionally charged minefield. Regrettably, for the past 2,000 years, the name of Jesus has been linked with Christian anti-Semitism. The cross sometimes stirs up anxieties and apprehensions within us. Jews think of the Crusades, the Good Friday pogroms, and other massacres, when thousands of Jews were murdered, under the cross, in the name of Jesus.

Jesus, himself a Jew, would be appalled if he knew about the atrocities perpetuated in his name in the centuries following his death. Fortunately, in the last three or four decades, Christian-Jewish relations have greatly improved. Thus, Jews can now take a more dispassionate and objective look at the figure of Jesus. Let us emphasize that Jesus was born, lived, and died as a Jew. He was never anything but a Jew.

Jesus was a devoted son of the synagogue. He sat at the feet of some illustrious Rabbis of his time and dazzled them with his genius and brilliance. He taught Jewish ideals and values. Jesus was also a hero among the oppressed Jewish masses living in Palestine at the time of the Roman occupation. Many Jews looked to Jesus to free them from this harassment and oppression. The Roman authorities were naturally threatened by Jesus. They regarded him as a dangerous revolutionary, and, therefore, they crucified him.

However, it was Paul, not Jesus, who founded Christianity. Paul did not even know Jesus while he was alive. Paul was a Jew, whose original name was Saul. About thirty years after the crucifixion, Paul traveled to Damascus, now capital of Syria. En route, he caught a vision of the risen Jesus. He then concluded that he could reach God solely by placing his faith in Jesus. He no longer needed to observe the laws of the Torah.

Influenced by Greek thought, Paul insisted that everyone was born with a sinful condition. It was inherited from Adam, who disobeyed God. The only way we can rid ourselves of this sinful blemish is to accept the saving power of Jesus, whom Paul regarded as God made flesh. He directed his newfound faith primarily to Gentiles, not to Jews. He gave the non-Jews a way to connect with God, without following the mandates of the Torah.

Therefore, why don't Jews believe in Jesus? The truth is that Jews can accept the Jewish Jesus, as one of the eminent religious teachers of his time. As a Jew, Jesus lived by the requirements of Torah. It is the Christian Christ that Jews can't embrace. First of all, to Jews, God cannot assume a flesh-and-blood form. To us, God will always remain intangible and indivisible.

There is also another significant consideration. When Jesus was born 2,000 years ago, Jews had already been in a covenant with God for the previous 2,000 years. That covenant is permanent. To provide an opportunity for non-Jews to covenant with God, Paul offered a new possibility: the notion of a Christian Christ. In other words, Jews have all they need in the first covenant through Torah. The second covenant through Jesus was intended for Gentiles. It was to enable them to bond with God. Both covenants are equally valid: one for Jews, the other for Gentiles. So much for the Jewish stance on Jesus.

Finally, the third question: "Are Jews a race?" This is a particularly sensitive question, especially since the time of Hitler. He spoke of the Aryan master race. Hitler regarded Jews as part of a sub-human race that needed to be exterminated. The truth is that Jews don't constitute a race. Admittedly, most Jews today are Caucasians.

Yet, Jews are represented in every major racial community. There are not only Caucasian Jews, but also Oriental Jews and Black Jews. When I was a Jewish chaplain in Korea, I encountered several Koreans who were Jewish. Admittedly, they were not born Jewish. However, upon converting to Judaism, they became as authentically Jewish as anyone born into an all-Jewish family.

Similarly, in the last few decades, over 25,000 Black Jews left Ethiopia to settle in Israel. They have been Jewish for centuries. In a few major cities of our nation, there are also Black Jewish congregations. In fact, an African-American woman, living in Denver, enrolled in Hebrew Union College to study to become a rabbi.

Thus, if Jews are not a race, what are they? Jews are not a nationality, because Jews are represented in almost all the major nationalities of this world. There are American Jews, French Jews, Russian Jews, Turkish Jews, Greek Jews, Italian Jews, Mexican Jews, etc. What, then, are Jews?

The best definition of Jews I have encountered is that of Dr. Mordecai M. Kaplan: "Jews are a people, with an evolving religious civilization." Yes, Jews are more than a religious group. Jews are community with religion at its essential core. Jews also have languages, like Yiddish. Jews have foods, like gefilte fish. Jews have dances, like the hora. Neither Yiddish, nor gefilte fish, nor the hora are religious in nature. Yet they are elements of Jewish civilization. In short, Jews are part of a religious entity, but so much more.

So here are my attempts to answer the three questions most often posed to me in my encounters in the wider community. Inquirers want to know about the afterlife, Jesus, and race. It is essential that Jews explain themselves clearly to others. So much of the world's violence and bloodshed comes from a misunderstanding of each other's religious views. I feel a mission to teach about Judaism to people in the wider community. By doing so, I try to do my part in advancing fruitful dialogue between peoples and ultimately world peace.

The Myth of the
Judeo-Christian Tradition

Some years ago, a group of governors met in Fontana, Wisconsin. All went well until the final moments of the gathering. As the sessions were to close, Kirk Fordice, who was the governor of Mississippi, went to the podium. He then boldly declared that America is a Christian nation. At that moment, South Carolina's governor, Carroll Campbell, ran to the microphone. He feared that the remark of Governor Fordice might offend many people, so he tried to soften it.

Governor Campbell implied that Governor Fordice was essentially correct and that we are a Christian nation. However, he wanted to clarify it. He explained that the value base of our country comes from our Judeo-Christian heritage. After leaving the podium, Governor Campbell whispered to the Mississippi governor: "I just wanted to add the 'Judeo-' part." Governor Fordice snapped back: "If I wanted to do that, I would have done it."

The fact is that both governors were wrong. This is not a Christian country, even though the majority of citizens in the United States are of Christian origin. This is a country made up of people of a large variety of religions, as well as those with no religion at all. Each religious group is important. Each has significance.

Furthermore, the Judeo-Christian tradition is a myth. Critics have called it a clever device designed to promote ecumenical public relations. The term Judeo-Christian also reveals a profound ignorance of the true convictions of both Christians and Jews. It shows a blatant disregard for those unique and distinctive qualities that make Judaism and Christianity the great religions that they are.

Of course, in a very general way, Christians and Jews do share some values in common. Both Judaism and Christianity want people to behave ethically and morally, to live Godly lives. However, we approach this goal in much different ways.

A few examples. Judaism believes that human beings are born free of sin. Christianity, on the other hand, maintains that people are essentially sinful when they come into the world. They must be cleansed of that taint by professing their faith in Jesus.

Furthermore, Judaism believes that the center of religious life is the family and home. Christianity, however, maintains that the church is the center.

Then too, Judaism, though it does embrace a belief in life after death, stresses that the most important phase of one's existence is between the time one is born and the time one dies. Christianity, by contrast, emphasizes the afterlife, or life in the next world.

These basic differences between Judaism and Christianity would, of course, affect the way we behave toward other people, the way we respond to injustice, and the way we look upon our homes and our religious institutions. Using the expression "Judeo-Christian" ignores these realities.

Skipp Porteous, a former Pentecostal minister, well understands the difficulty with using this expression. He insists that the term Judeo-Christian "denies the uniqueness of Jewish history, experience, and faith." He calls it "false and misleading."

There is a second problem with the term besides its dishonesty. The expression Judeo-Christian is exclusive. Using it, we are asserting that America's religious groups consist only of Protestants, Catholics, and Jews, and no one else. This might have been an appropriate model for the 1950s. It is now out-of-date.

In America today, numerous people from the Far East and the Near East have settled in the United States. We now have many more religious communities than just Jews and Christians. There are Buddhists, Hindus, Bahais, Sikhs, and many others. In fact, in the United States today, there are more Muslims than Episcopalians.

The organization which had been known as the National Conference of Christians and Jews has appropriately undergone a change of name. It is now known as the National Conference of Community and Justice, which is more inclusive. It acknowledges the presence of multiple religious communities in our country, each deserving recognition.

Finally, besides being inaccurate and exclusive, the term Judeo-Christian has been coopted by the Religious Right. When Jerry Falwell founded the Moral Majority, many American Jews were troubled. Falwell tried to allay their fears. He began to use the term Judeo-Christian to attempt to soften Jewish opposition to his program.

Falwell and his cohorts argued that "Judeo-Christian" means that Christianity is based on Judaism. What they didn't mention is that, to them, Judaism is the parent religion, and Christianity is the child. Now that the child has outgrown its parent, it doesn't need the parent any longer. Christianity can now take the place of Judaism.

When the Christian Right speaks of Judeo-Christian values, most Jews would not endorse these values. Its followers invoke this term to oppose abortion, to fight gay rights, to block sex education programs, and to promote prayer in public schools. In fact, in a horrendous address that Pat Buchanan delivered to the Republican National Convention, he himself spoke of Judeo-Christian values. When religious zealots, like Jerry Falwell, Pat Buchanan, and Pat Robertson, use this term, they subtly denigrate Judaism and glorify Christianity.

Thus, the phrase Judeo-Christian blurs legitimate differences between Judaism and Christianity. It cuts out many religious groups that are now growing in numbers and strength in America. It also serves as a dangerous euphemism to promote the agenda of the Christian Right. Let us no longer use it.

Judaism is a precious religion to Jews. Christianity is a cherished religion to its followers. Each is a correct faith for its own adherents. Each religion, at its best, adds to the glory and beauty of our spiritual life in these United States. By avoiding the term Judeo-Christian, we will not compromise the uniqueness of Judaism and of Christianity, but rather we will enhance the integrity of both of them.

Should Jews Proselytize?

Most of us feel uneasy with the thought of missionaries. We imagine revival tents, gospel hymns, promises of eternal life in the bosom of Jesus, and threats of punishment and damnation for failing to embrace him. Missionaries carry a posture of self-righteousness. They appear holier-than-thou. Among the more fanatical and rabid, we can find gross intolerance, and even bigotry, which often leads to disastrous consequences.

Such might have been our reaction when we heard the call of Rabbi Alexander M. Schindler to bring the faith of Judaism to the non-Jew. Rabbi Schindler was the president of the Union of American Hebrew Congregations, the association of Reform synagogues in the United States and Canada.

In December 1978, in Houston, at the Board meeting of the UAHC, Rabbi Schindler galvanized the Board to pledge to plan a special program to bring the message of Judaism to any and to all who wish to examine or embrace it. The resolution they adopted states: "Judaism is not an exclusive club of born Jews. It is a universal faith with an ancient tradition which has deep resonance for people alive today." A special task force of thirty members was appointed to consider this and other recommendations for implementation and to report back to the spring 1979 meeting of the UAHC Board.

In his address, Rabbi Schindler dispelled some of our apprehension regarding missionaries. The campaign he proposed would avoid sensationalism. Rabbi Schindler assured us: "I do not envisage that we conduct our outreach program like some kind of traveling religious circus. I envisage, rather, the unfoldment of a dignified and responsible approach: the establishment of information centers in many places, well-publicized courses in our synagogues and the development of suitable publications to serve these facilities and purposes."

The appeal was to be directed only to the unchurched among the Gentiles. There was to be no attempt to undermine the allegiance of those who are already loyal to another religion.

Furthermore, in this campaign, we would not hold out the assurance of salvation to those who adopt Judaism. We would not promise perpetual bliss to those who would embrace our religious faith. In fact, Jews believe that the good and noble of all peoples can attain fulfillment.

Our motivation for seeking converts would be entirely different. We would not go forth to save souls. Rather, we would try to prevent Jewish extinction in America. There are now about 6,000,000 Jews in the United States. Yet, there is an impending problem with shrinkage. The rate of intermarriages in which the couple retains no ties with Judaism is soaring. Young Jewish couples, adhering to zero population growth, are not producing children. Some say that within a hundred years, the Jewish population in America may sink to as low as 10,000. In short, Rabbi Schindler suggested mass conversion as a possible guarantee for Jewish survival.

For years we have been taught that Jews have not proselytized actively. In fact, when a non-Jew approaches a rabbi to request admittance into Judaism, the rabbi is urged by tradition to respond somewhat negatively. Rabbis are to bring the person in with one hand while pushing him/her away with the other. They are to rehearse the woes and sufferings of the Jewish people over the centuries. They are to prepare the would-be proselyte for the vulnerability inherent in the life of the Jew. Only if the convert realizes that being a Jew can mean possible discrimination and persecution do rabbis begin to train that individual for conversion.

However, this ambivalence toward potential converts is a rather recent development. In the days of the Maccabees, about 2,000 years ago, Jews aggressively missionized. The production of the Septuagint, the translation of the Hebrew Bible into Greek, was part of this missionary drive. The intention was that once non-Jews understood the genius of Hebrew scriptures, they would abandon their former faith and become Jewish. So zealous was the Jew in proselytizing that the author of the Gospel of Matthew accuses the Jew of going to the ends of the earth to find a single soul for conversion.

Jews were eminently successful in their outreach to the Gentile. By the beginning of the Christian era, there were 4,000,000 converted Jews, constituting 10% of the population of the Roman Empire.

Soon, forces within and without dampened this Jewish missionary zeal. Christianity became the official religion of the Roman Empire. Antiochus Pius, the Roman emperor, forbade non-Jews to be circumcised. Since traditional Judaism requires circumcision for conversion, their proselytizing efforts were, necessarily, inhibited.

Later, Christian rulers ordered Jews to discontinue this plan of conversion. Both the proselytizer and the convert were subject to the death penalty if they disobeyed. The Islamic rulers who conquered much of Europe and the Middle East centuries later dealt in similar harsh ways with converts to Judaism and those Jews who converted them.

Then, too, many who converted to Judaism defected from the ranks of our people when it became disadvantageous to be a Jew. Amazingly, with all the warnings and penalties, and with all the backsliding, active conversion of the non-Jew continued until the sixteenth century, though with waning enthusiasm.

Rabbi Schindler's plan emerged from a different world view. It came out of a context of liberty. According to him, now that people are free to convert and fear no punishment, Jews should take advantage of this opportunity in order to save the Jewish people from disappearing.

Rabbi Schindler's proposal has much merit. Adding converts would strengthen Judaism. Many native-born Jews today, even those who are active in their synagogues, are essentially secularists. They are proud of our identity. They may be passionate supporters of the State of Israel; they want their children to remain Jewish. Yet their religious devotion is often wanting. They pray infrequently. They observe few rituals. The credo of the contemporary American Jew is: "I'm a good Jew but not very religious."

Those who enter Judaism from the non-Jewish world will approach Judaism as they did Christianity—primarily as a religious expression. They are not as concerned with ethnic preoccupations. Such is the reason that converts are among the most fervent participants in the spiritual life of a Jewish congregation. They are the ones who often have to coerce their biologically Jewish spouses to come to services. They are the ones who demand that their families celebrate the Holy Days at home. A host of converts will revitalize and reinvigorate the religious life of Judaism. They will spark a veritable Renaissance of Jewish religious practice in our Temples and synagogues.

Yet, there are some inescapable problems with his proposal. How can Jews who do not rank religious Judaism as a high priority in their daily lives be expected to persuade others of its value? Protestant missionaries are effective in their evangelical pursuits because they are consumed with the love of their religion. A luke-warm devotion will not win many adherents to Judaism.

Furthermore, in aggressively seeking converts, we may attract some who are emotionally disturbed and who are seeking solace in Judaism for the wrong reasons. They may have deep-seated psychological problems. We need to help and support these troubled individuals in their times of anguish. However, by encouraging them to become Jewish, we are dealing only with the symptom while allowing the actual problem to fester. In the Jewish community of which they may become a part, they can become a serious burden instead of a source of strength. We have a responsibility not only to the prospective proselyte, but also to the community of Jews. We must be careful not to allow conversion to become a substitution for psychotherapy.

In addition, unfortunately, some Jews incorrectly believe in a racial Judaism. They erroneously maintain that Judaism can be transmitted only through the bloodstream. In spite of all of our admonitions never to remind converts that they were once Gentiles, in spite of our insistence that a Jew by adoption is equal to the biological Jew in all respects, some Jews unjustifiably look upon the convert as a second-class citizen. Until they renounce this deplorable attitude about Jewish bluebloods, until we become less exclusive, we will not be ready for any active missionizing program.

I personally maintain that a program to convert the non-Jew in order to preserve the Jewish presence in America should be a last desperate step. Instead, our goal should be to attract non-practicing Jews to become Jewishly active. We should reach beyond the walls of the synagogue to those Jews who have persistently refused to become a part of synagogue life. In Los Angeles, my colleagues report that only 20% of the Jews of that city hold a membership in a Temple or synagogue. In San Antonio, years ago, almost every Jew belonged to a Temple or synagogue. Today, only 53% have joined.

Obviously, we are not meeting their needs. In dialogue with them, we need to find out why. It is more than just a question of money. We pay for what is precious to us. Let us listen to them, and discover the reason that in their lives Judaism has become so trivial and inconsequential.

Only if we overcome repeated failures at kindling the devotion to Judaism on the part of Jews should we design plans to bring the teaching of Judaism to the non-Jewish world.

Our religion, I agree, has much to offer. In a world of mind-manipulation engineered by the Jesus freaks, the Moonies, and Hare Krishna, we Jews teach freedom of thought.

In the age of deteriorating home life, we Jews stress family solidarity.

In a time of growing irrationalism and superstition, we Jews offer intellectual openness.

In a time of callousness and indifference, we Jews uphold human dignity in a just society.

We should bear these gifts first to the many Jews who, until now, have spurned or neglected them. It is our hope that they will discover the satisfactions and the benefits that Judaism provides.

Raising an Interfaith Child

Many interfaith couples struggle with the perplexing question of how to raise their children religiously. Often they want to cover all their bases. Therefore, they rear their children in neither religion, but expose them to both, and then let the children choose when they are adults.

Other interfaith parents bring up their children with both faiths simultaneously. In their homes they celebrate both Jewish and Christian holidays. In the case of a male child, they want to hold a *B'rit Milah*, or a ritual circumcision, and then later a baptism, so as to commit the child to both Judaism and Christianity from the beginning. Actually, I don't know of any responsible rabbi or *mohel*, or ritual circumciser, who will agree to preside over a *B'rit* if they know that a baptism has preceded or will follow the ritual circumcision.

Sometimes the reason for raising the children in two religions at once is that each of the parents is deeply committed to his or her own faith and desires to transmit it to the child. In other words, neither parent wants to give up a claim to that child's religious identity.

Other parents in mixed unions are apathetic about religion. They are involved in an "interfaithless" marriage. However, they hope to appease both the Jewish and the Christian grandparents. Therefore, they want the child to undergo both a *B'rit* and a baptism. Sometimes the Christian wants to play it safe for fear that, if the child is not baptized, the child might be doomed to damnation.

Parents who subject their child to ritual circumcision and baptism may erroneously believe that Judaism and Christianity are essentially variations of the same religion and that no fundamental differences exist between them. To them, Christmas trees or Hanukkah menorahs, hot-cross buns or latkes, colored Easter eggs or roasted Seder eggs—these are matters of taste, not principle.

Indeed, Judaism and Christianity are similar in so many ways. Both stress ethical living. Both draw inspiration from Hebrew Scriptures. Both affirm an allegiance to God. Yet, on certain fundamental points, the distinctions between Judaism and Christianity are profound. Some beliefs are not compatible with each other, contrary to what the Jews for Jesus and the Messianic Jews may stridently claim. Such is particularly true of the birth ceremonies in each tradition.

Christians perform baptism because many believe in the idea of Original Sin. Adam and Eve rebelled against God, who forbade them to eat of the Tree of Knowledge. As a result, Adam and Eve caused every human being in subsequent generations to enter the world with an Original Sin. Original Sin is a condition of birth. It is congenital. There is no human remedy to remove the primal taint.

Among some Christian faiths, like the Roman Catholic, infant baptism is a must. It removes this inherited stain. Without baptism, the soul of that infant will remain unredeemed and defiled. In fact, a child remains a non-Christian, even if born to Christian parents, until that baptism is performed.

Unlike baptism, *B'rit Milah*, or ritual circumcision, does not obliterate Original Sin. In fact, Judaism maintains that the infant is born innocent and without blemish or taint. In Judaism, a person sins when he or she does something sinful, not because that person was born into sin. Everyone does sinful things, because all of us are fallible as human beings. Yet, Judaism provides mechanisms, like Yom Kippur, to help rid ourselves of sin.

Furthermore, even before the ritual circumcision, a male infant is considered a Jew if he is born to Jewish parents. Circumcision is performed, not to remove sin nor to establish Jewish identity, but to seal the covenant God made with Abraham into the flesh.

Thus, ritual circumcision and baptism cannot be performed on the same child. As Rabbi Harold Schulweis observes: "Circumcision and baptism are not knife-or-water options, but ritualized dramas of values. They affect our relationships to God, world, and self." Respect for each other's faiths does not demand that we homogenize our different religious traditions. Each religion must uphold its own uniqueness and its own integrity.

Raising a child in two faiths or neither faith ultimately leaves the child confused and plagued with tangled roots. I maintain that the child of a mixed marriage should be pledged to one specific faith, and that decision should be made before the child is born. It should not be delayed. Naturally, as one anxiously concerned about the continuation and survival of Judaism, I hope the child will be brought up as a Jew.

To raise the child in neither or both faiths makes it temporarily easy for the parents. After all, at that point, neither has to sacrifice anything in the marriage. But to do so will eventually inflict a terrible injustice on the child. It will force a child to select one religion over another. In the child's mind, that means choosing one parent over another. This is an unfair burden to lay upon a child.

Also, raising the child in neither or both faiths leaves a child in limbo, with a clouded sense of self. I think of Benjamin Disraeli, who became prime minister of Great Britain during the reign of Queen Victoria. Though he was born Jewish, his father arranged his conversion to Christianity when he was almost a Bar Mitzvah celebrant. Though religiously an Anglican, Disraeli still remained connected to his Jewish roots but often felt adrift. Victoria once asked him: "Which Testament is yours?" Disraeli replied: "I am the blank page between the Old Testament and the New Testament."

Disraeli's haunting statement leads us to conclude that children need to feel a sense of belonging, to tie their fate and destiny to a particular group. Such is crucial for a child's ultimate well-being, identity, and security.

Blessings in Judaism and Christianity

Often, at a dinner, the host will approach me and ask: "Rabbi, before we start eating, will you please bless the bread?" Actually, I don't know how to bless the bread. What I can do is offer a blessing over the bread. Yes, there is an important distinction between the act of blessing the bread, which is Christian, and that of pronouncing a blessing over the bread, which is Jewish.

John Shelby Spong, one of the most exciting religious writers today, explains the difference brilliantly. Spong was the Episcopal Bishop of Newark, New Jersey. He has written several volumes on uncovering the Hebrew roots of Christianity.

Spong points out that Judaism looks positively at the world and all of the creations within it. God declared them to be good during the first days of creation. They continue to be the objects of God's love, because things in the physical universe are basically good. God intended for us to appreciate them. Therefore, when we sit down to eat bread, we bless God, not the bread. It is God, who, in goodness, makes that bread possible. Such is true about all other objects, like the Torah and Sabbath candles, over which we recite blessings, as well.

Bishop Spong points out that classical Christianity, by contrast, having come under strong Greek influence, traditionally has seen the physical world and its various parts as evil. Therefore, in classical Christianity, bread is unclean, because it is a part of the material universe. It remains defiled until certain words are said, certain formulae are recited, and certain signs are performed. In classical Christianity, then, to bless something means to cleanse it, to purify it, to rid it of its taint and blemish.

Yes, our approaches vary considerably. We Jews intone blessings for three entirely different reasons. The first one is illustrated by the story of two beggars. Both were soliciting charity from passersby on a busy city street. Both were hapless and forlorn-looking figures. Yet one of them seemed far more successful than the other. People were dropping nickels, dimes, quarters, and even dollars into the cup of the one, while generally ignoring the other.

Someone watching this scene nearby soon discovered the reason. The card of the unsuccessful beggar read: "I am blind." However, the card of the successful one stated: "It is May, and I am blind." This second beggar called the attention of each passerby to the beauty of the springtime that his blindness had robbed him of seeing. Thus, the first reason that we offer blessings in Judaism is to keep us in a constant state of awareness of God's gifts to us, that we may tend to overlook and ignore.

In the Talmud, Rabbi Judah prescribes that when a person is walking and sees beautiful trees swaying in the air, that person should stop there and say: "Blessed is the Lord, for having created a world, in which nothing is lacking, and for having made living things and beautiful trees and plants to delight the human heart." (b. *Berakhot* 43b)

Indeed, in Judaism, traditionally we are enjoined to utter 100 blessings a day to God for seemingly mundane happenings. Some of these are eating bread and other kinds of food, drinking wine, seeing a previously unknown species of an animal for the first time, viewing the ocean, beholding a rainbow, and even awakening successfully from sleep.

The Rabbis remind us that to enjoy anything in this world without first offering a blessing is like robbing the sanctuary. Thus we must acknowledge everything we enjoy in this world as a special offering of God. It remains God's property until we acquire ownership by reciting a benediction. The blessing is to keep alive in us a sense of wonder, awe, astonishment, and surprise at God's never-ending goodness.

The second purpose of offering blessings is revealed in the tale of Samuel Morse, who developed the Morse Code. Before the age of telephones, radios, televisions, and computers, messages were transmitted by dots and dashes. These dots and dashes were arranged in an intricate way to spell words and to convey the most complex of ideas.

When Samuel Morse completed his first message across the wires, it did not say: "Look how great a genius I am to have invented this remarkable system." Rather, he wrote: "What God hath wrought!" Morse ascribed his creativity and his inventiveness not to himself, but to God.

Thus we offer a blessing to learn humility. Our hands and our minds might have accomplished something extraordinary. Yet God is the one who is ultimately responsible. During our meals, we often eat bread. It is true that the bread is the end product of many previous steps, all involving human activity: growing the wheat, cutting it down, making the flour, kneading the dough, shaping the bread, and baking the bread. And yet before partaking of it, we thank God, not the human agents who were involved in its production, for bringing forth this bread from the earth.

There is yet another purpose of offering blessings: to enlarge our souls. So many of us go through life mechanically and prosaically. Each day we immerse ourselves in trivialities, in petty issues, and in inconsequential goals. We are afflicted with stress, mixed with boredom and monotony.

How well the poet, William Wordswoth, captures this sad state of affairs in his lament:

> The world is too much with us; late and soon,
> getting and spending, we lay waste our powers:
> Little we see in Nature that is ours;
> we have given our hearts away, a sordid boon . . .

The function of a blessing is to correct this condition. It is to enlarge and enrich our lives, to lift up our spirits, to broaden our vistas, to raise our sights.

It is communicated in a story about a man who had gone without food for several days and needed money to end his starvation. Someone noticed his plight and gave him five dollars. The donor asked him how he intended to spend the money. He replied: "With three dollars, I'll buy food. With the remaining two, I'll purchase flowers. The food is in order to live; the flowers are in order to make life worth living." Indeed, how grateful we are that Judaism has given us the opportunity to bless God in order to make our souls great and to make our lives worth living.

Hanukkah: More Like
Thanksgiving than Christmas

There are a few times in a century that Hanukkah begins during Thanksgiving weekend. Personally, I am thrilled on those occasions when Hanukkah coincides with Thanksgiving. I think that it helps us to resist the temptation to identify Hanukkah too closely with Christmas.

I will admit that there are some similarities between Hanukkah and Christmas. Both occur on the 25th day of the month. Hanukkah starts on the 25th of the Hebrew month of Kislev, while Christmas begins on the 25th of December.

In addition, both Hanukkah and Christmas are holidays of light. Both are probably based on an even older winter light festival before Judaism and Christianity even began. When the days became short, ancient peoples feared that darkness would overtake them permanently. Therefore, they lit bonfires and torches to assure themselves that there would be light in the midst of the encroaching darkness.

These two holidays of Hanukkah and Christmas probably grew out of a common pagan celebration of light. Today we mark Hanukkah with the menorah, a symbol of light. In the Christian community, light is the dominant feature of the Advent wreath, which is kindled weekly for four weeks before Christmas, as well as the Christmas tree.

But yet, beneath these superficial similarities, the minor Jewish holiday of Hanukkah and the major Christian holiday of Christmas have little in common. They celebrate two entirely different historical events. Hanukkah marks a triumph over religious persecution, while Christmas recalls the birth of the Christian savior.

However, there is a strong link between Hanukkah and Thanksgiving. Both Hanukkah and Thanksgiving celebrate the efforts of religious groups to preserve their spiritual identity. The holiday of Thanksgiving recalls the Pilgrims, who came to these shores in revolt against the Church of England. This state church persecuted them for refusing to subscribe to the doctrines of the dominant Anglican faith. The Pilgrims had to leave England in order to carry on their religious traditions as they believed.

Similarly, the Maccabees in Palestine valiantly fought against the paganism which their Syrian Greek overlords tried to impose on them. Antiochus sent his soldiers to Jerusalem to convert the Holy Temple into a pagan shrine and to outlaw the practice of Judaism.

Antiochus set up altars and idols throughout Judea. He forbade Jews to follow their sacred traditions, like Shabbat, circumcision, and the dietary laws. He insisted that the Jews of Palestine bow down and sacrifice to these idols. The Syrian Greeks took the Torah, spattered it with pigs' blood, and then burned it.

Essentially, Antiochus gave Jews a choice: either convert to Greek idolatry or die. Most Jews went along with Antiochus. However, a minority, known as the Maccabees, fought against the Syrian Greeks and rescued the Holy Land from idolatry. Like the Pilgrims, the Maccabees were religious non-conformists. Both resisted the coercion of the leaders of the dominant culture and insisted on worshiping God as they believed to be right.

It would be a mistake, however, to call Hanukkah and Thanksgiving holidays of religious freedom. The Maccabees fought for the right of the Jewish community to practice Judaism according to the dictates of the Torah. However, they would not tolerate non-observant Jews within their community. The Maccabees were zealots. They would not allow any

Jew within their group to violate Jewish law, in a flagrant way, by eating pork or by smoking on the Sabbath.

Similarly, the Pilgrims, also known as the Puritans, wanted rights only for their community, not for individuals within the community. They were intolerant of any member of their community whose beliefs or practices were deviant. They enforced a rigid observance of Sunday as the Sabbath. They originated the Blue Laws. They also created a sexually repressive society. They even conducted the Salem witchcraft trials to deal harshly with those whom they considered sinners.

It was only with the Enlightenment 200 years ago that the notion of individual religious freedom, as we understand it today, emerged. The idea that one could worship any God that he or she pleases or not believe in any God at all would have been foreign both to the Maccabees and the Pilgrims or Puritans.

Thus, we must conclude that both Hanukkah and Thanksgiving are not holidays of religious freedom. They are holidays of religious survival. Both celebrate the stubborn refusal of religious groups to submit to the ways of the majority. Both represent the victory of spiritual integrity and continuity in a world hostile to their messages.

Jews and the Anti-Christ

One the most popular children's public television shows is "Teletubbies." Actors dressed in colorful, oversized costumes portray the four "Teletubbies." They are called "Teletubbies" because a television screen is built into each of their protruding stomachs. They cavort in the tranquil green hills and the warm sunshine of a peaceful place called Teletubby Land.

Each Teletubby is garbed in a different color. Dipsy is green. Laa-Laa is yellow. Po is red. Tinky Winky is purple. Yet right-wing Christian televangelist Jerry Falwell singled Tinky Winky out for his special wrath.

Falwell accused the producer of this show of designing Tinky Winky to be a gay role model. Falwell marshaled these three pieces of evidence as proof: Tinky Winky's color is purple, the color of gay pride. In addition, the antenna on the top of his head is shaped like a triangle, the gay symbol. Furthermore, Tinky Winky, though a male, sometimes carries a red purse.

Steve Rice, an executive with the company that licenses "Teletubbies," charged that Falwell's claims are silly. He explained that Tinky Winky's purse is actually a magic bag. Such an apparel item does not make a person gay. Rice went on to say that reading sexual innuendoes into a children's show is not only sad; it is also absurd and offensive to attack something that is designed to be a sweet and innocent production for preschool children.

Falwell's remarks unleashed a tidal wave of ridicule and parody in the media. Cartoonists and talk-show hosts, like Jay Leno and Conan O'Brien, had a great time lampooning Falwell. Barry Lynn, the executive director of the Americans

United for the Separation of Church and State, wrote that he awaits the day when Falwell will go after the other Teletubbies. He may even attack the green Dipsy as a symbol of the radical environmentalist movement and the red Po as a sign of Communism.

Perhaps Falwell is unaware that purple, identified with gay pride, is also the official color of the vestments of Roman Catholic cardinals. When a priest is elevated to the rank of cardinal, people say that he has been "raised to the purple."

Falwell's assault on Tinky Winky was actually the second of his recent offenses within a short time period. Earlier that year, he spoke at a prayer breakfast for the National Religious Broadcasters' convention in Nashville, Tennessee. Fifteen hundred people were in attendance. The breakfast, which included some Jewish leaders as guests, featured prayers for Jerusalem.

In his address, Falwell told the breakfast participants that he believed that Jesus will return to earth in ten years. Then he added that the Anti-Christ, a sign of supreme evil, will precede Jesus. After Jesus returns, he will defeat the Anti-Christ. Falwell then added the "zinger." He emphasized that the Anti-Christ must be a Jewish man and that he is alive today. Falwell's remarks set off an avalanche of criticism from Jewish and ecumenical leaders. They feared that Falwell's comments could inspire assaults on Jewish men.

Falwell quickly responded with a press release. He denied that he was an anti-Semite and apologized for offending anyone. He made clear, however, that his apology was not for the substance of his comments. Rather, it was for his lack of tact and judgment in expressing them as he did. Most of the Jewish leaders accepted his words of contrition. I believe they might have let him off the hook too easily.

Falwell, after all, revived a false, but lethal, medieval stereotype about Jews. Linking the Anti-Christ with a Jew is one of the most dangerous historical myths. Some, like Falwell, do believe that, before the second coming of Jesus, a time of chaos and confusion will sweep the earth. It is called a period of Tribulation.

At that time, the Anti-Christ will appear. The Anti-Christ does not always mean one opposed to Christ, as the prefix "anti-" implies. It can also mean an alternative to Christ. The Anti-Christ will be a clever, cunning, conniving, and charming figure. He will have all the answers to the world's problems. Eventually, this Anti-Christ will turn out to be the most vicious monster the world has ever known.

According to some versions of this poisonous medieval tale, the Anti-Christ had a soiled beginning. He was born to a mother who was a Jewish prostitute and to a father who was the devil. The Anti-Christ is contrasted with Jesus, whose parents were a Jewish mother, who was a virgin, and a father, who was God. Comparisons between Jesus and the Anti-Christ in this myth continue. Though the Anti-Christ was born in Babylonia or Persia, he, like Jesus, was raised in the Galilee. However, unlike Jesus, sorcerers and witches specializing in black art trained him.

Like Jesus, at age thirty, he went to Jerusalem to reveal himself to the Jews as their Messiah. His powers of persuasion, his superficial saintliness, his ability to perform magical feats, and his vast wealth won the Jews to him. He finally succeeded in convincing them that he was their Messiah. Jews then followed him, even though eventually he would cause their deaths.

Like Jesus, the Anti-Christ preached and taught for three and one-half years. Then he tried to imitate Jesus' resurrection. He had hoped to ascend to heaven, borne by demons. Some day the angel Michael will come to destroy him at Armageddon, which is the battleground of the war between the forces of good and evil. His Jewish followers will continue to believe in him, even while they are being annihilated. After that time, Jesus will make his second appearance.

We can see how sinister a claim Falwell made. Not only was the Anti-Christ born of the union of a Jewish whore with the devil. Also, by embracing him, rather than the real Christ, as the Messiah, Jews will lose their lives. This will be their punishment.

We in the Jewish community must be on guard against people like the Falwells. Let us not be misled by their fervent support of the State of Israel and by their generous contributions to Jewish causes. Their theology dictates that Jews must live in an independent state, whose borders are defined in the Bible. Jews should not surrender even one inch of their land. Only then will their Messiah come. Unfortunately, Israel's former prime minister, Binyamin Netanyahu, and other leaders of the Likud party court these people.

They overlook the fact that, when the Messiah does come, the Falwells believe that then Jesus will take over the State, rebuild the Temple, and reign in Jerusalem. Jews will finally see the light and accept Jesus as the true Messiah. Because these ultra-right Christian groups strongly oppose the peace process, they have won the hearts of Israelis who likewise want to overturn the Oslo Accords. I am appalled that, whenever Netanyahu came to the United States, during his incumbency, he met with Falwell and others, while he refused to be photographed with any group of Reform rabbis, for fear of censure from his ultra-Orthodox Jewish supporters.

I am glad that Falwell and his ilk speak only for a segment of the Christian community. There are so many more Christians who oppose his message and know how harmful it is to inter-group relations. There are Christians, like Dr. Norman Beck, of Texas Lutheran University, who has written and spoken extensively on confronting honestly the anti-Jewish portions of the New Testament. He and others are struggling with these verses so they do not bring further harm to Jews.

I know Christian leaders who are pained that the Holocaust began in Germany, one of the most Christian countries. They realize that the hatred that their clergy taught in their churches about Jews paved the way for Nazism. These are the Christians that we Jews must embrace and befriend. Let us open our hearts and our minds to them and know who our true allies are.

Grace: Christian and Jewish Understandings

One of my most talented colleagues in the ministry in San Antonio is Max Lucado. An evangelical Christian leader, Max is a prolific author and a gifted preacher. A few years ago, he wrote a book, entitled *In the Grip of Grace*. Max has an amazing ability to illustrate difficult theological ideas with homey and pithy illustrations. One of these is grace. Grace is God's love for us which we do not necessarily deserve. To describe grace as an evangelical Christian, Max relates an unsettling autobiographical tale. He received a disturbing letter from his former insurance company.

The letter informed Max that he was being dropped as a client. On Max's record were some speeding violations, as well as a serious collision, when he carelessly backed into a vehicle in a parking lot. His wife, Denalyn, had been part of the same auto insurance policy. Her driving record was not much better than Max's. She, too, had been caught speeding, and she also had rear-ended a car at a stop sign.

After receiving this disturbing letter, Max thought that he could provide a good defense of his and Denalyn's accident. It is true that he did run into another car in the parking lot. Yet, he did face up to his responsibilities. He could have been a hit-and-run driver, something that he considered doing. However, he decided to confront the owner. He walked into the building adjacent to the parking lot, approached the owner, and reported what he had done. Shouldn't Max be given some credit for his honesty?

And then there is the case of his wife, Denalyn, who rear-ended a car. He thought that the insurance company could be more considerate of all of her circumstances. After all, she was giving a bottle to their baby, Sara, while at a stoplight. Sara had dropped the bottle on the car floor and was crying. Denalyn, as a good mother, bent over to pick the bottle up. In the process, she hit the car in front of her. Couldn't the company see this accident as an honest mistake of a conscientious mother and not hold it against her?

After reviewing these rationalizations, Max continued to be puzzled by the harsh action of the insurance company in not retaining him as a client. Max learned the hard way that insurance coverage has strict limitations. We, then, must wonder if God's insurance has similar limitations.

Max asks us to imagine getting a letter from Heaven informing us that we have reached our quota of sins. We have been guilty of excessive greed. Our prayer life has been anemic. We have gossiped excessively. We have been unfaithful to the cardinal doctrines of our religion. God could now tell us that the protection that God has to offer also has limits. It is no longer available to us. We must find some other form of coverage.

At this point, Max launches more fully into his explanation of grace from his Christian evangelical perspective. Suppose, Max asks, the founder and CEO of the insurance company chooses to be kind and merciful to Max. He wants to keep Max, in spite of his numerous mishaps on the road, as a client. To do so, the head of the insurance company can close his eyes, grant Max amnesty, and clear Max's driving record, as well as his wife's. This possibility presents two serious problems, however. First of all, it would compromise the integrity of the insurance company. It would cause the company to lower its standards.

Secondly, this president's action would not inhibit Max from making serious errors on the road in the future. In fact, he might even be encouraged to make more. Why should Max drive carefully if there is no accountability? If the president of the insurance company would be willing to overlook

Max's behavior behind the wheel, why should Max bother to be cautious on the road?

The challenge for the head of the insurance company, then, is how can he be kind to Max, and yet address the fact that Max made serious mistakes as an automobile vehicle operator? The president could call Max into his office and tell him that he found a solution to this thorny dilemma. He could reveal to Max that he checked the records of other clients and found one person with a spotless past. This individual had never speeded nor was he ever in a collision. Not even a parking ticket was issued to him.

The president could inform Max that this person had volunteered to trade records with Max. Max's name could be placed on that individual's file and *vice versa*. The company would now hold this other client accountable and fault him for what Max did. Max was flabbergasted by this seemingly generous proposal. Max asked the president, "Who in the world would offer to do such a thing?" The president said, "Me."

In human terms, we know that there is no CEO of any insurance company who would make such a magnanimous offer. No executive of any stature would switch his own clean record with the blemished record of one of his clients. However, Max informed us that God had done so through Jesus. Jesus gave his followers his own perfect record in exchange for their blemished record. By his death, Jesus atones for their sins.

In this system of Christian grace, God doesn't condone their sin nor does God compromise any standards. God doesn't ignore their transgressions. Instead of blaming them for their sins, God, through Jesus, assumes their sins and sentences himself. By believing in Jesus, who switches insurance records with them and pays their premiums, they now have a paid-up, irrevocable insurance policy called grace. Even if they are undeserving, God, through Jesus, has given them a way to wipe away their sins, according to Max.

The Christian understanding is valid and appropriate for

Christians, and I respect it, as such. As a Jew, however, I would tell the story about Max's auto insurance differently. I would have the president or CEO of the insurance company summon Max to his office. Under no circumstances would he trade his clean record for Max's blemished one. Rather, he would tell Max that Max now has the opportunity to check his driving record carefully and to show that he is truly regretful for his mistakes and mishaps as a driver. After Max does so, Max must promise the president never to repeat them.

The president must now believe that Max is truly sorry about his past record. He must be convinced that Max intends to be scrupulously careful on the road in the future. The president then informs Max that he has one more step to take. He must prove that he is willing to act on that commitment to reform himself behind the wheel. Only then will the president clear Max's record of all past violations. In other words, no one can switch records with Max. Only Max himself, through his acts of regret and reaffirmation, can be absolved of his spotted record.

Thus, we Jews generally understand grace as something that we earn, not something that God freely gives us without any action or merit on our part. Such is the dominant view of grace within the Jewish tradition. There is also a recessive view, however. Here we receive unmerited consideration from God.

On the High Holy Days, for instance, we stand before God and freely admit we are undeserving when we pray: "Our Father, our King, be merciful to us and answer us. Even though we have no merit, treat us with justice and kindness and save us." We can pray in this fashion on the High Holy Days because we depend on *zekhut avot*, the merit of our ancestors. We are unworthy. Yet we inherited from Abraham, Isaac, and Jacob, and other religious giants, a rich legacy of spiritual capital. We, indeed, are conscious of our errors and are unworthy of God's pardon. Still, we can withdraw some of the untapped rewards from the estates of these forebears in order to win God's favor.

In other words, Max could approach the president of the insurance company and claim that, even though his driving record is blemished, his departed loved ones, who were faithful clients of the company, had pure records. He could ask that he be given credit for their excellent driving performance.

In this recessive view, is also a concept of vicarious atonement, in which innocent parties suffer for the sins of the guilty, as Jesus does for Christians. In ancient times, the High Priest would drive a goat, carrying the community's blemishes, into the wilderness. Then, too, there is the legend of the *Lamed Vavniks*. In each generation, there are thirty-six (the numerical values of the Hebrew letters *Lamed* and *Vav* total thirty-six) righteous, pure, and self-effacing individuals who are harassed and persecuted in order to atone for the sins of others who are guilty.

In short, then, we Jews generally believe that grace is based solely on our own actions for which we alone must perform. We must earn God's love through our obedience to the commandments. In other words, our driving records are our own responsibility.

In rare instances, however, God does wipe away the offenses from our blemished record—not because of any improvement in our own behavior, but because of the outstanding performance of our distinguished ancestors or the willingness of others to suffer for the consequences of our misdeeds. In these cases, God shows us special love by enabling us to begin anew with a fresh start without any positive action on our part.

V

Jewish Beliefs and Practices

Kabbalah Lite

Some time ago, Madonna, the noted entertainment star, hosted a Kabbalah cocktail party. The Kabbalah is the name we give to our Jewish mystical literature. Madonna is just one of scores of screen and stage personalities who, of late, have been attracted to the study of Kabbalah.

Other big names include Roseanne, Barbra Streisand, and Elizabeth Taylor. All of them have "made it" by external standards. They have amassed money, fame, power, and influence. However, they are obviously unsatisfied and unfulfilled in their personal lives. They are looking to the esoteric wisdom of the Kabbalah for answers.

Their quest is part of a widespread American Jewish hunger for the spiritual. Many searching Jews grew up in the 1950s and early 1960s. American Jewish life in those days seemed to center on building new edifices and supporting Israel. No one paid too much attention to the needs of the soul.

Today, a growing number of sensitive Jews are clamoring for the mystical and the transcendent. Many of them are not aware that within Judaism are rich resources to fill their spiritual void. Thus they turn to Zen Buddhism and other Eastern religions for nourishment. Those Jews, however, who want to explore matters of the spirit within the confines of Judaism are flocking to purveyors of the Kabbalah. In fact, the exploration of the Kabbalah has become a national Jewish passion, if not a fad. How should we respond?

We must point out that, for centuries, learned and pious Jews ignored the Kabbalah. Some were even fearful of it. In his novel *As a Driven Leaf*, Rabbi Milton Steinberg adapted the Talmudic tale of the four Rabbis who met frequently to study mysticism. They were Ben Azzai, Ben Zoma, Elisha ben Abuyah, and Akiva.

The results were disastrous. The Talmud records that Rabbi Ben Azzai went mad. Rabbi Ben Zoma died. Elisha ben Abuyah, the hero of Steinberg's novel, became a heretic and abandoned Judaism. Only Rabbi Akiva remained spiritually intact. Some Jewish scholars were convinced that Jews become mentally unfit after pursuing mystical studies.

This apprehension was reinforced 400 years ago. Shabbetai Zevi, a hypnotic and charismatic personality from Turkey, began to study the Kabbalah in great depth. From his intensive studies, he drew the conclusion that he was the Messiah. He regarded himself as the one elected by God to end the persecution of the Jewish people and to return them to the Holy Land. He traveled from country to country, including the Holy Land, and successfully convinced whole Jewish communities the world over of his Messianic claim.

Some Jewish mystics believed that the Messiah would actually appear in 1666. In that year, they challenged Shabbetai. They asked him to try to dethrone the mighty Sultan in Constantinople. Shabbetai rose to the challenge. When Shabbetai arrived in Constantinople, he and his entourage were imprisoned. But even behind bars, Shabbetai was allowed to receive huge delegations of Jewish communities the world over. He was tremendously popular.

The Sultan quickly saw that Shabbetai was a threat to his throne. He gave Shabbetai a choice: conversion to Islam or execution. Standing before the Sultan, Shabbetai Zevi lost heart and became an apostate. He put on a fez to demonstrate to the Sultan that he had now embraced the Islamic faith.

With his conversion, a mass wave of disillusionment swept over thousands of his loyal followers. After Shabbetai's notorious betrayal, which they blamed on the Kabbalah, the Rabbis made a strict rule: only married men over forty who were Torah and Talmud scholars would be allowed to study

Kabbalah. This pursuit was to be limited to people of advanced years, solid learning, and impeccable character.

In addition to this threat of the potential dangers of studying Kabbalah, respected Jewish scholars until recently considered the Kabbalah to be of minimal value. They were largely attracted to rationalism, not mysticism. This was particularly true of Reform leaders. In fact, when I was a rabbinical student at Hebrew Union College-Jewish Institute of Religion in Cincinnati, which is the American seminary of Reform Judaism, I never studied the Kabbalah.

It was the great German-Jewish scholar Gershom Scholem who began to reshape this viewpoint. He tried to bring respectability to the study of the Kabbalah through his comprehensive research into the history of Jewish mysticism while teaching at Hebrew University in Jerusalem. But even Scholem had trouble convincing his colleagues of the worth of his work.

The Jewish Theological Seminary, where Conservative rabbis are trained, invited Scholem to lecture on the Kabbalah in the mid-1940s. Professor Saul Lieberman, a world-renowned Talmudist and the foremost member of the Seminary faculty at that time, was asked to introduce Dr. Scholem. In doing so, he mentioned that, for several years, Seminary students had been clamoring for a course in the Kabbalah. He told them: "At a creditable academic institution like ours, it is improper to offer a course on *narishkeit* (nonsense). But the history of *narishkeit* (nonsense), that's different. That's scholarship. With that in mind, I present to you Dr. Scholem."

This negative stance of Professor Lieberman and other Jewish scholars does not resonate with modern Jews today. Many have positive feelings about the Kabbalah, even though they know little about it. And this is the major problem.

So much of Kabbalah study today is superficial. Many who teach it today have not even read a page from the original texts. The Kabbalah requires immense learning and vast scholarship to understand and teach it properly.

The Kabbalah is based on a work called the Zohar, which means "light." In the 1200s, Moses de Leon, a Spanish Jew, discovered the Zohar. De Leon claimed it had been composed by the eminent ancient Rabbi Shimon bar Yochai to win its acceptance. However, most scholars believe that de Leon was the real author. It is written in Aramaic, a language similar to Hebrew, in which most of the Kaddish is formulated. The Zohar is a running mystical commentary on the Five Books of Moses. It contains the keys to unlocking the secrets of God. By delving into it properly, one can begin to unravel Divine mysteries.

The Zohar is based on the idea that God is the *Ein Sof*, which means "without boundaries." As the *Ein Sof*, God is inaccessible and unknowable. However, God does make the Divine self known through a series of ten *Sefirot*, or emanations. It is through the spheres that the individual can make contact with God.

Most organized tours to Israel include a trip to the famous synagogue of Rabbi Isaac Luria in Safed. This synagogue is known for its elaborately crafted gilded Holy Ark. Isaac Luria, also called "*Ha-Ari*," or "The Lion," added a new dimension of understanding of the Zohar. He believed that the Prophet Elijah visited him and brought him new insights into the mystical tradition. According to *Ha-Ari*, before the spheres were formed, God, the *Ein Sof*, had to withdraw in order to leave room for the spheres to emerge. This withdrawal is called *Tzimtzum*. Rabbi Luria also believed in reincarnation. He taught that every soul, especially that of a sinner, must return to this world in the body of another person in order to be further purified.

As we can see from this very brief overview, the study of Jewish mysticism is not for dabblers or dilettantes. It is for those who want "Kabbalah **Light**," not for those who seek "Kabbalah Lite." The Kabbalah requires deep concentration and immense learning.

In the meantime, there are many other Jewish literary sources, like the 150 Psalms, which demand much less technical expertise. These ancient poetic words of inspiration can bring us the kind of spiritual satisfaction we are seeking. The search for the big answers of life in Jewish sacred writings is commendable. However, I hope interested persons will seek them in documents they can confront and comprehend with integrity.

The Meaning of the *Mezuzzah*

A story is told about a wealthy Jewish Englishman who bought a spacious home with more than fifty rooms. He then invited a corps of workmen to decorate the place. After the task had been completed, the Jewish owner remembered that he had forgotten to add *mezuzzot* (plural of *mezuzzah*) to the doors. He went out and bought fifty of them and asked the workmen to affix them to the various rooms in the house.

The owner was concerned that the decorators wouldn't do their job properly and would chip the paint. He left the house and in a few hours returned to find that all the *mezuzzot* were properly installed. He was so thrilled that he gave the decorator a bonus. As the decorator was leaving, he said: "I'm so glad that you're happy with the job that we did. By the way, we took out all the guarantees that were in those little boxes and left them on the table for you."

In this humorous tale, we find a common misconception about the nature of the *mezuzzah*. The container, regardless of how artistically designed it is, is not the essential part of the *mezuzzah*. The essential part is the small piece of parchment inside of it.

The rules about producing this parchment are clear and precise. On it, a scribe, like the one who writes the Torah scrolls, inscribes two passages from the Book of Deuteronomy in twenty-two lines. One of these is the *Shema*. The *Shema*, in its extended form, tells us to write the words of Torah "upon the doorposts of your house and upon your gates." The other section from Deuteronomy outlines God's rewards if we follow the commandments. On the reverse side of the parchment, the scribe pens the word *"Shaddai,"* which means "the Almighty One."

The parchment is then rolled into a cylinder with the word *"Shaddai"* on the outside. It is inserted in a case, often made of metal, wood, or ceramic. The *mezuzzah* is then placed on the main doors of every room of the home, except the bathroom, kitchen, laundry room, garage, and areas of that nature. It is set on the top third section of the upper right doorpost as one enters the home or the room. It is fastened onto the doorpost with screws, nails, or glue, after a proper blessing is recited.

It is always set at a 45-degree angle, if possible. The reason is the result of a debate between two eminent Rabbis about 900 years ago over the proper positioning of the *mezuzzah*. One insisted that it be set vertically and the other horizontally. The rabbinical court called upon to resolve this disagreement did not want to favor one authority over the other. Thus they compromised by mandating that the *mezuzzah* should be placed diagonally, with the top pointing inward. Reform Jews generally consider it sufficient to place a single *mezuzzah* on the main entrance door of the home and do not require *mezuzzot* on the other doors.

Mezuzzot are placed only on the doors of permanent dwellings. Therefore, one would not add a *mezuzzah* to the entrance of a Sukkah, which is only used for one week during the year. Synagogues have inherent holiness, so no *mezuzzot* are needed on their doors, though they are permitted. Traditional Jewish law requires that the *mezuzzot* must be inspected at least once every seven years. Some authorities require it even more often than that. They have to make sure that the text is still intact and has not eroded, thus making it unfit for use.

Jews have sometimes looked upon the *mezuzzah* as a magical symbol. They consider it almost like a ceremonial police force, to protect them from outside harm. In fact, they read the word *Shaddai*, which means the Almighty One, as an acronym for the three Hebrew words: "*Shomer Daletot Yisrael*—Guardian of the Doors of the People of Israel."

Several years ago, Israeli schoolchildren riding in a bus were killed in a horrible accident. The chief rabbi of the town in which they lived declared that the accident happened because many of the *mezuzzot* in that town were not kosher. He based this on the primitive belief that the *mezuzzah* should emit mysterious vibes to ward off evil. Some people today go so far as to place *mezuzzot* on cars in the hope of preventing mishaps on the road.

Moses Maimonides, considered to be the greatest Jewish mind of the last millennium, condemned this kind of superstitious practice as nonsense. He reminded his followers that the *mezuzzah* has one purpose: to emphasize the unity of God and the need to love and worship God. He warned against turning it into an amulet for their selfish interests, to satisfy their desire to preserve their worldly goods.

What about the untraditional use of the *mezuzzah* as part of a necklace? It depends upon the purpose for which it is used. If one wears it as a good-luck charm, I would not favor its use. However, as an expression of Jewish self-pride and self-identification, I have less of a problem with it.

Occasionally, a Christian will admire the symbolism of the *mezuzzah* and ask if it would be appropriate to affix one to the doorpost of his or her home, especially since it contains Scripture verses sacred both to Judaism and Christianity. While this sentiment is well-intentioned, the proper setting of a *mezuzzah* is only a Jewish one.

In fact, one of the reasons Jews place a *mezuzzah* on their doorposts is to identify their dwelling as a Jewish home, as the ancient Israelites did with the blood of a lamb. In the Book of Exodus, we read that they gathered to slaughter a lamb in preparation for Passover. God ordered them to take the lamb's blood and place it upon the two doorposts of their home, as well as the horizontal bar connecting them.

God was about to go through the land of Egypt to slay the firstborn males. When God would see which homes were daubed with blood on their doorposts, God would spare them. Would not an all–knowing God be able to tell which homes were those of Israelites without any outward identifying sign? Of course. However, God wanted the Israelites to do something tangible to proclaim themselves outwardly as Jews. Such is one of the main reasons we have *mezuzzot* today.

There was a time when American Jews hesitated to place a *mezuzzah* on their doors, because they feared that the practice was "too Jewish." They wanted to maintain a low-profile and be inconspicuous. Thankfully, today, Jews embrace their identity more securely. Thus, *mezuzzot* are much more common on the doorposts of Jewish homes.

But even more important than affirming one's Jewish identity is the need to see the *mezuzzah* primarily as a religious symbol. It designates the Jewish home as a small sanctuary, as a spiritual citadel, a sacred space. The *mezuzzah* should remind those who live in that home and those who pass through its doors that Godly values, as imparted in the Jewish tradition, are to be practiced there.

Though only a short blessing needs to be offered, often we conduct a brief ceremony to consecrate a new home. In one such ceremony from *Gates of the House*, the aims of the *mezuzzah* are eloquently articulated:

> We affix the *mezuzzah* to the doorposts of this house with the hope that it will always remind us of our duties to God and to one another. May the divine spirit fill this house – the spirit of love and kindness and consideration for all people ... Fortify our resolve to make it now and always, a Temple dedicated to You. Let it be filled with the beauty of holiness and the warmth of love. May the guest and the stranger find within it welcome and friendship ...

The Star of David: How Jewish Is It?

The official congregational seal of Temple Beth-El in San Antonio, Texas, is in the form of a circle. The name of the congregation appears on the circumference. A star dominates the center. When I first saw it, I was surprised to note that the star has five points, like that on the Texas flag, instead of six. From this, I concluded that the founders of the congregation in 1874 wanted to identify more as Texans than as Jews.

After studying the history of the six-pointed Star of David more carefully, I am now not certain that my conclusion was correct. It was only at the very end of the 19th century that the Star of David had become an unequivocally Jewish symbol. Until then, it was not exclusively Jewish. Thus, in 1874, when Temple Beth-El was founded, the *Magen David*, or the Star of David, might not yet have been identified solely with Judaism.

The words *Magen David* literally mean the "Shield of David." It supposedly represents the symbol of six points on the armor that King David, the famed warrior, wore in battle. However, I can find no evidence of this claim.

In fact, 2,000 years ago, the six-pointed star was used both on Jewish and non-Jewish buildings. The synagogue in Capernum, in Israel's Galilee region, was built in the third century. There we can find a six-pointed star next to a five-pointed star and a swastika, which also is an ancient symbol. The six-pointed star was rarely used in ancient Jewish works of art. If art dealers see a Jewish artifact with a six-pointed star, and that artifact is more than two centuries old, they suspect it is a forgery.

In those early days, if there was any distinctive Jewish

symbol at all, it was the menorah, the seven-branch candelabrum. The menorah became the sign of the mission of the Jewish people, for Jews are mandated to become a "light to the nations." For centuries, many non-Jews living in the Middle East and North Africa thought the six-point star had magical powers which would bring them good luck.

In the Middle Ages, hostile governments often required Jews to wear badges identifying them as Jews. These badges were not usually the six-pointed star. For some unknown reason, by the end of the nineteenth century, most synagogues had featured a six-pointed star to identify them as Jewish houses of worship, just as a cross marks the structure as a church.

In 1897, the World Jewish Congress met in Basle, Switzerland, and adopted the six-pointed star as its emblem. Since then, the *Magen David* has become universally acknowledged as a Jewish sign. In 1948, the six-pointed star was chosen to dominate the blue-and-white flag of the new State of Israel. Nonetheless, the official seal of the State of Israel features the menorah.

In modern times, some Jewish thinkers, like Franz Rosenzweig, have tried to give religious significance to the interlocking triangles of the star. They claim that the top triangle points upward to indicate our obligations toward God, while the bottom one points downward to signify our duties to our fellow human beings on earth. Others say that the three sides of each triangle represent the three groups of Jews in ancient Temple times: the priests, the Levites, and the Israelites.

All this is speculation. What is certain, however, is that in the twentieth century, the Star of David has become an exclusively Jewish symbol, so much so that Nazis forced Jews to wear this star on their clothing. The star in Nazi Europe became their yellow badge of shame. While wearing it, they were subject to all forms of humiliation and harassment in public places. The Nazis arrested those Jews caught without it and sent them to death camps.

Now that we acknowledge that the star is an exclusively Jewish symbol, we were stunned by the scandal that erupted in August 1998 in Gulfport, Mississippi. Ryan Green, son of a Jewish father and a Christian mother, is a fifteen-year-old student at Harrison Central High School in Gulfport. During the summer, his Jewish grandmother gave him a pendant with the Star of David as a sign of his Jewish heritage.

Ryan was raised in both Judaism and Christianity. Yet this carrot-topped, freckled-face teenager wanted to wear his grandmother's gift to school on the first day of classes. One of his teachers suggested that he place it inside his shirt. Nonetheless, he wore it again to class the next day, and school officials ordered him to remove it.

Shortly thereafter, the school superintendent, together with all the members of the school board, prohibited Ryan from donning his Star of David. They quoted a policy that forbids students from dressing with gang symbols. There were two gangs in Gulfport, and both were largely inactive. One sported a six-pointed star, and the other a five-pointed star.

This stupid decision labeling the Star of David as a gang symbol sent shock waves through the Jewish community. It also angered staunch defenders of civil rights. Possibly a few centuries ago, it would have been possible to give alternate interpretations to the Star of David. However, in recent decades it has been clearly established solely as a Jewish symbol.

Critics accused school officials of promoting anti-Semitism and of stifling religious liberties. A week later, the school board, in response to much pressure, unanimously rescinded its decision and voted to exempt all religious symbols from its anti-gang policy. This didn't satisfy the American Civil Liberties Union of Mississippi. The ACLU filed a complaint in federal court against the school board.

The American Jewish Congress, one of the three major national Jewish defense organizations, also pointed out that the school board did not bar crosses even though they were on the list of gang symbols. It seems that a Jewish symbol was singled out. The county sheriff explained that no gang uses the cross as its symbol. He was not convincing. Thus, the effect of the policy, contrary to the protestations of the school officials and the county sheriff, was anti-Jewish. It is not an action that we can defend as a safety issue. We should not let gangs define what our Jewish symbols can mean.

What lessons can we learn from this incident? First of all, we take pride that Ryan Green stood up for his rights at a time of life when peer pressure is intense, especially in a community where there are probably just a handful of Jews. We admire his courage in fulfilling the admonition of Hillel, who said that: "Where there are no men, strive to be a man." (M. *Avot* 2:5) Ryan realized that there are times when one must be a non-conformist and go against the tide.

Secondly, we learned that it is not what symbols once meant but what they have come to mean today that is all important. For example, it would be almost inconceivable today to hold a Jewish wedding without the breaking of the glass. It would not seem like a Jewish wedding to us. The breaking of the glass probably started out as a superstition. The ancients believed that hovering around the wedding canopy are evil spirits, threatening to overturn the joy of the bride. By shattering the glass, we scare away those evil spirits.

Today that explanation is not compelling. Today we understand the breaking of the glass is not only a way of giving a special Jewish distinctiveness to a wedding ceremony; it also illustrates that, in the midst of joy, we should remember that life has its darker side.

Similarly, the Star of David, though once possibly a pagan sign, is today a token of Jewish identification. It demonstrates that Jews belong to a heritage and a people with whom they can be proudly identified.

The Controversy over Circumcision

Until a few decades ago, several Reform Jewish congregations in the East and Midwest held their main worship service of the week on Sunday morning. This custom was not unusual in cities like New York, Chicago, Cleveland, Pittsburgh, St. Louis, and Philadelphia. It never spread to Texas or to other parts of the South, however.

These northern Temples, however, were careful to use a weekday morning liturgy and not the Sabbath morning service for their Sunday worship. These Temples still acknowledged that Shabbat was on Saturday. In fact, some of these Temples even held a small chapel service for the faithful few who came on the seventh day instead of Sunday.

We may also be surprised to know that in the 1800s, some extremist Reform Jewish leaders actually tried to make Sunday the official Jewish Sabbath, an attempt that failed. Similarly, these radical Reformers attempted to abolish ritual circumcision, but they lost this fight as well.

It is true that, at that time, Reform leaders had abolished most long-standing Jewish observances. They eliminated such Jewish traditions as keeping kosher, wearing skullcaps, and sitting separately in the synagogue. Nonetheless, as radical as they had become, they tenaciously held on to the Saturday Sabbath and to circumcision. Both the Saturday Sabbath and circumcision are different from other hallowed Jewish practices. They symbolize the covenant, the pact between God and the Jewish people. To reject these two symbols of the covenant would be like tearing the heart out of Judaism.

Actually, the Reform leaders of the previous century were not the first Jews who hoped to do away with circumcision.

Two thousand years ago, many Jews in Palestine wanted desperately to assimilate. They were upset that their circumcisions made them look different from non-Jewish males. They were living under Antiochus Epiphanes, the Syrian Greek leader, who turned the Holy Land into pagan territory.

The Syrian Greeks held public gymnastic exercises. Those men who took part had to be nude. The Greeks thought that the unadorned and unimproved human body was the acme of natural beauty. These Palestinian Jews submitted to a painful operation to hide the evidence of their circumcision. They wanted to look like everybody else. Only the Maccabees resisted this trend and persisted in circumcising their children. However, the Maccabees represented a tiny minority. Yet, fortunately, their point of view finally won out.

Even today, some Jewish parents, who want to do things the natural way, object to circumcision for their sons, partly because of medical reports. For the last few decades, physicians' organizations have, from time to time, asserted that removing the foreskin of an infant boy has no hygienic value. It is medically unnecessary, they claim.

These same parents have also come to believe that circumcision inflicts traumatic pain on the baby. On a talk show on national television, one man, obviously of Jewish origin, insisted that he could still remember the terrible suffering that his circumcision caused him when he was eight days old.

Actually, reputable physicians across the nation today argue that circumcision is medically beneficial. Penile cancer and urinary tract infections are tremendously more frequent in males who are not circumcised. They also emphasize that the pain the child experiences has no long-term negative effects.

Dr. Elliot Leiter is a prominent New York urologist who speaks enthusiastically about the many benefits of circumcision. He has been associated with the Beth Israel Medical Center and the Mt. Sinai School of Medicine in New York. Dr. Leiter presents a convincing case. He explains that the foreskin has very few nerve endings and is far less sensitive than

most people think. Also the spinal pathways that carry messages from the extremities to the brain mature very slowly.
They are far from fully developed when the infant is eight
days old.

It is reassuring to hear these solid medical facts. Yet, the
bottom line is that we Jews, even in Reform Judaism, believe
that circumcision, irrespective of any medical opinions, is a
supremely significant and essential religious act. In Hebrew
we call the rite *B'rit Milah,* the covenant of circumcision.

Through this procedure, a Jewish male infant does not become a Jew. He is already a Jew. Rather, the infant has sealed
into his flesh a sign of the covenant, the bond between the
Jewish people and our God.

In Genesis 17, God tells Abraham to circumcise every
male on the eighth day after birth throughout all the generations. This eighth day requirement is repeated in Leviticus
12. It is so important that even if the eighth day occurs on
Shabbat or Yom Kippur, the circumcision must still be done.
Jewish law does not permit the *B'rit Milah,* as a religious rite,
to be performed before the eighth day. However, some
Reform Jewish parents do prefer to have their sons surgically
circumcised on the second or third day after birth and
arrange for a religious naming ceremony at a later date.

Many medical experts strongly believe in the wisdom of
the eighth day. They maintain that the ability of the blood to
clot reaches its optimal level on the eighth day. Yet Jewish tradition is realistic. If the child is suspected of a serious illness
or a genital deformity, circumcision may be postponed well
beyond the eighth day. It must wait until a physician pro-
nounces the child to be physically ready for such a procedure.

In the Orthodox belief, a father must circumcise his own
son. He can, however, designate someone else to do this *mitzvah* for him. Thus the *mohel,* the specialist in the art of circumcision, acts as the father's agent in this ritual. Dr. Leiter
believes that the circumcisions performed by a *mohel,* who is
competent, certified, and experienced, is at least as safe, if
not safer, than those done by physicians.

In fact, a non-Jewish British urologist recommends that surgeons consult the handbooks that are used for the training of the *mohel* as a model of good sense and sound surgical procedure. Many do not know that Queen Elizabeth and Prince Philip engaged a *mohel* to circumcise Prince Charles when he was a baby.

Most *mohalim* (plural of *mohel*) are Orthodox. Several years ago, the Reform movement began to certify physicians who could serve as Reform *mohalim*. A few years later, the Conservative movement began to do the same. Both groups require these physicians to undergo extensive training so that they will become familiar with the history and the laws of circumcision.

When a *mohel* is not available, most Reform and Conservative rabbis will participate in the *B'rit Milah* as the officiant, together with a physician, preferably a Jewish one, who performs the surgery. A circumcision can be done in a hospital, a doctor's office, a home, or even the Temple.

Why do we Jews attach so much importance to circumcision? Because we believe that the survival of Jewish people depends on it. In Europe, very few non-Jews undergo circumcision. Therefore, during the Hitler period, Nazis could distinguish the Jewish males from the non-Jewish ones. Yet the German Jewish community, as acculturated as it was, continued to insist on circumcision for their male children.

By contrast, in the former Soviet Union, religion had been banned since 1917. Circumcision was forbidden. Therefore, most Russian Jewish males were not circumcised. Judaism in that country was gravely threatened, as a result.

Thus the *B'rit Milah* has a way of assuring our continuation as a people. Even Benedict Spinoza, the towering Jewish philosopher who was ex-communicated by the Jewish authorities in Amsterdam for his heretical views, believed strongly in circumcision. He once said: "Such great importance do I attach to circumcision, the sign of the covenant, that I am persuaded that, by itself, it is sufficient to guarantee the existence of the Jewish people forever."

What Has Happened to Confirmation?

In the long sweep of Jewish religious history, spanning 4,000 years, Bar Mitzvah is a relatively young ceremony. It became popular sometime during the Middle Ages. In those days, a young man who religiously came of age would thoroughly prepare a lesson on a complex unit of the Talmud. He would then deliver a learned address, or *derashah*, on it, to demonstrate his proficiency. Often a small celebration followed.

As the years progressed, the young man no longer presented a scholarly message. Instead, he chanted a small section of the weekly Torah portion. He also intoned the entire Haftarah, i.e., the corresponding verses from the Hebrew prophets. In some places he would conduct the major parts of the service as well. Often he would deliver a speech, sometimes not of his own composition. Today there are many variants in the ways different synagogues mark a Bar Mitzvah.

Actually, the term Bar Mitzvah refers to a chronological age, not a ritual. When a boy reaches the time of his religious majority at thirteen and one day, he becomes a Bar Mitzvah, with or without a ceremony. In Orthodox and Conservative Jewish congregations, this is the time that the young man is required to observe all the commandments of the Torah. To mark this occasion, he receives a pair of *tefillin*, or phylacteries. He is expected to don them every weekday during his morning prayers. He is also eligible to be counted in the *minyan*, the required quorum of ten for public worship.

When Reform Judaism was born in the early 1800s in Germany, its leaders wanted to abolish Bar Mitzvah. The reason is that Reform, from its inception, has been ardently com-

mitted to the equal roles of men and women in Jewish religious life. These Reform founders found that Bar Mitzvah
was discriminatory. It was open only to males, not to females.
Incidentally, the Bat Mitzvah, the female counterpart to Bar
Mitzvah, did not come into being until 1922.

They had a second problem with Bar Mitzvah. They were
eager to transmit advanced religious concepts to their followers. They believed that one had to be at least fifteen or sixteen in order to grasp them. To address these two concerns of
sexism and religious immaturity, they invented Confirmation.
They borrowed the idea from the German Lutheran Church.
However, they adapted it to Jewish life and invested it with
Jewish content. The Reform luminary Israel Jacobson introduced the first Confirmation ceremony in Seesen, Germany,
in 1810.

Unlike Bar Mitzvah, which centers on an individual,
Confirmation is a group ceremony for young men and
women. It takes place usually at the end of the tenth grade.
For many decades, Confirmation supplanted Bar Mitzvah in
the majority of Reform congregations. It became the sole life-
cycle ritual in the religious development of a Jewish adoles-
cent. Several Reform congregations did not even permit a
Bar Mitzvah to take place in their sanctuaries until the late
1960s and early 1970s. Confirmation was the focal point of
their concerns.

The goal of the entire Religious School curriculum was
Confirmation. In most Reform congregations, the senior
rabbi personally taught the class and encouraged a question-
ing posture on the part of the students. The rabbi tried to impress upon them that they could no longer be satisfied with
being Jews just because they were born that way. They must
study and probe adult Jewish values and ideals. They must
prepare to stand before the congregation and declare that
they are now Jews—not only by birth, but also by conviction.

Confirmation is traditionally held on the festival of
Shavuot, celebrating the time that God gave the Torah to the
Jewish people. The reason is persuasive. Just as our Israelite

ancestors received the Torah at Mt. Sinai four millennia ago, so today do these young people declare their allegiance to our Torah.

Confirmation used to be a major congregational event. Congregants attended the service, whether a family member was being confirmed or not. In numerous Reform Temples, Confirmation was almost as important as Rosh Hashanah and Yom Kippur. I think of those years from 1917 to 1963, when Abba Hillel Silver was rabbi of The Temple, in Cleveland, one of America's premier Reform synagogues. Confirmation at The Temple was so popular and the capacity in the huge 1,800-seat sanctuary so limited that one was required to have a ticket to attend the service.

The ceremony was most moving and impressive. Young men and women, attired in white robes, marched down the aisle, often while singing hymns like "Father, See Thy Suppliant Children." A standard feature of the service was the floral offering, reminiscent of the Shavuot festival offering in olden days. On that sacred occasion, the Israelites brought the First Fruits of their harvest to the Temple in Jerusalem. A couple of students who were proficient in Hebrew read the Ten Commandments from the Torah scroll.

The highlight of Confirmation was the rabbi's individual blessing. He called each Confirmand before the open Ark and whispered some sublime thoughts tailored to that young person. He concluded his message by raising his hands over the Confirmand's head and pronouncing the Priestly Benediction.

Over the past few decades, all of this has fundamentally changed. Confirmation is losing ground. Virtually every Reform congregation in the country permits Bar and Bat Mitzvah. In fact, in the majority of cases, there has been a 180-degree shift. Bar and Bat Mitzvah seem to be replacing Confirmation. There has been a troublingly high dropout rate after Bar and Bat Mitzvah. In congregations with fifty to sixty Bar and Bat Mitzvahs a year, the Confirmation classes may number a mere ten or fifteen. In addition, the

Confirmation ceremonies themselves have lost their spiritual drama and pageantry and have become rather prosaic and uninspiring.

What accounts for this reversal of priorities? First of all, today the majority of Reform congregants who were born Jewish come from Orthodox or Conservative backgrounds. While they were growing up, Confirmation was nonexistent or unimportant. Secondly, many consider the Confirmation ceremony too formal and rigid. Today, the mood in Reform is more informal and casual. Third, some are disturbed that Confirmation was borrowed from non-Jewish sources. That fact should not trouble us.

In fact, hardly any Jewish ritual was originally Jewish. For example, on the anniversary of the death of a loved one, we observe a *Yahrzeit*. Before the sixteenth century, the word *Yahrzeit* was never mentioned. The name is based on a similar German word, used in the Roman Catholic Church to denote the occasion for honoring the memory of the dead. Burning a candle on this occasion is also Catholic. However, like Confirmation, we Judaized the candle by viewing the flame as a symbol of the human soul. In short, we Jews are not great originators; instead, we are outstanding creative adapters.

Fortunately, in some congregations, especially those with a Classical Reform heritage, Confirmation is still important, though not as significant as it once was. They still incorporate much of the pageantry of the past. In addition, their Bar or Bat Mitzvah celebrants must pledge to continue their religious studies through Confirmation.

However, even in these congregations, one development has become unsettling. Confirmation is no longer seen as a public event, even though it is intended to be such. Generally, only the parents and a tiny handful of close relatives who live in the local area attend the service. Rarely do out-of-town grandparents bother to come to Confirmation. Regrettably, Confirmation has lost some of its appeal.

I still dream that this situation some day will be reversed, if only to affirm the historic Jewish value of community.

Judaism stresses the group over the individual. Confirmation is a group ritual rather than an individual one. Then, too, Confirmation is not designed to be a private event, only for the Confirmands and their immediate families. It should be a congregation-wide celebration of its youth, supported and attended by its members.

Priests, Rabbis, and Rebbes

Over the centuries, the Jewish people have been led by priests, rabbis, and rebbes. Each of them arose to meet the circumstances of the generations they were serving. In this connection, I recall an incident after my first year at Hebrew Union College. That summer I was the Jewish chaplain at a Boy Scout camp near Muskegon, Michigan, that served the greater Chicago area.

A large number of the scouts attending that summer were Roman Catholics. On several occasions, some of them, in all innocence, would address me as "Father Stahl." I had to explain to them tactfully that Jewish religious leaders today are not priests but rabbis. However, at one time our religious community indeed was led by priests.

In the Book of Exodus, the Jewish priesthood is first introduced. The priests were intermediaries between God and the people. They conveyed God's blessings to the congregation. They presided over the sacrifices of animals. Incidentally, animal sacrifices were not unique to Jews. All ancient peoples worshiped in this way but did so irresponsibly. Their worship included sexual orgies and was intended to appease many gods. The Jewish people needed priests, however, to make sure that these animal sacrifices would be stripped of all their pagan features and be directed only to the one God.

Jewish priests wore special garb: an ephod on white linen; a breast plate, with the twelve tribes represented; an oracle, called the *Urim* and *Tummim*, over the breastplate; and a mitered hat, with the words "*Kadosh Ladonai*—Holy unto the Lord" inscribed on it.

At one time, almost any Israelite male could be a priest. A priest could be the head of a family or a clan, such as the first-born son. He could even be the king himself. The category then began to narrow.

King Josiah decreed that only Levites, members of the tribe of Levi, could be priests. Later, eligibility for the priesthood became even more stringent. One not only had to be a member of the tribe of Levi; he also had to be a descendant of Zadok, who was the High Priest at the time of King David.

A caste system developed. At the top was the High Priest. He entered the Holy of Holies on Yom Kippur, pronounced God's actual name, and pleaded for forgiveness for the sins of his people. Under him were the regular priests. They were the descendants of Aaron, and members of the tribe of Levi. Lower yet were the other Levites, who assisted these descendants of Aaron. They took care of the exterior of the sanctuary, as well as the courts and the furniture. At the bottom were the commoners, or Israelites.

Priests tended to make peace with corruption. They had a penchant for accommodating the unsavory status quo. Many of the towering prophets, like Amos, Hosea, Isaiah, and Micah, verbally attacked the compromising priests. The prophets criticized the priests for being too concerned about formal Temple ritual—the sights and smells of the sacrifices and the sounds of the sacred songs—while they cared too little about good conduct. For example, Amos, speaking in God's name, thundered:

> I loathe, I spurn your festivals. I am not appeased by your solemn assemblies. If you offer Me burnt offerings, or your meal offerings, I will not accept them. I will pay no heed to your gifts of fatlings. Spare me the sound of your hymns, and let Me not hear the music of your lutes. But let justice well up like water; righteousness like an unfailing stream. (Amos 5:21-24)

The priests eventually became insensitive aristocrats, especially during the Roman occupation. They lost touch and fell out of favor with the masses of the Jewish people. The priests wanted to ingratiate themselves with Roman officials. The priests were the ones who opposed Jesus, because they regarded him as a traitor against the Roman government. The Jewish masses sided with Jesus, however.

Jewish religious leadership changed drastically in 70 C.E., when the Second Temple was destroyed. Animal sacrifices were no longer possible. As a result, the priests had no functions to perform. They were now unemployed. New leadership was needed in the Jewish community, and the rabbis emerged.

Unlike the priests, the rabbis had to earn their position through study. They did not inherit it. Any adult Jewish male could train to become a rabbi. A rabbi, unlike a priest, is not an intermediary between the people and God. Technically, the rabbi is not a clergyman. The rabbi is an ordinary Jew who, through intensive study, has acquired a deep knowledge of Jewish law and lore.

After the Temple fell, the synagogue became the chief place for public Jewish worship. Unlike the Jerusalem Temple, the synagogue never was the exclusive place for public worship. Wherever ten Jews gather, they can offer Jewish prayers, even outside a synagogue. Such is still true today. The rabbi, unlike the priest, does not need to wear special garb to set him apart from the people. The change from Temple and priest to synagogue and rabbi was revolutionary. It represented a movement from elitism to democracy in Jewish leadership.

Rabbis and synagogues took the place of the priests and the Temple. However, in reality, rabbis and synagogues had already existed, even while the priests were still officiating in the Temple, several centuries before 70 C.E. Interestingly, after the Second Temple was destroyed, the Rabbis assigned a place for the priests. The Rabbis assured the priests that they and their descendants would always enjoy some special prerogatives, but they would also be bound by some restrictions.

Today, many descendants of the original priests live in

America, with last names like Cohen, Kahn, Kagan, Katz, Kaplan, etc. There are also offspring of the Levites, the associate priests, whose last names are Levy, Levine, Levitt, etc. Today, when the Torah scroll is read in an Orthodox or Conservative synagogue, the Kohen, or priestly descendant, is awarded the first of the seven honors, or *aliyot*.

The priest also participates in the ceremony of *pidyon haben*, the redemption of the first-born son. According to Exodus 13:1-2, the first-born Israelite sons were to be dedicated to God and to serve the priests. However, with five shekels they could be redeemed. This redemption is effected through a priest.

In the more traditional wings of Judaism, there are many things that the priestly descendant, even today, cannot do, however. He cannot marry a divorcée. He may not come into contact with the dead, except in the case of a close relative. In other words, he cannot attend a funeral, go to the house of the deceased, or enter a cemetery, except for the death of a close relative.

The Rabbis promised the priests that on some distant day, when the Messiah arrives, they will be fully functioning again. The Third Temple will be built and the animal sacrifices restored. Reform Judaism, with its commitment to full egalitarianism, no longer recognizes the special distinction of first-born males or priestly descendants.

The Rabbis grew out of a group known as the Pharisees. Pharisees are much maligned in the New Testament for being too rigid and legalistic. They were actually the opposite. The Pharisees were the progressives, the party of the people, the promoters of democracy. Leadership among the Pharisees was based on learning and character, rather than birth.

However, the priests did make one last ditch effort to keep control. Their party was known as the Sadducees. The Sadducees were the fundamentalists, the conservatives, and the elitists. They accepted the Torah literally, whereas the Pharisees interpreted it liberally.

There was another difference between the two groups.

The Sadducees did not believe in the resurrection of the dead, nor anything else that was not found in the Five Books of Moses. However, the Pharisees insisted that some day the dead will arise again. The Pharisees were so committed to this notion that they made the idea of resurrection one of the few required beliefs in Judaism. In due time, the Sadducees lost out to the Pharisees. As heirs of the Pharisees, the rabbis grew to become the dominant heads of the Jewish community.

Rabbis then and now must be primarily students and teachers. Learning the Torah is designed to be a lifelong process. The title of rabbi has always been earned strictly through the acquisition of knowledge. The rabbi was expected to marry. Many Jewish families, in fact, wanted their daughters to marry rabbis.

One originally did not earn his living as a rabbi. For this reason, many of the early rabbis pursued other occupations. Several were woodchoppers, builders, blacksmiths, tailors, and water carriers. They were expected to spend only one-third of their day on their secular work. The rest was to be devoted to study. However, they did not consider their secular career as a means for their self-growth or personal fulfillment. Secular work merely enabled these rabbis to acquire enough material sustenance in order to free them for study.

Only in the Middle Ages did they begin to receive monetary compensation for serving as rabbis. Actually, the rabbinate did not become a full-time profession earning remuneration until the fifteenth century. But eventually, some rabbis became overly distant and haughtily intellectual. Like the ancient priests, they lost touch with the masses, especially those in Eastern Europe. Thus new leaders were needed.

There then emerged a third category of Jewish leadership: the rebbe of the Hasidic community. The rebbe did not replace the rabbi but co-existed with him. Hasidism began in the eighteenth century in Eastern Europe. A spiritual and economic depression had infected the people in these lands. The Cossack massacres, when over 100,000 Jews were killed, caused untold suffering and sadness.

In addition, many Jews found the Talmudic scholarship of the rabbis inaccessible, incomprehensible, and unsatisfying, The rabbis were not responsive to the spiritual yearnings of the masses. These masses hungered for mystical teachings that would assure them of new hope, happiness, and closeness with God. They craved a religion that would be simple, direct, comforting, and unsophisticated. The Eastern European rabbis were remote and austere and could not touch their hearts.

Responding to these needs, Hasidism was born. Its founder was Israel Baal Shem Tov, also known as the Besht. The Besht taught that God wanted sincere devotion, zeal, and heartfelt joy more than serious scholarship. The Besht insisted that worship must be cheerful. We serve God best by rapture and ecstasy, not by sober intellectualism. Prayer should express rapture. The Besht argued that wooden or perfunctory prayers are worse than no prayers at all.

Soon various Hasidic sects proliferated. There are even today the Satmar Hasidim, the Belz Hasidim, the Lubavitcher Hasidim, the Gerer Hasidim, etc. Each sect is headed by a different rebbe. Each sect has its loyal followers. The rebbe acquires his position by heredity, as well as by training. The son of a rebbe, if he is worthy, usually becomes the next rebbe of a particular sect.

The Hasidim initially encountered strong opposition. Their greatest enemy was a noted Lithuanian rabbi, Elijah Gaon of Vilna. He excommunicated the Hasidism, in 1796, with these bitter words: "Woe unto the evil renegades who have brought forth a new law and religion ... let no one pity them." His bitter words sound almost like the invectives Orthodox rabbis in Germany and Hungary hurled in the nineteenth century, when they denounced Reform Judaism.

A bitter battle raged between the Hasidim and their opponents. The acrimony was somewhat quelled when a great Hasidic rebbe, Shneur Zalman, succeeded in raising the status of Hasidism. He founded the Chabad movement, which restored the intellectual component that earlier Hasidim had rejected. After the death of Elijah Gaon of Vilna, Hasidism captured even more of the hearts of many Jews throughout Eastern Europe.

Today, the rebbes of the Hasidim enjoy unchallenged obedience from their followers. The rebbe stands between the people and God. Today the authority of someone like the late Lubavitcher Rebbe, Menachem Schneerson, is far stronger than that of the modern rabbi. After the Persian Gulf crisis, Rabbi Schneerson told his people that the Messiah is here, ready to be revealed. A group of his followers today believe that he is the Messiah.

But rebbes did not replace rabbis. Instead, in the non-Hasidic community, two kinds of rabbis emerged. Externally, we can identify the two main groups by examining their headgear. Those with black hats represent the Old World rabbinate. Those with small skull caps or no head covering at all are modern rabbis. How did the modern rabbinate develop?

In the nineteenth century, in Western Europe, the ghetto walls broke down. Jews began to live among their non-Jewish neighbors. The rabbinate underwent a major change, especially in Western Europe and in the United States. At one time the rabbi governed both religious and civil matters. Now his role became restricted to religious concerns. Civil law was in the hands of the secular court.

Even today, Old World rabbis study in a yeshiva to prepare for their ordination. Their course areas are almost exclusively Talmud and rabbinic codes. A secular college education is not required nor is it even desirable. Such is still the case in places like Monsey and Williamsburg, New York, and Meah Shearim, in Jerusalem—the centers of the black hat rabbinate.

The modern rabbi studies in a seminary. The curriculum is broader. Rabbis now learn homiletics, education, and human relations, as well as Bible and Talmud. They are also required to receive a university education. In Germany and Hungary, before World War II, most ordained rabbis held Ph.D.'s.

Except among the black hat ultra-Orthodox, most rabbis in Western Europe and in the United States have become clergy persons. Such is true not only in the Conservative and Reform movements, but even in the mainline Orthodox. The rabbi now is more than just a scholar and teacher. The rabbi has to perform many of the tasks common to Protestant ministers, such as visiting the sick, preaching sermons, supervising the religious school, overseeing the administration and the programs of the synagogue, etc. Often these tasks rob the rabbi of precious hours needed for study.

Since 1972, women have been ordained as rabbis, first in Reform and Reconstructionist Judaism and later in the Conservative movement. In fact, about one-half of today's ordination classes of the major non-Orthodox rabbinical seminaries are female. These modern rabbis, male and female, are the religious leaders to whom most religious American Jews relate. They come out of a similar world and speak the same language.

I have briefly described three kinds of religious leaders in Judaism. The first of the three were the priests, who inherited their position. They supervised the sacrifices of animals in accordance with the Torah. They eventually became aristocrats and lost touch with their people. Then eventually the Temple was destroyed, thus putting priests out of commission.

The rabbis then took over. While priests inherited their position, the rabbis earned it by learning and study. As long as the rabbis were responsive to the people, they were the unquestioned leaders of the community. When certain rabbis became too intellectually remote, they spawned the Hasidic movement with its various rebbes. Today, rebbes, who inherit their position, enjoy tremendous allegiance. They are viewed, like the ancient priests, as almost superhuman figures, linking the people to their God.

Yet the rabbinate was never superseded. Instead, it split into two categories. Some rabbis shunned the modern world and "learned" at an old-world yeshiva. Under the influence of Western culture, most other rabbis train at a seminary, rather than a traditional yeshiva. They have become clergy people. They share many responsibilities in common with their Christian counterparts.

Priests, rabbis, or rebbes—all have been key leaders of the Jewish people. They have arisen to meet certain Jewish spiritual and societal needs of their people throughout Jewish history. That bond of these leaders with their people is so essential for their effectiveness.

Phillips Brooks was a famous nineteenth-century Protestant minister and one of the great orators of his day. Brooks describes such an idyllic relationship between a community and its religious leader. With the change of the word "minister" to "rabbi" and with the making of his language gender inclusive, he speaks of the kind of union that I think is possible even today between a rabbi and his or her congregation:

> The . . . relation, then, between the rabbi and the congregation is plain. They belong together. But neither can absorb or override the other. They must be filled with mutual respect. He/she is their leader, but his/her leadership is not one, constant strain, and never is forgetful of the higher guidance upon which they both rely.
>
> It is like the rope, by which one ship draws another out into the sea. The rope is not always tight between them, and, all the while, the tide on which they float is carrying them both. So it is not merely leading and following. It is one of the very highest pictures of human companionship that can be seen on earth . . . It is too sacred to be thought of as a contract. It is a union which God joins together for purposes worthy of God's care.

Vegetarianism:
Religious Option or Requirement?

The first diet prescribed in the Bible was quite restrictive. On the sixth day of creation, after God had formed the first human being, God ordered that our foods be limited to vegetables and fruits.

Later, God liberalized our culinary choices. After the flood that struck Noah and his generation, God permitted us to eat meat, as long as there was no blood in it. In other words, originally God wanted us to be vegetarians. Centuries later, God allowed us to become carnivorous.

Nonetheless, in recent years, vegetarianism is making a strong comeback. At one time it was just a fringe phenomenon. Now it has become mainstream. I must admit that vegetarians do advance a strong case for their way of life. They argue that eating meat, with its high levels of cholesterol and saturated fat, can ultimately lead to heart attacks, strokes, cancer, and other serious maladies.

Vegetarians also assert that vegetarianism helps the environment and conserves its resources. Twenty times more land and ten times more energy and water are required for meat-eating diets. We feed 70% of the grain grown in the United States to animals, which are destined for slaughter.

At the same time, 20,000,000 people die each year of hunger. Would it not be better, the vegetarians ask, to feed this grain directly to human beings rather than to reserve it to produce meat? What a wasteful allocation of resources that only exacerbates hunger and poverty!

And finally, vegetarians argue that refraining from meat

demonstrates mercy and compassion to animals. They insist that we should not have to kill some of God's creatures in order to satisfy our hunger.

I must concede that these arguments are compelling. Indeed, vegetarianism does enhance bodily hygiene. It does express a greater concern for the poor and needy. It does heighten sensitivity to the pain and suffering of animals. Yet, if we read our Bible carefully, we will note that vegetarianism was never intended for the real world. Vegetarianism was the dietary regimen prescribed for the realm of Paradise, where human beings did not have to take the life of an animal in order to sate their appetite.

However, in the real world, after the flood, God acknowledged that powerful instincts, drives, and lusts drive human beings. Realistically, then, most human beings crave meat. In fact, when the Israelites wandered through the desert, after leaving Egypt, they subsisted on vegetarian manna, which fell from heaven. They found that diet unsatisfying and boring. They yearned for the fleshpots of Egypt and demanded meat.

God became so angry at our people for clamoring for meat that God told them: "You shall eat flesh not one day nor two days nor five days nor ten days nor twenty days, but a whole month, until it comes out of your nostrils and it will become loathsome to you." (Num. 11:19-20). In other words, God informed them that God would satisfy their cravings with sickening abundance.

Allowing the eating of meat is a compromise, a concession to our human passions. Eating meat represents a resolution of the tension between the ideal and the real, and has become an acceptable part of our diet. However, Jewish tradition urges humaneness in producing meat. Judaism has always emphasized *tza'ar ba'alei hayyim*, avoiding pain to any living creature. Animals do feel. They experience fear. They suffer. They hurt. They grieve. We must be understanding of their condition.

Scripture orders us not to muzzle an animal when that animal is plowing because the animal may be hungry and may need to graze. To restrain a dumb animal from eating under these circumstances would be cruel and heartless. Similarly, we may not harness a stronger ox with a weaker donkey together.

Furthermore, Jews are enjoined to say, "*Tithadesh*," literally meaning, "May you be renewed," or in a paraphrased version, "Wear it well," when observing someone who has acquired a new article of clothing. However, if that person has obtained new leather shoes, new leather garments, or a new fur coat, this expression is not offered, because a living creature had to be killed for those dress items to be manufactured.

Those who follow the Jewish dietary laws are to learn such sensitivity to the suffering of animals. If we are to take the life of an animal for food, we must do so as painlessly as possible. The *shohet*, or ritual slaughterer, must wield the knife that severs the jugular vein quickly. There must be no delay, halting, or prolonging the act. His knife must be razor sharp, smooth, and free from any notches.

He must bear in mind, at all times, the sacred responsibility that he is undertaking. He must maintain an awareness of the potential cruelty that he could be inflicting. Even after he has completed the act, he must pour the blood that flows from the slaughtered animal upon a bed of dust and cover it with the dust so as to hide his shame and embarrassment for killing a living creature.

There is a rabbinic legend about an old *shohet* who died. A possible successor was brought into the community to be examined for his qualifications. After the people tested the new *shohet*, someone who was not present asked someone who was, how the *shohet* did.

The man replied that the *shohet* had followed the procedure scrupulously. He had offered the correct prayers. He had sharpened his knife properly. He had even moistened the blade. He had fulfilled every regulation meticulously. Yet the man who was present added a note of disappointment. He indicated that this new *shohet* differed from the old one who died, because the old one used to moisten the blade with his tears.

Even though many do not observe the kosher laws, they still need to be pained by animal suffering. Even though the traditional Jewish dietary laws do permit the eating of *pate de foie*, as well as veal, we might consider avoiding these foods.

Pate de foie is a delicate meat paste, made of fattened goose liver and truffles. It is produced by inhumane means. To obtain it, the farmer holds the neck of the goose between his legs and pours corn down its throat with one hand. With his other hand, he massages the throat as the corn goes down its neck. When that is not effective, the farmer resorts to a wooden plunger. The object is to grow the liver of the goose to such an enormous size that sclerosis develops and thus this delicacy is the result.

Veal also comes to our table after the animals that produce it are tortured. Within hours after birth, baby calves are separated from their mothers. They are chained by their necks for the rest of their lives in wooden crates that are less than two feet wide. They can never stand freely on their legs. They can never have enough room to turn around to see the sunlight. For seven days a week, twenty-four hours a day, they must endure darkness. The baby calves are fed a liquid diet with no iron content and are given no exercise. They are to be kept anemic and free from iron to ensure the pale color and tenderness of veal.

Sometimes their craving for iron becomes so great that they lick the iron fittings on the stall and even their own urine. When they leave their pen for slaughter, they sometimes drop dead from exhaustion on the way.

Thus, *pate de foie* and veal are delicacies that are products of barbarism. Eliminating them from our menus is a step that we should seriously consider.

Even though we are allowed to partake of meat in the real world, we should not focus only on the real world. While inhabiting the real world, we should always keep the vision of the ideal world before us.

In that ideal world of the future, the Messianic age, the prophets tell us that we will return to a vegetarian diet. It will be a time when we can survive and thrive without having to destroy the life of another in order to do so. That is really how life is supposed to be.

Reform Judaism's Three Enduring Contributions

After a devastating earthquake in Los Angeles in the mid-1990s, the Commission on Social Action of Reform Judaism sent a message to all Reform synagogues about a relief fund that the Reform movement had established for the earthquake victims. For many Reform Jews living near the epicenter, the loss was colossal. Their homes, their businesses, and their Temples were either destroyed or extensively damaged. Fortunately, there were no casualties among the Jews of Greater Los Angeles, but some injuries were sustained.

I was fascinated, as well as elated, when I learned about the system by which funds would be distributed. The committee in charge planned to allocate the monies it collected to Reform congregations and their members that needed assistance in the Greater Los Angeles area. However, the funds would not be limited to the Reform movement, or even to the Jewish community. They would also be given to individuals and agencies which provide direct assistance to other earthquake victims, regardless of race, religion, or ethnic origin.

This gallant and universalist response to the earthquake is a glowing example of one of the three major contributions of Reform Judaism, i.e., Reform Judaism has urged its followers to attend to the welfare both of Jews and non-Jews. We Jews have always taken good care of our own. We joined fellow American Jews in standing up for the rights of Russian and Ethiopian Jews. We raised impressive sums to bring them out of their lands of oppression and to resettle them in Israel and other lands of freedom.

And yet the impulse to help the poor and oppressed non-Jew has generally not been as strong among us. Many American Jews still harbor painful memories of anti-Semitic assaults: of Cossacks and pogroms, of street urchins chasing us and yelling, "Sheenie" and "Christ killer."

I am reminded in this connection of a visit of the noted German Jewish philosopher Hermann Cohen to a Polish synagogue during the High Holy Days. The cantor began to sing the expansive words of Isaiah: "My house shall be called a house of prayer for all peoples." As he was doing so, he started to weep profusely. Hermann Cohen thought it was touching that the cantor was so deeply moved by the idea of peoples from many faiths joining together in worship.

After the service, Cohen confronted the cantor to confirm his impression. He asked the cantor: "Why did you cry?" Much to Cohen's shock, the cantor replied: "How can I help but cry when I think that some day our Temple, the place of holiness and glory, may be filled with *goyim* (non-Jews)?"

By contrast, we Reform Jews look forward, with eager anticipation, to that Messianic day foreseen by Isaiah when peoples of all religious backgrounds will be able to worship God in the same setting. We teach that we must be concerned not only with Jewish needs but also with the misery and pain of all humanity. Reform rabbinical and congregational groups pass resolutions and initiate programs and projects concerning not only Israel but also nuclear disarmament, environmental responsibility, and racial justice—issues that affect people in general and not just Jews in particular.

In addition to fostering outreach to Jews and non-Jews, Reform Jews have made a second major contribution: Reform Judaism has pioneered the equality of the sexes from its very beginning. Traditional Jewish law favors the male gender. It was men who wrote the rules of the Torah, some of which severely restrict the rights and privileges of women. With our commitment to democracy, modern Jews needed to correct these inequities and Reform boldly took up the task.

Reform congregations dropped the *mehitzah*, the divider

segregating men and women in the synagogue. Reform rabbis rewrote the *ketubah*, the Jewish marriage contract. The traditional version outlines the obligations the husband owes the wife in the event of his death or their divorce. The wife is merely a passive recipient. In the Reform marriage certificate, both husband and wife are now equal partners, with mutual obligations and responsibilities. Reform Judaism also permitted women, as well as men, to act as witnesses in signing the *ketubah*.

Furthermore, Reform Judaism dropped the requirement for a Jewish divorce, in which a husband gives a wife a *get*, a bill of divorce. Reform Judaism objects to this requirement which binds a woman to her husband, but not her to him. Technically, he can remarry without a *get*, but she cannot. The basic premise of the *get* is unfair. Thus, we Reform Jews, affirming the equality of men and women, assert that civil divorce suffices.

Furthermore, though the event was much too long in coming, Reform Judaism was the first movement in Jewish religious life to ordain women as rabbis in 1972.

In addition to gender equality, Reform Judaism must be credited with a third contribution. It saved Jews for Judaism. Were it not for Reform Judaism, our Jewish community today would be infinitely smaller.

Let us recall what happened in the early 1800s in Germany. Germany was one of the first communities to release Jews from the ghetto. Jews were now coming into contact with cultures and values of the Western world. In response, they were abandoning Jewish observances and, in many cases, converting to Christianity. There was an "epidemic of baptisms" among German Jews at this time.

Until 1823, the German government forbade Reform Judaism and recognized only the strictest of Orthodoxy. After that time, it granted legitimacy to Reform. Shortly thereafter, the rate of conversion to Christianity dramatically declined. Why? Until 1823, German Jews had two choices: Orthodox Judaism or Christianity. There were no other options. When an alternative like Reform emerged, the choices were no longer either black or white. Thus most German Jews elected to stay Jewish.

We know that in the last 200 years, when Jews are presented with the alternatives of Orthodoxy or something else, whether that something else be Christianity or secularism, they will choose that something else. For example, though Reform and Conservative Judaism does exist in Israel on a small scale, Israelis think that their sole choices are Orthodoxy or nothing. Most select nothing.

On the other hand, almost all of historic American Reform congregations have among their membership ranks, many who are descended from the founding families of those congregations, going back to the mid-1800s.

Therefore, it is important to appreciate these three towering contributions of Reform Judaism. So many Reform Jews unfortunately do not. Two-thirds of today's Reform Jews were not raised Reform, and many have little knowledge about the nature and history of Reform Judaism. Several have joined Reform Temples for reasons other than the ideology of Reform Judaism.

A growing number of Reform Jews, unfortunately, also have inferiority feelings about being Reform. They feel fraudulent. They support Orthodox institutions, which they regard as more genuinely Jewish than the Temples with which they are affiliated. Their image of piety is not a Reform Jew at prayer, but a *hasid*, who is garbed in a large black hat, an oversized *tallit*, and *tefillin*.

I have great respect for Orthodox Judaism and those who adhere to it, but at the same time, I do not consider Orthodoxy as *the* authentic form of Judaism. Rather it is *an* authentic form of Judaism, just as Reform is an authentic form of Judaism. Reform Jews should swell with pride when assessing what Reform Judaism has accomplished: It has advanced concern for the needs, hopes, and dreams of both Jews and non-Jews alike; it has guaranteed both men and women equal religious privileges; and it has ensured Jewish survival.

The chief architect of American Reform Judaism, Isaac Mayer Wise, spoke optimistically over a hundred years ago when he expressed his hopes for Reform Judaism:

> What the Reform group proposes, it proposes for the welfare of future generations. It wishes to prevent the endless desertions from Judaism ... It wishes to banish the hideous indifference that has taken hold of a large portion of the Jewish community. It wishes to inspire Jews with a new love for their religion ...

Today, I think Reform Jews have, at least partially, fulfilled Isaac Mayer Wise's dream. I hope that we will continue to do even better, as we go forward into the future.

VI

Some Who Made a Difference

Abraham Joshua Heschel

By the late 1930s, the Nazis had closed the doors of all rabbinical seminaries in Germany. There is a little known story about Dr. Julian Morgenstern, president of the Hebrew Union College, America's seminary of Reform Judaism in Cincinnati. He had invited a number of eminent Jewish scholars and rabbinical students to leave Germany to continue their academic work at the college.

One of these professors was Abraham Joshua Heschel, a charismatic thinker, writer, and religious leader. For five years, from 1940 until 1945, Heschel taught philosophy and rabbinic literature at the college.

He was always grateful to Dr. Morgenstern for rescuing him from death. He once said that Morgenstern was "the least appreciated man in American Jewry." Yet, Heschel, an observant traditional Jew, was never religiously at home in the Classical Reform environment of the Hebrew Union College of the 1940s and felt that he needed to move on.

Fortunately, for him, in 1945, Heschel was asked to join the faculty of the Jewish Theological Seminary, the bastion of Conservative Judaism in New York, as professor of Jewish ethics and mysticism. Two Hebrew Union College students, Samuel Dresner and Richard Rubinstein, who were deeply influenced by Heschel's thought, followed him to the Seminary. They were later ordained there. Both eventually became respected Jewish thinkers and writers.

Heschel remained at the Seminary until his death, twenty-seven years later. Dr. Ismar Schorsch, the current chancellor of the Seminary, has called Heschel "the most important Jewish thinker of the modern period."

Abraham Joshua Heschel was born in Warsaw in 1907. He was a descendant of numerous Hasidic dynasties. He spent his formative years learning at a traditional yeshiva, like all Eastern European Jews with his religious background.

At age twenty, he entered a new world of thought. He enrolled at the University of Berlin to obtain his doctorate. He also studied at the Hochschule fuer die Wissenschaft des Judentums, Berlin's liberal rabbinical seminary, where he later taught Talmud.

In 1937, Martin Buber, the famed Jewish philosopher, named him his successor at the Lehrhaus in Frankfort. This was the city's central agency for adult Jewish learning. The following year, the Nazis deported Heschel and all Jews of Polish citizenship back to Poland. Fortunately, six weeks before the Nazi invasion of Poland in 1939, Heschel was able to leave Poland for London. There he established the Institute of Jewish Learning. The following year, he moved to Cincinnati.

Heschel's life was a combination of paradoxes. First, he was a scholar in the Western tradition. He wrote scores of scientifically sound works on the classics of Judaism, like the Biblical prophets, the writings of Maimonides, and the Kabbalah. On the other hand, he also penned numerous volumes of a non-academic nature on the spiritual crises and questions which the modern Jew confronts, with titles like *Man Is Not Alone, God in Search of Man*, and *Man's Quest for God*.

Then, too, in his personal ritual practice, Heschel was almost Orthodox. Yet, at the same time, he was deeply committed to strengthening ties with peoples of other faiths. In 1964, Heschel met with Pope Paul VI. As a result, Heschel influenced the Second Vatican Council to issue strong statements in support of Jews and Judaism. The following year, Heschel became the first Jew ever to be appointed to the faculty of the Union Theological Seminary in New York. This is one of the foremost Protestant theological schools in the United States.

Furthermore, Heschel was not only a prolific scholar but also a courageous social activist. He ardently believed that prayer and study could not be separated from communal involvement. Heschel cut a striking figure with his white beard and crown of wavy hair, his small but imposing bearing, and his passionate and determined manner of speaking. When he cried out for justice, one could almost hear the echoes of God in his voice.

In 1965, Heschel went to Selma, Alabama, to march with Martin Luther King in the struggle for civil rights. Someone who marched with him questioned why this eminent scholar came to Selma instead of remaining in his ivory tower in New York. Heschel's reply was profound: "When I march in Selma, my feet are praying." Later that year, Heschel helped to found an interreligious clergy and lay group to oppose the involvement of our United States government in the war in Vietnam.

When Heschel died in 1972, our country was convulsed by rebellions against the establishment. Riots were erupting on major American college campuses. Scores of disenchanted young people blamed the country's imperfections on their elders, whom they considered hypocrites. These youth wanted to bring about a just society. In 1972, we were undergoing a period of turning outward. I don't recall ever hearing the word "spirituality" in those days.

Now the mood of our times has shifted 180 degrees. We are now looking inward. Spirituality has become almost a buzz word. More and more people want to connect with God. In this search, Heschel can be an enormous resource.

Michael Lerner, editor of *Tikkun*, wrote that Heschel was the first person he had ever met who took God seriously. Heschel noted that in our quest for God, we will experience what he called "radical amazement," an overwhelming sense of awe and wonderment. This core religious moment, however, is immediate and non-verbal. It cannot be expressed in language or imprisoned in rational theological categories. To Heschel, God was not a philosophical abstraction. Heschel's God was a living reality, the personal Deity of our patriarchs, Abraham, Isaac, and Jacob.

Heschel believed God takes a passionate interest in those God created. He spoke about "Divine pathos," which means that God suffers with God's creatures when they are in pain and demands a commitment to social justice to alleviate their plight.

Heschel also noted that other peoples build their cathedrals in space. We Jews, by contrast, build our cathedrals in time. The Sabbath is the Jewish quintessential cathedral in time.

Though English was not Heschel's native tongue, he mastered English and became an exemplary wordsmith. His eloquent writings are savored not only by Jews; they also serve as reflections in Catholic convents and in Baptist study groups.

Dr. Fritz Rothschild, who was his colleague at the Seminary, made the following perceptive observation about Heschel's writings:

> We find ourselves confronted with a style that exhibits a beauty and vividness of phrase rarely found in scholarly works. The idea appears in aphoristic insights ... spiritual gems ... His easy flowery prose hides subtle and complex thought processes that are ours to discover, only if we delve beneath the smooth surface and study each passage in depth.

Anne Frank

On *Yom Hashoah*, Holocaust Day, we commemorate the deaths of six million Jews who died in Nazi Europe until May 1945, when the death camps were liberated. Anne Frank missed the liberation by one month. In late February or early March of 1945, shortly before her sixteenth birthday, Anne Frank died of typhus and malnutrition in Bergen Belsen.

To mark the fiftieth anniversary of her death, in 1995, Doubleday Publishers issued a new, definitive edition of her diary. It contains about 30% more material than the original book that Otto Frank, her father, edited shortly after World War II.

These additional entries were excised by her father and by a prudish Dutch publisher because they contained some highly critical passages about her mother. They also featured a few frank descriptions of her emerging sexuality, such as her ripening feminine anatomy and her menstrual cycle.

This new edition gives us an even deeper understanding of this remarkable teenager who hid in a secret annex in Amsterdam to escape the detection of the Nazis. It provides us with textures and nuances of her character not found in the original edition. We also gain an even greater appreciation of her keen observation powers, her writing skills, her sense of humor, and her self-awareness.

About a month before Anne went into hiding in 1942, her parents presented her with a red-and-white plaid diary for her thirteenth birthday. Reading her words, we become amazed at how quickly Anne had to grow up. Her circumstances forced her to move swiftly from childhood through adolescence to become an adult prematurely by the age of fifteen. She almost skipped her teen years. Here is Anne's insight into her life before and after she went into hiding:

> When I think back to my life in 1942, it all seems too unreal. The Anne Frank who enjoyed that heavenly existence was completely different from the one who has grown wise within these walls. Yes, it was heavenly. Five admirers on every street corner, twenty or so friends, the favorite of most of my teachers, spoiled rotten by Father and Mother, bags full of candy and a big allowance. What more could anyone ask for? ...
>
> I'd like to live that seemingly carefree and happy life for an evening, a few days, a week. At the end of that week I'd be exhausted, and would be grateful to the first person to talk to me about something meaningful. I want friends, not admirers. People who respect me for my character and my deeds, not my flattering smile. The circle around me would be much smaller, but what does that matter, as long as they're sincere? ...
>
> Looking back, I realize that this period of my life has irrevocably come to a close; my happy-go-lucky, carefree school days are gone forever. I don't even miss them. I've outgrown them. I can no longer just kid around, since my serious side is always there ...

This remarkable young woman also graphically portrays the tensions that strained relations among her and the seven others who shared a hiding place on the top two floors of her father's pectin and spice factory. The other residents of the annex were her parents, Otto and Edith Frank; her sister, Margot; Mr. van Daan, her father's business partner; Mrs. van Daan; Peter van Daan, their sixteen-year-old son; and Mr. Dussel, a dentist.

To remain in such cramped quarters for days and months on end and going out only rarely on a risky shopping expedition is bound to engender mental anguish. Here is how she depicts it:

> My mind boggles at the profanity this honorable house has had to endure in the past month. Father walks around with

his lips pressed together, and whenever he hears his name, he looks up in alarm, as if he's afraid he'll be called upon to resolve another delicate problem. Mother's so wrought up, her cheeks are blotched with red. Margot complains of headaches. Dussel can't sleep. Mrs. van D. frets and fumes all day long; and I've gone completely around the bend. To tell you the truth, I sometimes forget who we're at odds with and who we're not . . .

Anne is open and candid in her appraisal of her fellow annex residents. She finds Mrs. van Daan and Mr. Dussel particularly obnoxious and insufferable and does not hesitate to disclose her animosity. At times she is merciless in her description of her mother. For the most part, she has warm feelings toward her father, her sister, and Mr. van Daan, and eventually develops a romantic attachment for Peter.

Some readers may be surprised to discover how assimilated the Frank family was. They had come from Germany to Holland in the early 1930s because of the growing power of the Nazis. We learn in this diary that the only Jewish holiday that Anne and the others in the annex celebrated was Hanukkah, when they lit the candles. However, with far greater enthusiasm, they observed St. Nicholas Day. Anne never mentions Passover nor the High Holy Days at all.

Furthermore, Anne shows marked tendencies as an early feminist. She writes that she needs to accomplish real work as a woman. She can't imagine having to live like her mother, Mrs. van Daan, and all the women who go about their work and then are forgotten.

She emphasizes that she needs to have something besides a husband and children to whom she can devote herself. She wants to be useful or bring enjoyment to all people, even those that she has never met. She emphasizes that in this way she wants to go on living even after her death.

In Anne's written accounts, she vividly reveals two strong opposite inclinations. First, her foreboding continually intensified as she peeked through the annex window to see Nazi soldiers rounding up Jews for deportation, as she heard frequent air raids over Amsterdam, and as she listened to BBC radio reports about Jews who were being gassed. But, on the other hand, Anne still could not suppress her other impulse, her fierce zest for life.

Anne's diary ends three days before August 4, 1944. On that day, an S.S. sergeant and at least three members of the Dutch security police, who were armed but dressed in civilian clothes, pulled up in a car in front of the factory. Someone must have turned in those eight people hiding in the annex. All eight were arrested and eventually sent to concentration camps. Otto Frank was the only one of the eight to survive. He spent his last years in Switzerland, where he died in 1980.

After the family was deported, Miep Gies found the diary. She was a faithful employee who had immeasurably helped the eight residents of the annex during their years of seclusion. The Nazis had ordered everyone to stay out of the annex after the arrest.

However, Gies defied orders. She went in to retrieve anything of value. She saw the cover of the diary on the floor of Otto and Edith Frank's bedroom. Its pages were scattered. Miep collected everything and planned to keep the diary until the family would be released.

At a ceremony honoring Gies when she was eighty, she recalled: "I wanted to see Anne's smile, to hear her say: 'O Miep, you saved my diary.'" Miep kept it in an unlocked drawer in the office to avoid suspicion. When Anne's father left the concentration camp, Miep gave it to him. Soon thereafter, he arranged for its editing and publishing.

We are boundlessly grateful that Anne Frank bequeathed to us this legacy just before her descent into hell began. She was a precious soul, who never ultimately succumbed to cynicism or despair. She maintained her faith in others, as she wrote in one of her last entries: "I still believe, in spite of everything, that people are good at heart."

Oskar Schindler

The Book of Esther features the arch-villain Haman, who was the genocidal ancestor of Hitler. He convinced King Ahasueres to issue a decree ordering the destruction of all the Jews of Persia. In that dramatic saga, no righteous Gentile ever rose up to save Jews from their annihilation. Fortunately, because of the urging of her cousin, Mordecai, help came from the Jewish Queen Esther, and all the Jews of Persia were spared.

The story of Europe's Jews, as we know, did not end so happily. Six million of them met their cruel and callous deaths. Most non-Jews either supported Hitler's "Final Solution" or they remained silent onlookers. However, there were those few righteous Gentiles, *hasidei umot ha-olam*, who stood out as brave rescuers. At great risk to their own lives, they selflessly and courageously saved Jews from the jaws of Nazi destruction.

One such titan was Oskar Schindler, a lapsed Roman Catholic. His hedonistic lifestyle would make him a most un-likely hero. One writer called him a "tarnished angel." Schindler was an incurable womanizer. He was notoriously unfaithful to his wife, Emilie, who was also a righteous Gentile in her own right.

Emilie loved to recount the time that she had admonished a Nazi for throwing a crystal glass in praise of Hitler in her dining room. She also recalled with pride her helping to open a frozen cattle car full of dying Jews in sub-zero weather.

Yet, Emilie suffered numerous indignities with Oskar, to whom she remained officially married until the end of his life. While in Poland, Oskar kept a German mistress, had occasional affairs with his Polish secretary, and enjoyed a number of flings while running his factories.

In 1957, Oskar left Emilie in Argentina, where they had settled. He went to West Germany, where he wanted to seek compensation for his war losses. Emilie reported that the first thing he did when got to Germany was to cash in his return ticket. He never ever lived with Emilie again until his death in 1974.

Oskar was also a heavy drinker, with a special fondness for cognac. He moved to Cracow, Poland, late in 1939, from his native Czechoslovakia. Initially, he arrived as an opportunistic businessman. His goal in Cracow was not to save Jews, but to make a fortune.

The Nazis shortly before had occupied Cracow, where Jews had lived and flourished for 600 years. Here, Schindler wined and dined Nazi officials. He always wore an enamel swastika bull's eye pinned to his lapel. Schindler was a gifted con-artist and charmer, a high liver and a smooth talker. He managed to convince the wealthy Jews of Cracow to give him the necessary capital to buy a once profitable enamel pot factory.

The Nazis had recently confiscated it from its Jewish owners. Schindler had hoped to operate the factory and to manufacture mess kits and other items for the Nazi war effort. Here he hired Jewish slave labor. He withheld their wages and turned those sums over to the S.S., but kept steep profits for himself.

Schindler's conscience was forcefully pricked as the Cracow ghetto was being liquidated. Watching on horseback with his girlfriend atop a hill, Schindler became sickened by the bloody and brutal massacres that he witnessed below. Nazi soldiers were indiscriminately firing at Jews and herding them into transports.

In the movie *Schindler's List*, the black-and-white screen is relieved at that point by a spot of bright color, to which Schindler's attention is drawn. Here he saw a little blonde girl dressed in a scarlet coat. He suddenly understood that ultimately this little girl's fate would be no different from that of the other doomed Cracow Jews.

At that moment, Schindler underwent a fundamental transformation. Schindler now became the courageous rescuer of the Jewish victims of Nazism. Cleverly and cunningly, he began to dispense hundreds of generous bribes and gifts to Nazi officials to keep Jews alive.

Schindler followed the evacuated Jews from Cracow to the Plaszow concentration camp, which was run by the sadistic and ruthless Amon Goeth. Like Schindler, Goeth had a voracious appetite for the good life, for women, and for liquor. Each morning, for sport, Goeth went to the porch of his villa to shoot randomly at a few Jewish prisoners. He kept, as his Jewish servant, Helen Hirsch, whom he hurt and humiliated in spite of the fact that he loved her. Schindler was able to win custody of Helen by beating Goeth in a game of cards.

In fact, Schindler plied the monstrous Goeth with liquor and bribes to get Goeth's permission to take some of his Jewish laborers back so that he could continue factory production. While working in Schindler's Plaszow factory, Jews were treated humanely. They lived on a diet of approximately 2,000 calories a day, something unheard of among the masses of starvation-ridden Jewish victims of Nazism. Schindler's humanity stands in stark contrast to Goeth's barbarism.

Plaszow was about to be evacuated and the Jews sent to Auschwitz. Schindler then drew up his famous list. He arranged to buy his Jews from Goeth with suitcases of money and to transport them to Schindler's hometown of Brinnlitz, Czechoslovakia, where he was about to open a new factory camp. Here his metamorphosis as a savior of Jews became complete. Schindler no longer was concerned about amassing wealth.

During this period, he learned that a train of 300 Jewish women en route from Plaszow to Brinnlitz was accidentally rerouted to Auschwitz, where they were about to be gassed. At this point, Schindler intervened by bribing Nazi officials with diamonds to ensure that all 300 women would be returned to him.

While operating the munitions factory at Brinnlitz, Schindler cleverly managed to convince Nazi inspectors that he was fulfilling all production requirements. Yet everything made at that factory was deliberately defective. Not a single shell the factory produced was worth anything. By the end of the war, Schindler had impoverished himself by giving handsome bribes in order to save Jews.

Both Thomas Keneally, in his novel *Schindler's List*, and Steven Spielberg, in his screenplay by the same title, produced masterful works. Neither of them, however, gives any reasons for Schindler's heroic behavior. They never explain why Schindler, the bon vivant and insatiable adulterer, was so driven to deliver Jews from Nazi extermination.

However, each of these artists presents a fundamentally different view of Schindler. Spielberg portrays Schindler, to the very end, as a "good Nazi," a term which is really an oxymoron. Throughout the movie, Schindler wears his Nazi lapel pin. He never renounces his ties with the Nazi party.

In fact, on V.E. Day, Schindler gathers together all the *Schindlerjuden*, those Jews whom he saved, to deliver a moving speech. In it, he basically asserts that he is really like any other Nazi. He tells them: "I am a member of the Nazi party. I am a munitions manufacturer. I am a profiteer of slave labor. I am a criminal. After midnight, I'll be hunted." After he finishes his talk and the Schindler Jews thank him profusely, he adds his regrets that he did not do more to save Jews.

Keneally, on the other hand, meticulously researched Schindler's life and career. He never quotes this speech. Among the transcripts from that V.E. Day, no such speech can be found. Keneally depicts a different Schindler. This Schindler was so nauseated by the Nazi bestiality that he observed during the evacuation of the Cracow ghetto that he became a confirmed anti-Nazi. After that episode, he essentially renounced Nazism. Schindler says, in Keneally's novel:

"Beyond this day, no thinking person could fail to see what would happen. I was now resolved to do everything in my power to defeat the system."

It is true that in the novel, Schindler wears his Nazi lapel pin to the end. Yet he does so not because of any allegiance to the Nazi cause. To him, the pin is most likely a device to gain entree into the offices of the S.S. in order to save Jews.

Spielberg's view of Schindler's goodness is relative. In other words, Spielberg implies that, compared to other Nazis, Schindler was decent, but still a Nazi. In Keneally's novel, however, Schindler's humanitarianism is absolute. Keneally is telling us that by any standard, Schindler, the ex-Nazi, would be a towering ethical giant.

Following the war, Oskar suffered numerous financial reverses, first in Argentina and then in Germany. By 1961, Oskar was again bankrupt. Hearing of his problems, the *Schindlerjuden* living in Israel wanted Oskar to visit Israel at their expense. It was the first of seventeen trips that Oskar made each year to Israel.

That year, 1961, was the time of the trial of Adolf Eichmann in Jerusalem. On the day before the trial, a British journalist wrote a feature article. He quoted the opening words of the appeal of Israel's *Schindlerjuden* to come to the aid of Schindler: "We do not forget the sorrows of Egypt. We do not forget Haman. We do not forget Hitler. Thus, among the unjust, we do not forget the just. Remember Oskar Schindler."

Indeed, we must never overlook Oskar Schindler. We must never forget his courageous goodness. We must never ignore any of the rescuers, for that matter. We who live after the Holocaust need the assurance that, even within the darkness of violence, brutality, and barbarism, the bright sparks of kindness and goodness can shine. May Oskar Schindler's memory be a blessing.

Mordecai M. Kaplan

The Biblical Moses lived for 120 years. As a result, 120 has become the ideal Jewish life span. A customary salutation in both Hebrew and Yiddish is: "May you live to be 120." Mordecai M. Kaplan, father of Reconstructionist Judaism, died at the age of 102, in 1983. Two years before, when he reached 100, a visitor greeted him with the traditional wish that he live to 120. Kaplan replied: "I have had enough. Let some young man use the 20 years."

His answer was typical of his inimitable quips. For example, he once reflected on the fickle nature of denominational loyalties among American Jews in these words: "Many Conservative Jews become Reform at the drop of a hat."

Kaplan's career spanned most of the twentieth century. He probably understood the psychology of American Jews during that century better than any other Jewish thinker. Kaplan was the twentieth century's most daring, creative, courageous, and imaginative Jewish theologian and ideologue.

Kaplan was born in Lithuania in 1881. He was eight when he moved to New York. At the age of twelve, Mordecai Kaplan enrolled in the Jewish Theological Seminary, the school for training Conservative rabbis. During his seminary years, he received a master's degree from Columbia University.

He was ordained a rabbi at the seminary at the age of twenty-one. He took a position with Congregation Kehilath Jeshurun in Manhattan, which was Orthodox. Since members of Kehilath Jeshurun did not recognize his ordination from a non-Orthodox seminary, they called him "Minister." At the age of twenty-seven, in 1908, Kaplan was married. He and his bride went to Europe for a honeymoon. While in Europe, he received an Orthodox *semikha*, or ordination. Upon his return, he was one of the few English-speaking Orthodox rabbis at that time.

Even in his twenties, though his background, his credentials, and his ritual practices were Orthodox, his thinking was quite un-Orthodox. Kaplan began to doubt whether the miracles of the Bible actually happened and whether the Five Books of the Torah were really written by Moses.

Such seemingly heretical views were bound to create conflict with his Orthodox congregation. He left Kehilath Jeshurun to accept the invitation of the renowned chancellor of the Jewish Theological Seminary, Dr. Solomon Schechter, to become the first dean of the Seminary Teachers' Institute. Later Kaplan added to his duties the professorship of homiletics, which is the art of sermon construction, in the rabbinical school. He held these two posts for nearly fifty years.

In 1922, in New York, he founded the Society for the Advancement of Judaism, an institution which was to become the mother synagogue of Reconstructionism. In 1934, he published his *magnum opus, Judaism as a Civilization*, which became the authoritative reference work on Reconstructionist Judaism.

He also collaborated in the creation of a new Reconstructionist Haggadah. In 1945, he issued a radically new Sabbath prayerbook. In it, many of the traditional doctrines of Judaism were altered. The publication of this prayerbook aroused the anger of some ultra-Orthodox rabbis. They put Kaplan under the ban of *herem*, or ex-communication, and publicly burned the prayerbook.

Kaplan caused a revolution with his ideas in two fields: Jewish sociology and Jewish theology. In the realm of sociology, Kaplan gave a sound definition of Jews and Judaism, accepted by almost all Jews today. Judaism is not a race, because there are Jews that are part of the Anglo, Black, and Oriental races. Jews do not constitute a nationality, because there are

English Jews, French Jews, Argentinian Jews, and Russian Jews. Furthermore, Jews are more than just a religious community, in contrast to what Reform Jews believed some decades ago.

Kaplan maintained that Jews are people with an evolving religious civilization. The word "people" takes into account the ethnic dimension of Judaism. "Civilization" means that Judaism is more than a religion. It includes special folk dialects, like Yiddish and Ladino; ethnic foods, like bagels and blintzes; non-religious, but Jewish, art, music, and literature, such as the clever tales of Sholom Aleichem, the hora, and the exotic paintings of Marc Chagall.

Amidst all of the civilizational elements, however, religion does stand at its core. Religion has centrality. Yet, Judaism is not static and unchanging, but is dynamic and developmental. Thus the use of the word "evolving." Kaplan stressed the idea of an organic Jewish community. In fact, some claim that he was the real founder of the Jewish Community Center movement.

In addition to providing an apt definition of Jews and Judaism, he maintained that American Jews live simultaneously in two civilizations. Kaplan told the story about the time he lived in Paris when he was seven, one year before coming to America. From Paris, he boarded the ship to New York. The Sabbath was approaching.

Young Kaplan heard the announcement that there would be fireworks to mark Bastille Day, which was July 14. Kaplan wanted to see the fireworks, but his mother said he had to recite his Sabbath eve prayers. By the time he had finished, the fireworks were over.

He commented that, since then, he had been living in two civilizations: the Jewish and the non-Jewish. Kaplan believed that one should renounce any conflict between the two civilizations and live in both of them harmoniously and happily.

Though Kaplan was an avid Zionist, he believed that it was possible to create a vibrant Jewish life here in America.

He also insisted the American Jew celebrate American holidays, like the Fourth of July and Thanksgiving, with the same fervor as the Jewish holidays of Rosh Hashanah and Passover.

His sociological innovations created little stir. However, his theological views aroused intense controversy. Kaplan did not accept the traditional doctrine of divine revelation. Orthodox Jews believe that God dictated every word of the Torah to Moses at Mt. Sinai. The Torah must be observed in all of its legislative details. Kaplan adopted a view similar to that of Reform Judaism. He maintained that the Torah is a product of human beings. Its laws could be changed in response to new circumstances.

Kaplan himself was always a strictly observant Jew. Yet, he did recommend sharp departures from the Tradition for others. In fact, he eliminated the use of the word *Halakha*, or Jewish law, to describe required Jewish practice and substituted the expression "folkways and mores."

Furthermore, Kaplan abolished the concept of the "Chosen People." He claimed that it implies a notion of superiority. In fact, he created a new version of the Kiddush and the Torah blessings, with references to the "Chosen People" excised.

In addition, he revised our traditional thinking about God. He posited a naturalist view of God. To Kaplan, God was not a personal Deity but an impersonal force. Kaplan defined God as a Power within us and without us who makes for salvation. There have been some who have joked that Reconstructionists begin their prayers: "To whom it may concern."

Kaplan was a pioneer in advocating equal rights for women in the synagogue. As far back as 1922, his congregation, the Society for the Advancement of Judaism, called women to the Torah. Furthermore, Kaplan was the inventor of the Bat Mitzvah in Jewish life. He was the father of four daughters and no sons. He wanted to welcome his daughters ceremonially into the more mature responsibilities of Jewish life. In fact, the first Bat Mitzvah in Jewish history was his daughter, Judith Kaplan Eisenstein, who was a noted musicologist.

Kaplan never wanted Reconstructionist Judaism to become a separate movement, with its own rabbinical seminary, congregational association, and rabbinic organization, as is the case today. Kaplan hoped Reconstructionists would influence the then three existing denominations in Jewish life.

In his earlier years, Kaplan chided Reform Judaism for reducing Judaism to a religion and dismissing its civilizational elements. Yet Reform Jews, in recent decades, have embraced his thinking and philosophy. In fact, at the time of his death, Kaplan was an honorary alumnus of the Hebrew Union College and an honorary member of the Central Conference of American Rabbis, both Reform institutions, even though he spent almost his entire professional career with the Conservative seminary.

The Bible tells us that, until the end, Moses' eyes were undimmed and his vigor unabated. The same was true with Mordecai Kaplan. Until his mid-nineties, Kaplan was lecturing, writing, and traveling. On the occasion of his 100th birthday, a bibliography of his works was issued. He had produced over 700 items.

He taught us that one must never stagnate. Almost until the end, he was the daring innovator. I think of a story told about him as a professor of homiletics at the Seminary. He taught a particular course which met on Thursday and on the following Monday. On Thursday, he prepared his students for their responsibilities of delivering a sermon for the following class.

One Thursday, he gave an example of a very good sermon. A student who would be the first to deliver the sermon on Monday thought of himself as very clever. He carefully recorded Kaplan's sermon. He wrote it down. He memorized it. He delivered it word for word on Monday.

Kaplan critiqued the sermon. He shouted that the sermon was terrible. The student could have done much better. The student was naturally perplexed. The student said, "Dr.

Kaplan, you and I both know that these were your exact words last Thursday. How can you condemn them?" Kaplan looked at him squarely in the eye and said, "I've grown since last Thursday." Such is Kaplan's legacy to us: See life with new eyes every day.

Rembrandt

The second of the Ten Commandments enjoins us not to make any graven images. Generations of traditional Jews have interpreted this prohibition to mean that no fully developed human figures can be represented in art. In traditional synagogues, no likenesses of men and women are etched into stained glass windows. No statues or busts of leading Jewish personalities are housed in the synagogue, although some Reform congregations have relaxed these prohibitions. The most extreme traditionalists will not even sit for portraits or allow themselves to be photographed because of their stringent interpretation of this regulation against making graven images.

Yet, surprisingly, in the interiors of the ancient synagogues of Dura Europas, in Syria, and Bet Alpha, in Israel, we find numerous Biblical scenes containing human beings. In certain times in Jewish history, traditional Jews have been more liberal on this issue than others. One such time was Holland in the seventeenth century. It was here that Rembrandt, one of the greatest painters of human subjects, especially Jewish ones, lived.

Rembrandt was born in 1606 in Leiden, Holland. His father was a miller. His mother was the daughter of a baker. Rembrandt was raised in a Calvinist Protestant home. It was a home in which the Bible was venerated. Rembrandt frequently used Biblical subject matter in his paintings. He possessed the gift of reproducing human figures with rare insight into the inner world of those figures.

Eventually, Rembrandt moved to Amsterdam. He needed a large city which would provide him a suitable arena for him to express his vast talents. He received numerous commissions for portraits in Amsterdam. He chose to make his home in the heavily populated Jewish section of Amsterdam. He studied Hebrew, which was part of the Renaissance humanist tradition. In those days it was fashionable for all educated Christians to read the Hebrew Bible in the original.

Rembrandt led a tragic life. He was married twice and widowed both times. His only child, a son from his first marriage, died while he was still a young man. Rembrandt had severe financial reverses in his later years. Many of his customers did not like his work and began to withdraw from him. Rembrandt died at the age of sixty-two, a sad, forlorn, and lonely man. He was almost totally forgotten after his death until some years later, when his greatness was rediscovered.

Rembrandt was the first artist of consequence to portray Jews as people with human dignity. Others had presented them as ugly, greedy, and grasping creatures. Rembrandt simply refused to share the anti-Semitism of his fellow Christians.

Why was Rembrandt so positively inclined toward Jews? There are several possible explanations. First, the country of Holland treated Jews well. In other words, Rembrandt lived in a general climate of tolerance and acceptance. Holland, a short time before, had been under the domination of Catholic Spain. The Jews who lived in Holland were of Sephardic background. They came from Portugal, where they had been persecuted. They arrived a short time before Rembrandt was born.

The Dutch felt a kinship of common suffering with the Jews. Therefore, unlike other Europeans, they did not force the Jews to live in ghettos. The Jews chose on their own to inhabit the southern part of Amsterdam. Jews were also not required to wear armbands or other disgraceful identifying symbols.

Possibly there is another reason that the Dutch warmly embraced the Jews. They viewed the Jews as helpful in expanding Holland's vast commercial enterprises in foreign lands.

Furthermore, a large number of Rembrandt's clients were

Sephardic Jews. They had lived among Christians, had a positive attitude toward the graphic arts, and were wealthy. With their love of art and their financial resources, they became among Rembrandt's most dedicated and enthusiastic patrons. Most of the portraits that Rembrandt produced were commissioned by Sephardic Jews.

The Ashkenazic Jews, mostly from Poland, had lived apart from Christian communities. They had somewhat negative attitudes toward the graphic arts. They also had less wealth than the Sephardic Jews. Yet Rembrandt did not ignore them. He found them fascinating subjects for portraits.

There is yet another reason. Rembrandt's personal life was filled with agony and distress. He found Jews, especially Ashkenazic Jews, with their background of suffering, excellent candidates for portraiture. The Jews he encountered had been driven by misfortune. They had been harassed and removed from their homes. Their loved ones had been tortured and burned at the stake.

In their physical features, Rembrandt was able to detect a sad and tired expression, combined with a look of iron determination to remain faithful Jews and to await the future with hope. He saw in their faces better material for art than the coarser, more carefree, looks of the average Dutchman.

Some experts maintain that of Rembrandt's 200 oil portraits of men, 37 are Jews. In addition, he produced numerous oils, etchings, and drawings of Jewish couples and ghetto beauties. In his most celebrated oils on themes in the Bible, such as "Samson and Delilah," "Saul and David," "Sacrifice of Abraham," "Joseph's Dream," and numerous others, he obviously used Jewish subjects.

Evidently, Rembrandt turned to Jews not only as fascinating subjects for his artistic creations. We believe that he had a broader mission. He was committed to promoting a better understanding between the Jews and Christians of his day. One of the leading authorities on the subject of Rembrandt and the Jews was Franz Landsberger. Landsberger reminded us that Rembrandt "painted Jewish faces, not only for those who had ordered them as portraits, but as a champion of the Jewish people. This same impulse led to his etchings of 'The Jewish Bride' and 'The Synagogue.' The artist's purpose in these creations, far from being anti-Jewish, was the promoting of an unprejudiced interest in Jewish customs."

Rembrandt's house is still located in what was once the center of the thriving Jewish community of Amsterdam. We sadly note that the Nazis managed to exterminate the majority of Amsterdam's Jews in the gas chambers and crematoria that they built for this evil purpose. Yet Rembrandt's home stands as a symbol of the love of Jews. It occupies a place where, three centuries later, Jews became the casualties of Hitler's fury and hatred. We can only hope that such symbols, like Rembrandt's home, will become more numerous in the years ahead.

King Hussein

Many ordinary people become saints in death. In the synagogue lectionary during the spring, we read three successive Torah portions, bearing the names *Ahare Mot, Kedoshim,* and *Emor.* If we take these four words together, we can loosely translate them: "After death, say that they are saints."

This assertion reflects a profound traditional Jewish observation about the selectivity of the human memory. When people die, often their faults and shortcomings are forgotten and their virtues and assets are magnified. In death, the philanderer sometimes is remembered as a loving husband and the simpleton becomes a genius.

Such has been particularly true of the way that the Jewish community has praised the late King Hussein of the Hashemite Kingdom of Jordan after his death. King Hussein has been hailed as a "brave soldier for peace" and a "true friend of Israel and the Jewish people." To give an honest and balanced portrayal of King Hussein's life, however, let us candidly admit that he was not always a champion of peace or an ardent lover of Jews.

From the time of the creation of the State of Israel in 1948 until the Six-Day War in 1967, Jordan controlled the West Bank and the Old City of Jerusalem. During those nineteen years, King Hussein did not allow any Jew to enter the Old City nor to pray at the revered Western Wall. In fact, throughout those years, Hussein's soldiers desecrated ancient Jewish cemeteries by using them for latrines. They also converted Jewish tombstones into concrete slabs to pave roads. Furthermore, Hussein permitted over fifty historic synagogues in Old City of Jerusalem to be converted into stables.

In 1967, he went against the clear warnings of Israel's leaders. He joined other Arabs in their war against Israel and, of course, lost. Then, six years later, in 1973, during the Yom Kippur War, he sent his Jordanian troops to fight alongside the Syrian army. King Hussein also supported Saddam Hussein, the villainous leader of Iraq, in the Persian Gulf War.

Admittedly, King Hussein sponsored or allowed these obscene actions, not necessarily because of any hatred of Israel or the Jewish people, but out of practical considerations. In short, during the forty-five years of his reign, King Hussein took the steps that he thought would be necessary, both to retain his kingship and to avoid his assassination.

In fact, he was the first ruler of the Hashemite dynasty to die of natural causes. A pivotal moment in his life occurred in 1951, when he was just fifteen years of age. He entered the Temple Mount in the Old City of Jerusalem with his grandfather, King Abdullah, who was then the reigning monarch of Jordan. There, at the Temple Mount, a Palestinian nationalist shot and killed King Abdullah, while his grandson stood beside him. It was a metal plate on Hussein's chest that saved him from death.

Talal, who was Abdullah's son and Hussein's father, succeeded Abdullah to the throne. Yet, he had to abdicate six weeks later because of mental illness. In the following year, in 1952, at the tender age of seventeen, Hussein was proclaimed King of Jordan.

The bitter memory of his grandfather's tragic death and the sure knowledge that his own life was never safe from Arab gunmen determined many of his political decisions. In short, King Hussein did what he thought was necessary to retain power and to avoid death. To his credit, he skillfully managed to keep Jordan free from the most extreme forms of political intrigue that are so rampant in the Arab world.

King Hussein was a clever politician. He covered all his bases. He courted various Arab rulers, while building up secret close relationships with Israel since the mid-1960s. In his last several years, possibly for more than just pragmatic reasons, Hussein went public with his desire to make peace with Israel.

Like the late Anwar Sadat of Egypt before him, he decided that, after a lifetime of warring against his neighbor, there was logic and value to pursuing peace. So, in 1994, under King Hussein's skillful leadership, Jordan became the second Arab country to sign a peace treaty with Israel.

Thus, in assessing King Hussein's legacy, we should not forget his heinous actions in the past. Nonetheless, we must acknowledge the fact that he was one of the most eloquent and sanest voices of reason in a part of the world notorious for its brutality, butchery, and strife. Indeed, his actions toward Israel in the years just before his death have been impressive.

With his rich, sonorous voice, emanating from his small-framed body, which he always carried with great elegance and dignity, Hussein delivered a moving and touching tribute to the late Prime Minister Yitzhak Rabin at his funeral in 1995. He also traveled to Israel to pay a call on the families of seven Israeli schoolgirls from Naharayim, who were shot by a deranged Jordanian soldier. Then, in his last few months, already severely weakened by terminal cancer, Hussein left his sick bed to attend the Wye Conference with the hope of bringing Yasir Arafat, of the PLO, and Benjamin Netanyahu, of Israel, closer together.

Certainly, King Hussein did make his blunders and mistakes, and sometimes they were tragic ones. Yet, his enduring legacy will be one of a peacemaker, a title he richly deserves. He demonstrated his ability to transcend bitterness and animosity and work steadfastly toward reconciliation and harmony.

After his death, the American Jewish Congress paid tribute to King Hussein. The concluding words of its statement are so fitting:

We hardly thought that we would be using this phrase again so soon; it has come to have for us a precious and singular meaning. King Hussein was an intimate partner with Yitzhak Rabin in the tireless pursuit of peace. And so, with all respect, we can think of no more fitting way to say farewell than, "Shalom, Chaver."

Felix Mendelssohn

Several years ago, Jiri Weil, a Czech Jewish writer, penned
a novel titled *Mendelssohn on the Roof*. Weil graphically portrayed an ambitious and inspiring S.S. officer during the Nazi
occupation of Prague. This officer had received orders to remove the statue of the Jew, Felix Mendelssohn, from the roof
of the Prague concert hall. The problem, however, was that the
roof was filled with numerous statues of renowned composers.
None was labeled or identified by name. Therefore, he had to
figure out which statue was Mendelssohn's.

The officer recalled that he had learned, in his course on
"Racial Science," that Jews have big noses. Therefore, he ordered the workmen to pull down the statue with the biggest
nose. As he stood watching the statue with the biggest nose
toppling from the roof of the concert hall, he panicked. He
discovered, all too late, that it was that of none other than the
famous German composer, Richard Wagner.

This story conveys a double irony. First of all, Wagner was
not only not a Jew; he was also a rabid anti-Semite. He wrote
scathing attacks on Jews, especially Jewish musicians. Not surprisingly, Wagner was Adolf Hitler's favorite musician.

In his prolific writings, Wagner even made disparaging
comments about Felix Mendelssohn. He tried to prove that
the life and works of Mendelssohn clearly demonstrate that
no Jew, however gifted, cultured, and honorable, could create
art that moved the heart and soul.

What is tragically apparent about Wagner's assessment of
Mendelssohn is that Mendelssohn, for most of his life, was a
practicing Lutheran. It is true that Felix Mendelssohn was
born in 1809 in Hamburg, Germany, to two Jewish parents.

His grandfather, Moses Mendelssohn, was an eminent rabbi and philosopher. Moses had urged German Jews, upon leaving the ghetto, to stay faithful to Judaism, while embracing German culture and thought. In fact, he remained a practicing Orthodox Jew throughout his life.

However, five of his six children eventually became Christians. One of them was Abraham Mendelssohn, the father of Felix. Abraham was a successful banker and businessman. Felix's mother, the former Leah Salomon, came from a prominent German Jewish family of considerable means. Abraham and Leah produced four children: Fanny, Felix, Rebekah, and Paul.

When Felix was six, his parents had them baptized in the Lutheran church, though they themselves, for the time being, remained Jewish. This was the era that many German Jews had gained their freedom from the degradation of the *shtetl*. They wanted to participate fully in the glories of German culture. They believed that Judaism, with its history of torment, persecution, and abuse, was an antiquated and self-defeating form of religion, an obstacle to their integration into the wider community.

When Felix was confirmed in the Lutheran church at age fourteen, his father wrote him a revealing letter. He stated that he and Leah had brought up their four children in Christianity because, to them, it was the faith of the most civilized people. Also, by 1812, German Jews were promised full civil equality if they converted to Christianity. These German Jews were seeking "tickets of admission to European culture," in the words of the poet Heinrich Heine. Thus, their adoption of Christianity was motivated by a zeal for social and professional advancement. It did not grow out of any deep religious conviction.

Jakob Salomon, Leah's brother and Felix's uncle, had already converted to Christianity several years before. He took the new name of Bartholdy to mask his Jewish identity. Bartholdy was actually the name of the owner of a large garden in Berlin that Jakob had bought for himself. Someone cleverly quipped that Jakob had acquired his new ancestry "by purchase."

When Felix was a teenager, his parents were finally baptized as Lutherans. They also took the name Bartholdy and dropped the name Mendelssohn. They wanted Felix to do the same. Felix was always an obedient, well-mannered, and compliant son, but here he drew the line. His father, in fact, ordered calling cards for him with the name "Felix M. Bartholdy." Felix refused to use them. He insisted on retaining the name Mendelssohn. His father remonstrated with him by arguing: "There can't be a Christian Mendelssohn any more than there can be a Jewish Confucius." Nonetheless, Felix held his ground.

Though Felix was a committed Christian, he never seemed to be embarrassed by his Jewish roots. In fact, his Jewish background was not much of an impediment in his musical career. He was probably considered the greatest musical genius of the nineteenth-century school of German romantic music. Some say that he was the most impressive musical prodigy since Mozart.

He gave his first public concert at age nine. At sixteen, he wrote his famous "Octet," and by seventeen he completed his "Overture" to Shakespeare's "Midsummer Night's Dream."

He also brought the works of Johann Sebastian Bach, which had been neglected for almost a century, into public prominence. Mendelssohn achieved great popularity and acclaim throughout Europe, especially in London. Only the people of Berlin, the city where he spent most of the formative years of his life, did not seem to appreciate his musical prowess.

Mendelssohn never showed any of the stereotypical eccentricities associated with artists. He was always charming and gracious. He was a good son, a devoted brother, a loving husband, and an affectionate father. Unfortunately, he did not live long enough to accomplish all he could have. In 1838, Felix Mendelssohn died at the age of thirty-nine, after suffering two strokes. Some say that the death of his beloved sister, Fanny, who was also a musical giant, a few months before, had demoralized him and robbed him of his incentive to live.

For the most part, Felix Mendelssohn lived and died a Christian. At his Christian funeral, attended by multitudes of admirers, a six-hundred-voice choir sang "Christ and the Resurrection." Felix was buried in the cemetery of Holy Cross Church in Berlin. Today, a huge cross marks his grave.

All of these outward trappings of Mendelssohn's commitment to Christianity did not impress the Nazis. To them, he was always a Jew. Almost a century after his death, they besmirched his memory as a Jewish composer. They forbade his music to be played. They ordered that the huge statue of him in Leipzig be taken down and destroyed. They also closed the Mendelssohn banking house and ordered all the Mendelssohn descendants still living in Germany to leave the country.

I reflect with pain upon Mendelssohn's bifurcated identity. His fate proves how almost impossible it is for Jews to reject their religious roots. First of all, technically, Jewish law does not recognize any conversions out of Judaism. If a person is born a Jew or converts to Judaism, that person's Jewish religious identity becomes permanent and irrevocable.

But even some Christians find it difficult to accept a Jew who embraces Christianity as anything other than a Jew. Leaving Judaism involves more than giving up just a religious system. It involves abandoning a heritage, a culture, a tradition, and, yes, even an extended family. A far more honest and healthier course of action is to be proud of one's Jewish roots, learn as much as one can about them, and live in peace with them.

Billy Graham

The 2002 Academy Awards ceremony had a Jewish spin. Shortly before, rumors began to circulate about John Nash, the schizophrenic mathematics genius who was the hero of the movie *A Beautiful Mind*. We learned that he once was a rabid anti-Semite. Critics faulted the producers of this film for omitting this important fact, as well as other key details in Nash's life.

Nash's defenders do acknowledge that a few years after he was diagnosed with this devastating mental affliction, he did claim to feel threatened by Jews and the State of Israel. He also believed that he was the Messiah.

Akiva Goldman was the writer of the screenplay. He is the son of two Jewish psychologists, who work with emotionally disturbed children. Goldman was fascinated by the biography of Nash he read. In the film, he wanted to show that, when people suffer delusions, their minds totally betray them. In short, Goldman is claiming that Nash's alleged anti-Semitism does not reflect his true convictions. It was the product of his deranged mind.

About the same time, another shocking revelation broke into the news. The National Archives made public thousands of tape recordings of conversations of the late President Richard Nixon, who was notorious for his slurs against Jews. On some of these tapes were exchanges between him and famed evangelist Rev. Billy Graham.

In 1972, Graham agreed with Nixon that our nation's problems lie with the satanic Jews. Both accused Jews of dominating the media, one of the oldest anti-Jewish canards. Graham went on to blame Jews for putting out pornographic materials. He told Nixon that the Jewish stranglehold has to be broken or the country will go down the drain. He admitted to Nixon that Jews do not really know his true feelings about them.

When Graham learned about this revelation, he flatly denied saying anything defamatory about Jews, either publicly or privately. Yet there is no question that Graham's famous Southern drawl is unmistakably the one heard on those tapes.

Graham, advanced in years and suffering from the ravages of Parkinson's Disease, swiftly issued a four-sentence apology. He also claimed that he had no memory of those 1972 conversations with Richard Nixon. Many Jewish leaders were unconvinced by his denials. Abraham Foxman, national director of the Anti-Defamation League, acknowledged that, for decades, we have viewed Graham as an American icon, the closest public figure we have to an American spiritual leader. However, Foxman added that Graham had been playing a charade all these years. Having been so close to so many presidents, who knows what else he might have told them about Jews?

How shall we deal with these disclosures about Graham's anti-Jewish diatribes? We can't ascribe them to mental derangement, as we can in the case of John Nash. Obviously, it was with a clear and sane mind that Graham denigrated the Jewish people.

Until we learned of these ugly assertions, we Jews had looked upon Billy Graham as a man of impeccable character, unlike many of today's evangelists who are notorious for their sordid behavior. The title of William Martin's biography of Graham described him as *A Prophet with Honor*. Indeed, Billy Graham was a symbol of moral rectitude.

Furthermore, Billy Graham has never become financially enriched by his Crusades. He receives a modest compensation from the Billy Graham Evangelic Association, located in Minneapolis. From the moment that this association was established in 1950, Billy Graham was put on a salary. He does not accept any additional love gifts or honoraria from admirers.

Billy Graham has also been a faithful husband to Ruth, his only wife, whom he married in the early 1940s. He refuses to be placed in compromising situations with other women.

However, his involvement in politics has repeatedly thrust him into an ugly predicament which has threatened to stain his character. Since the days of Dwight D. Eisenhower, Billy Graham has been a personal friend and confidant of American presidents. In his early years, he tried to influence the direction of government.

In fact, he, like many other Protestant leaders, including Norman Vincent Peale, feared the election of a Catholic president in 1960. He thus supported Richard Nixon over John F. Kennedy. Over the years, Graham and Nixon developed a very deep friendship.

In 1973, when the Watergate revelations were pouring in, Graham continued to defend Nixon. He claimed that he didn't believe that Nixon knew about this scandal and continued to vouch for Nixon's integrity. When mounting evidence did prove that Nixon was the major culprit in Watergate, Graham still refused to condemn his actions. To do so, in his judgment, was tantamount to deserting a close friend.

Possibly this is the background for his anti-Semitic vitriol in 1972. He wanted to "cozy up" to Nixon. I mentioned that the title of Graham's biography is *A Prophet with Honor*. Unfortunately, Graham is no prophet. He is unlike the Biblical prophets who boldly challenged kings and priests when matters of justice were at stake. Instead of taking Nixon to task for his hateful statements against Jews, Graham agreed with him. Instead of playing the role of a Biblical prophet who excoriated heads of state for their moral delinquencies, Graham took the cowardly route. Unfortunately, this was his posture with other presidents as well. He did not keep enough of a distance from them so that he could be an effective moral critic.

Also, I do not condone the insensitive way he prays at public gatherings. In his prayers at presidential inaugurations, in 1993, 1997, and 2001, he concluded his words in the name of Jesus and the Trinity. Christian prayers in Christian settings with Christian congregations are perfectly appropriate. However, offering sectarian prayers at public functions is offensive and exclusionary to many Americans.

Yet, if we examine Graham's life, we cannot find a single word or a single act in his public ministry that can be viewed as anti-Semitic. Until we learned about these despicable tapes, we have always seen Graham as a staunch friend of the Jewish people. In fact, after his first apology was not accepted, he issued a longer second apology, with an admission of guilt. Yet he said: "My remarks did not reflect my love of the Jewish people. I humbly ask the Jewish people to reflect on my actions on behalf of Jews over the years that contradict my words in the Oval Office that day."

In fact, he has always been a strong ally of the Jewish people. In the summer of 1996, as a Southern Baptist, Graham, like San Antonio's Rev. Dr. Buckner Fanning, disassociated himself from the Southern Baptist Convention resolution to target Jews for conversion. Quoting New Testament verses in the Book of Romans, Graham once said:

> I believe God has always had a special relationship with the Jewish people ... In my evangelistic efforts, I have never felt called to single out Jews as Jews.... Just as Judaism frowns on proselytizing that is coercive, or that seeks to commit men against their will, so do I.

Little in Billy Graham's background would have led him to embracing Jews. He was born on a dairy farm near Charlotte, North Carolina. His whole culture during his boyhood was rooted in a rural Protestant Christianity. He probably never knew a Jew in those early years.

Yet, over the decades, he has shown a strong affinity to Judaism and the Jewish people. For example, in the 1970s and 1980s, he managed to conduct crusades in the former Soviet Union, while the Communists were still in control. At the same time, he worked behind the scenes with Jewish leaders to advance the cause of Soviet Jewry. His goal was not to convert Jews but to rescue them from their cruel oppression and to bring them to lands of freedom.

Billy Graham has also been an avid champion of the State of Israel. In fact, his daughter, for a while, lived on a kibbutz. His Evangelic Association several years ago produced a documentary about Israel called *His Land*. In it, Graham shows respect for Judaism.

Furthermore, Graham was a friend of Golda Meir, the late prime minister of Israel. She hailed him as a "great human being, and outstanding spokesman for peace and rich brotherhood . . ." She commented that she would always remember him for his deep understanding of Israel's problems and for his support of Israel's struggle for peace for all the nations in that area.

Many prestigious national Jewish organizations have recognized his solidarity with the Jewish people. In 1977, Graham won the first interreligious award from the American Jewish Committee. The late Rabbi Marc Tanenbaum, the Interreligious Director of the AJC at that time, declared that most of the progress of Protestant-Jewish relations over the past quarter century was due to Billy Graham.

In a Letter to the Editor of the *New York Times*, Georgette Bennett, Tanenbaum's widow, recalled a marvelous story her husband told her about Graham's intervention in the 1973 war in Israel. Many others had also intervened. Yet it was only after Graham's phone call to Nixon that the president sent a military airlift to Israel. It was that dramatic action that helped to ensure Israel's survival.

How, then, shall we evaluate Billy Graham in the light of these anti-Jewish disclosures? We must acknowledge that he has made significant contributions to improving Christian-Jewish relations. He has also publicly supported the viability and security of the State of Israel and the Jewish people everywhere. Yet, in spite of these factors, now we regretfully have to look upon Billy Graham with ambivalence and even suspicion. We deplore Graham's covert bigotry voiced thirty years ago and, as a result, now see him as the Jewish people's tarnished hero.

The Four Chaplains on the U.S.A.T. *Dorchester*

Between my junior and senior years in high school in 1956, I attended the National Institute of the National Federation of Temple Youth at Saratoga, California, at a place now called Camp Swig. I met young people from Reform Jewish congregations throughout the country during this two-week leadership session. One of them was Rosalie Goode, whom I later learned was the daughter of the late Rabbi Alexander Goode. Rabbi Goode was one of the famed four chaplains who died heroically on the U.S.A.T. *Dorchester* in 1943. I later heard that Rosalie lives in Halworth, New Jersey. She was only three years old when her father lost his life.

Rabbi Goode was born in Brooklyn but grew up in Washington, D. C. His father was an Orthodox rabbi, as were his grandfather and great-grandfather. Alexander enjoyed a brilliant public school career. He succeeded both athletically and academically. He was not only a top student but was also an accomplished boxer, a gifted track star, a formidable wrestler, and a skilled tennis player.

One peak moment during his formative years occurred at Arlington National Cemetery when he was ten. He had walked there to witness the consecration of the Tomb of the Unknown Soldier. He was profoundly impressed by the fact that no one knew whether this soldier was a Jew or a Christian, or whether he was white or black. It made no difference. This insight left an indelible mark on him.

After graduating from high school, he went to the University of Cincinnati and Hebrew Union College to prepare to become a Reform rabbi. He excelled in his rabbinical studies and demonstrated tremendous scholarly potential. He wrote a number of high-quality essays in Jewish history and was ordained in 1937.

His first and only pulpit was Temple Beth Israel in York, Pennsylvania. In his six years there, his civic involvements were legion. He energetically plunged into the work of scores of boards and community organizations. As a champion of human equality, he refused to permit a Boy Scout troop in his Temple unless children of all denominations were welcome. Even with his manifold community and congregational responsibilities, he managed to complete his Ph.D. at Johns Hopkins University at the age of twenty-eight. He wrote his dissertation on the history of Jewish leadership in the Arabic period from 640 to 1258.

As World War II was beginning, Rabbi Goode was tormented by reports of the persecution of European Jews and by the horrors on the battlefields where American soldiers were fighting. In January 1941, he tried to join the Navy chaplaincy but learned that there were no vacancies. After the attack on Pearl Harbor on December 7 of that year, he applied for the Army chaplaincy and was accepted.

His first post was in Goldsboro, North Carolina, but he was restless there. He wanted to be in a place where the soldiers were fighting. He applied for reassignment and received orders to go to Greenland. He pleaded for a change as he was not convinced there would be enough combat action in the Arctic zone. As fate would have it, his request was refused. He had to go to Greenland after all, and the U.S.A.T. *Dorchester* was to take him there.

In January of 1943, he sailed for Greenland. On board were 902 servicemen, including soldiers, merchant seamen, civilian workers, and four chaplains. The *Dorchester* had once been a luxury cruise ship. Now it was an Army transport ship, one of three in that convoy.

When they were within 150 miles of their Greenland destination, Hans Danielsen, captain of the ship, got alarming information. German U-boats were sailing these waters and had already blasted several other ships. Captain Danielsen ordered the men to sleep in their clothes, with their life jackets on.

At 12:55 A.M., on February 3, an officer of a German submarine spotted the *Dorchester*. He issued orders to fire a torpedo. The hit was deadly and the ship was doomed. Water was engulfing it. Men were choking on the ammonia fumes pouring out of the refrigerator pipes that were shattered. Scores were killed. Many more were gravely wounded.

Panic swept over the crew. They knew that death was imminent. Many of the men jumped from the ship into the lifeboats that were accessible. However, they overcrowded these lifeboats until they almost capsized. Other lifeboats drifted far away from the ship before the soldiers could land in them.

The four chaplains on board tried to bring calm and hope to the frightened crew. Besides Rabbi Goode, George Fox and Clarke Poling, both Protestants, and John Washington, a Roman Catholic, ministered to those distraught men. These chaplains offered prayers for the dying and conveyed encouragement to those who would survive. As the crew members were crying, pleading, and praying, the chaplains were preaching courage.

John Mahoney, a petty officer, had forgotten his gloves and wanted to re-enter his cabin. Rabbi Goode stopped him. Mahoney told Rabbi Goode that he was freezing in the Arctic air but he had left his gloves in the cabin. Rabbi Goode responded: "Never mind. I have two pairs of gloves. Take these." Mahoney later realized that the rabbi had given him his only pair of gloves and that the rabbi had obviously decided to go down with the ship.

By this time, most of the men were at the top of the ship. The chaplains opened the storage lockers and started to distribute the life jackets that were there. They were short by four. The chaplains sacrificially decided to remove their own life jackets and give them to the four men who needed them.

The ship was now sinking rapidly. These four chaplains, with arms linked together and with fervent prayers on their lips, went down to their deaths. Word reached the United States about the magnitude of the tragedy of the *Dorchester*, during which 672 had died, and only 230 had survived. The American people also learned about the heroic and selfless feat of these four chaplains.

What these chaplains did was especially significant when we consider the mood of the times in 1943. Relations among religious communities were atrocious. Anti-Semitism was rife throughout the country. Relations between Catholics and Protestants were strained and hostile.

Yet, these four chaplains, representing the three major faiths at that time, transcended all this petty narrow-mindedness and lethal bigotry. In giving away their life jackets, Rabbi Goode did not call out for a Jew, nor did Father Washington ask for a Catholic, nor did Rev. Fox or Rev. Poling seek a Protestant. They gave them to the next soldier in line, regardless of that soldier's religious affiliation. All crew members were, to these chaplains, worthy children of God.

Rev. David Poling, of Albuquerque, a cousin of Chaplain Clarke Poling, summed up the significance of this event when he said: "Clergy of different backgrounds, drawn together in crisis, gave up their lives for others in the love of God. A threatening, challenging moment brought out the essence of their relationship—that they were brothers. It's a living parable that has affected the lives of many Christians and Jews ever since."

Madeleine Albright

Since the United States government was established over 200 years ago, only one, or possibly two, Jews, have served as secretary of state. The first is Henry Kissinger. Though he is Jewish, he is not particularly observant or affirmative of his religious legacy.

The other is Madeleine Albright. In the mid-1990s, she discovered that at least three of her four grandparents and perhaps a dozen other relatives were Jewish. In fact, they all died in Auschwitz and Terezin. Her parents, Josef and Mandula Korbel, had convinced her and her brother and sister that they were Czech Catholics.

Josef Korbel was a former diplomat who fled Czechoslovakia in March 1939. He maintained his disguise until his dying day. He taught at the University of Denver for almost thirty years after the war and none of his colleagues ever knew that he was originally Jewish.

Thus, though she is of Jewish ancestry, Madeleine Albright has always been a Christian, first a Roman Catholic, by her parents' choice, and later an Episcopalian, by her own choice. The question, however, remains: Is she really Jewish?

According to the strict interpretation of traditional Jewish law, if her maternal line is Jewish, then she is Jewish. However, most rabbis, of all Jewish denominations, would not automatically regard her as such. If, some day, she should decide to declare herself to be a Jew, she would need to undergo a process of study and a ceremony of reaffirmation.

Aside from these technical matters, however, is the fact that the revelation of Madeleine Albright's Jewish heritage evoked sharply different reactions from the Jewish community. Some Jews were highly critical of Albright. They maintained that a person who grew up in a provincial community and had been shielded from outside influences could become convinced of the disguise of his or her parents. It is hard to believe, however, that someone as worldly and sophisticated as Madeleine Albright, who at the time this story broke was almost sixty years old, would suddenly discover her Jewish origins. How naive does she want us to believe she is?

Since the prime victims of the Holocaust were Jews, should she not have suspected some Jewish ancestry, because three, and possibly four, of her grandparents and several other family members perished at the hands of the Nazis? After all, before coming to the United States, she did live with her Jewish cousin in London. Furthermore, she did choose not to reply to the communication of another cousin in Israel.

Others, however, argued that we should withhold judgment of Madeleine and her family. They invoked the Rabbinic dictum that we should not judge another person until we have stood in that person's place. In other words, we should not be quick to condemn someone, since we don't know how we would have responded under these same conditions.

Rabbi Irving Greenberg, one of the towering Orthodox Jewish thinkers of our time, espouses this position. Greenberg argues that Albright's parents had been highly assimilated Jews, like many other Jews in pre-World War II Czechoslovakia. They passed on none of the joy of celebrating Jewish holidays, of learning Torah, of sharing with the Jewish community. Thus, why should Korbel's children want to accept an identity which might lead to persecution, torture, and even annihilation?

Rabbi Greenberg recalls an exceptional French Catholic young woman who, about thirty years ago, was an *au pair* to the Greenbergs' five children. She once told the Greenbergs the reason that she was forced to leave France. Her mother had strenuously opposed her pending marriage to a Jew.

Her mother recalled passing by a train station and hearing the screams of Jewish children, wrenched from the arms of their mothers and fathers, as the Nazis were rounding them up and shoving them into trains bound for Auschwitz. Her mother swore that no grandchildren of hers would ever be exposed to such a horrible fate. Possibly this was the conclusion that Madeleine Albright's parents drew as they witnessed the mounting Nazi terror, from which they fortunately were able to flee.

Frankly, it is impossible to determine whether Madeleine Albright had been aware of her Jewish roots for a long time or had discovered them just recently. The evidence either way is skimpy. My problem with her response is the distance that she seems to be keeping from this important piece of her background. It is as though she has come upon something shameful in her family chronicles. She does not actually deny it, but she does seem hesitant to acknowledge it. One journalist described it so aptly when she wrote that Albright was "forced out of the closet."

In the postwar America in which she came of age, of course, it was not fashionable to be "too Jewish." As the noted Jewish thinker Deborah Lipstadt puts it: "It was a time for heavy-duty assimilation, for name changes and for nose jobs ... even the Holocaust was not talked about too loudly among American Jews in the 1950s." Thus, I do not want to judge Madeleine Albright's motives. However, I must admit my uneasiness with the enigmatic way she has dealt with the disclosure of her Jewishness.

I did see some evidence of a slight breakthrough, however. In March 2003, having left office, she addressed the annual convention of the Central Conference of American Rabbis, the international body of about 1,700 Reform rabbis. In introducing her, Rabbi Jerome Davidson mentioned that Albright's grandchild is a student in the Religious School of Temple Emanu-El of San Francisco and that she is donating her honorarium to the restoration of the Czech Jewish institutions devastated by the flood. In her address, she did demonstrate pro-Israel sentiments, but never acknowledged any Jewish ancestry.

Obviously, Madeleine Albright has focused only on the

pain of being Jewish. Others, fortunately, in similar circumstances to hers, have grasped the pride of being Jewish. One such person is Abe Foxman, executive director of the Anti-Defamation League. Before his parents fled the Nazis in his native Poland, they entrusted him to his nanny, who was Roman Catholic. She changed Abe's name, falsified his documents, and had him baptized. Abe Foxman was, for a time, raised in the Catholic Church.

After the war, his parents returned and reclaimed him. At that point, he reaffirmed his Jewish heritage, which had not been a part of his early childhood. Over the years, he has risen to become one of the foremost leaders of American Jewry. Unlike Madeleine Albright, Foxman has demonstrated that, in spite of a heritage of suffering, Jews have a magnificent legacy to embrace, live by, and pass on to their descendants.

Irving Berlin

In 1988, there appeared in the Bulletin of Temple Emanu-El of New York a congratulatory note to Irving Berlin, a member of the congregation, on his 100th birthday. I am sure that, to many, this bulletin announcement came as a double surprise.

First of all, it was not generally known that Irving Berlin was still alive. For over twenty-five years, Berlin had withdrawn from the public eye. In 1962, his last Broadway musical, "Mr. President," flopped after a six-month run. Since then, he had become a recluse. He guarded his privacy zealously.

When the weather was warm, he took a short walk around Beekman Place. He was usually assisted by a young woman or a doorman from the nearby building. Otherwise, he was never seen. He continued to communicate by telephone to a small circle of friends, but he granted no interviews to the media. He did not even appear at his gala centennial birthday tribute at Carnegie Hall.

The second surprise is that Irving Berlin was affiliated with a synagogue. He had conveyed the impression that he had little to do with organized Jewish life. Yet, his background was intensely Jewish.

He was born Israel Bailin in Siberia in 1888, the youngest of eight children. They lived in a village where their father was a *shohet*, a ritual slaughterer, and a cantor. He had only one memory of his life in Eastern Europe. When he was four, the Cossacks overran the village. His family hid under blankets in the nearby woods.

Shortly after this traumatic pogrom, his family left Russia

for America. They began to live in a dingy basement apartment on the Lower East Side of New York. Berlin recalled that his family spoke only Yiddish in those days. His mother never did learn to understand English. She kept a strictly kosher home. His father got a job as a *mashgiah*, a supervisor of kosher foods. His father also taught Hebrew and trained a choir at an Orthodox synagogue near their apartment.

Irving showed strong musical inclinations, even as a child. He sang in his father's synagogue choir. He went to the Yiddish theatre whenever he could afford it. At an early age, he demonstrated a keen ear for music. He could recall any melody he had ever heard.

When Irving was eight, his father died, and Irving began selling newspapers and delivering singing telegrams to earn a living. After two years of formal schooling, at age fourteen, Irving ran away from home. He began to work as a singing waiter in saloons and taverns.

At Pelham's Café, he served and entertained the patrons by singing parodies of current popular songs. It was here, at Pelham's Café, that he penned the words to his first published song, "Marie from Sunny Italy." The music was written by the saloon pianist. The song brought him the grand sum of $.37 in royalties.

However, on the sheet music of this song, a printer's error appeared. His name was recorded as Israel Berlin, instead of Israel Bailin. He thought that, even with Berlin, his name still sounded too un-American. Soon he took the name change a step further and made his first name Irving.

After he left Pelham's, a vaudeville star hired Irving Berlin to write a song for his act. Berlin wrote about Dorando, a renowned Olympic runner of that time. The vaudeville star didn't like the song and rejected it. Berlin then took "Dorando" to Ted Snyder, the noted publisher, who said that he would pay him $25.00 if he would compose the music as well. Berlin dictated the tune to one of Snyder's staff members. It was the first time that Berlin had created both the music and the words to a song.

What is amazing is that, with all of Berlin's genius, as a songwriter, he was never able to read or write music. He always needed a musical stenographer to record his original musical sounds on paper. Berlin also had limited piano skills. He could use only the black notes and always composed in the key of F-sharp.

Snyder published several of Berlin's songs and finally made him a junior partner. Eventually, Berlin left Snyder to form his own publishing company, Irving Berlin, Incorporated. This company quickly became a lucrative operation.

Throughout his prolific career spanning many decades, Berlin wrote at least 1,500 songs. Some of the best known are "Alexander's Ragtime Band," "Play a Simple Melody," "Blue Skies," "Always," "How Deep Is the Ocean?," "Doin' What Comes Naturally," and "There's No Business like Show Business."

Why have Berlin's songs become so popular and beloved by Americans from all sectors of society? Morton Gould, president of American Society of Composers, Authors, and Publishers, of which Berlin was a charter member, had a cogent answer. Gould explained that Berlin's songs have a sophisticated simplicity. People know precisely what he is saying. He distilled everything down to its essence. In his songs, Berlin expressed universal yearnings. Most people, for example, want "Blue Skies."

Three of Berlin's songs, however, give clues to the way Berlin viewed his identity as an American Jew: "God Bless America," "White Christmas," and "Easter Parade." "God Bless America" has become our unofficial national anthem. As an immigrant to these shores, Irving Berlin had always been a passionate American patriot. Berlin once commented that he loved to pay taxes because America had been so superbly wonderful to him.

Berlin expressed his gratitude to America philanthropically as well. He always donated his royalties from "God Bless America" to the Boy Scouts, Girl Scouts, and Camp Fire Girls.

These are quintessentially American organizations. The scouting movement earned almost a half million dollars from Berlin's generosity.

Berlin's songs are so typically American that they do not translate into other languages. It is difficult to make them understood in other countries, even English-speaking ones like Great Britain.

We must remember that Irving Berlin came to America when American society's ideal was a melting pot. It was a time when Jews were urged to shed all their ethnic and foreign characteristics and become like white Anglo-Saxons, as much as possible. The ideal was to look less Jewish and to talk less Jewish. Jews rushed into the entertainment business at that time. It was one of the few professions where anti-Semitism was relatively absent.

Yet, except for comedians, Jewish entertainers wrote and played for non-Jewish audiences and sanitized their material accordingly. In the 1920s and 1930s, Jewish film producers, like Samuel Goldwyn, Louis B. Mayer, and Adolph Zukor, ran Hollywood. Yet these movie moguls looked for actors who did not look or sound Jewish. Those who did had to Anglicize their names and undergo cosmetic surgery or else leave the movie industry.

Berlin adopted that same mentality of rarely reflecting his Jewish identity in his works. So assimilated had Berlin become that he composed two of his most popular songs for Christian holidays: "White Christmas" and "Easter Parade." In 1926, over the protest of her aristocratic Irish-Christian parents, Irving Berlin married Ellin Mackay in a civil ceremony. To my knowledge, he did not raise his children as Jews.

Yet, Berlin did not deny that he was Jewish. In fact, he contributed generously to Jewish causes. He was a member of Temple Emanu-El in New York. He was a supporter of the United Jewish Appeal and the State of Israel. He even wrote a tribute, "Israel," when the new state was proclaimed in 1948. At his funeral, a rabbi officiated.

For generations to come, however, Berlin will be remembered more as a passionate American composer than as a committed Jew. Jerome Kern said it simply and accurately: "Irving Berlin has no place in American music. He is American music."

Joseph Cardinal Bernardin

Shortly after the death of Cardinal Joseph Bernardin, Archbishop of Chicago, in 1996, Msgr. James Mahoney of New Jersey penned an eloquent tribute to him. In his church newsletter, Mahoney called Cardinal Bernardin the "most influential bishop in the history of the Catholic Church in our country." As a rabbi, I believe that Msgr. Mahoney's assessment of Cardinal Bernardin is fully accurate.

With the passing of Cardinal Bernardin, our country is bereft of a towering religious leader, for he demonstrated human greatness in unparalleled ways. For example, three years before Cardinal Bernardin died, Steven Cook, a former Catholic seminarian, accused him of sexually abusing him. Cook claimed this abuse had occurred several years before, when Bernardin was the Archbishop of Cincinnati. Cook's attempt to blemish the Cardinal's exceptional ministry and personal integrity failed.

Throughout the hearings, Cardinal Bernardin calmly but firmly denied these charges. Later, Cook himself admitted that these accusations were false, and the Cardinal then forgave him. A year later, Cook was dying of AIDS. Cardinal Bernardin, bearing no malice toward him, conducted a special mass for Cook. He also anointed him in an act of dramatic reconciliation.

Though the Cardinal absolved Cook, I am sure that the trauma of Cook's defamation extensively damaged Bernardin's sense of well-being. In fact, less than six months later, the Cardinal was diagnosed with cancer of the pancreas. For several months, the Cardinal had thought that he would remain in remission. However, he finally received the devastating blow. His physicians informed him that the cancer cells were now devouring his liver. They declared his case to be terminal and predicted that he had less than a year to live.

Rather than succumb to self-pity and despair, Cardinal Bernardin followed the Rabbinic admonition of living each day as though it were his last. He invested every second of his waking hours with profound meaning and significance. He pledged to use whatever time was left to benefit other priests and those people whom he was called to serve.

Cardinal Bernardin chose to die a public death. He was open and honest about the dying process throughout these last months of his life. In fact, on the day before he died, he saw the edited manuscript of his memoir, called "The Gift of Peace." In it, he dealt candidly with his preparations for death. He noted that when people are ill, they tend to turn inward and to focus on their own pain and suffering. They start to feel sorry for themselves and become despondent.

With his intense religious faith, he suggested that we do the opposite—that we think of others and their needs. He lived by his words. For example, he periodically went to Loyola University Cancer Center, now named after him, for chemotherapy.

With his characteristic humility, he insisted that he was just an ordinary priest and should not be shown special favors as a top-ranking cleric of the Church. Therefore, he always refused to use the private entrance of the clinic that was reserved for him.

Furthermore, he never left the clinic without visiting the other patients. He often followed up his visits with telephone calls, letters, and additional visits. He even made time to call on the parishes throughout the Archdiocese to anoint the sick.

Cardinal Bernardin was not only a compassionate pastor; he was also a master bridge builder. He was able to reconcile fundamental differences among high Church officials and to heal the rifts between the left and the right in the Church hierarchy.

What is especially noteworthy is that the Jewish community of Chicago adored and revered Cardinal Bernardin. He committed himself to strengthening relations between Catholics and Jews, from the moment that he arrived in Chicago in the 1980s. He established a guest lecture series on issues affecting Catholic-Jewish relations. He oversaw the introduction of Holocaust studies in all schools throughout the Archdiocese.

Of special note was his visit to Israel in March 1995. It was his only trip there. Accompanying him were seven Chicago Jewish leaders, among whom were three rabbis. While in Israel, the Hebrew University of Jerusalem conferred an Honorary Fellowship on the Cardinal.

His address on that occasion was courageous and bold. He chose to speak out against anti-Semitism from the Catholic perspective. He noted that, in recent years, the Catholic Church has undertaken important efforts to overcome its anti-Jewish past. It has acknowledged its guilt for its legacy of hostility toward Jews and Judaism. It has also repudiated as sinful any remaining messages of that legacy in contemporary Catholic teaching and practice.

He also freely admitted that the Nazis would not have enjoyed the popular support that they did, had it not been for the continuing influence of traditional Christian anti-Semitism on the masses of baptized believers in Europe. He mentioned Hitler's oft-quoted remark to church leaders who came to see him to protest his treatment of Jews. He told them that he was merely putting into practice what the churches had preached for nearly 2,000 years.

The Cardinal noted that since the Second Vatican Council, the Church's antagonism toward the Jewish people and the Jewish religion had lost its religious foundations. Yet, he insisted that much more needed to be done. There are still New Testament texts read during Holy Week that contain anti-Jewish teachings. Their poisonous effects need to be neutralized by extensive commentaries and sensitive translations.

Though he did not mention Pope Pius XII by name, he also said that the Church must now be prepared to deal frankly and candidly with the genuine failures of some leaders of the Church during the Nazi era. The Church must be prepared to submit its World War II records to a thorough scrutiny by respected scholars. Reflecting on the history of anti-Semitism and the Holocaust, he concluded his address by insisting that the Church must now engage in an act of public repentance for its anti-Semitic past.

After leaving Israel, Cardinal Bernardin continued to maintain close ties with the seven Jewish leaders who had joined him there. In fact, a few weeks before his death, he requested that these seven come together at the Holy Name Cathedral for a memorial observance.

So, on the day before the funeral, these seven Jewish officials, with the Cardinal lying in state a few feet from the podium, paid him a fond farewell. They reflected on his enormous contribution to Christian-Jewish understanding and urged continued support for the exemplary dialogue efforts that he led.

Isaac Mayer Wise

The Union of American Hebrew Congregations, parent body of Reform synagogues in the United States and Canada, was established in 1873. It was the brainchild of Isaac Mayer Wise. Wise was American Reform Judaism's leading organizational genius and chief architect. He founded two other Reform Jewish institutions that continue to this day. In 1875, he established the Hebrew Union College, the seminary for Reform Judaism, and in 1889, the Central Conference of American Rabbis, the Reform rabbinical association.

Wise's life was a fascinating one. He was born in 1819 in Bohemia, which is now part of the Czech Republic. His formal education was extensive and varied, but it was also somewhat eclectic and haphazard. He acquired an impressive knowledge of the Bible and Talmud as a child. At the age of twelve, he set out for a yeshiva in Prague and then studied at a famous rabbinical school in Jekinau. Eventually he attended the University of Prague for two years and the University of Vienna for one year. He was ordained a rabbi at the age of twenty-three.

At twenty-seven, he came to the United States to serve an Orthodox synagogue in Albany, New York. Almost from the beginning there were tensions in his relationship with his congregants. Wise tended to be impulsive, combative, and impatient in dealing with them.

He swiftly brought reforms into the worship service, but the people were not psychologically or religiously ready for them. He eliminated the chanting of the prayers and the Torah reading, and he introduced a choir. He banned the auctioning of *aliyot*, honors to ascend to the Torah, a practice which was common in Orthodox synagogues at that time. He also substituted Confirmation for Bar Mitzvah.

Tensions were reaching a boiling point between him and the leaders and members of his congregation. During his fourth year there, in July 1850, Wise ordered all his congregation's board members to close their stores on the Sabbath. One board member defied him. Wise gave him an ultimatum: either close the store or resign from the board.

The congregational president feared that Wise would denounce this board member from the pulpit and forbade him to preach. The congregation was split between Wise's detractors and his supporters. Paradoxically, the people who opposed Wise because of his reforms now objected to his demand that they close their businesses on the Sabbath. The officers and board members held a rump meeting on the morning of the eve of Rosh Hashanah and dismissed Wise.

However, Wise refused to leave and insisted on conducting High Holy Day services. As a result, he and the congregational president came to blows on the *bimah*. A riot broke out in the synagogue, and police had to be called in to quell the disturbance.

Wise and his supporters then resigned and founded a new congregation in Albany with Wise as the rabbi. Embracing his reforms, it grew rapidly and Isaac Mayer Wise remained its rabbi for four years, until 1854.

That year, Congregation B'nai Yeshurun in Cincinnati called him to become its rabbi for life. His ministry to them was far more harmonious than it had been to his first congregation in Albany. B'nai Yeshurun was quite traditional when he arrived. Yet Wise introduced his reforms more judiciously and slowly there. Under his leadership, in the 1860s, B'nai Yeshurun built the magnificent, Moorish-style Temple on Plum Street in Cincinnati, which is still in use today.

Relative peace did prevail within the walls of the Temple. However, Wise's life outside the Temple was filled with acrimonious ideological battles and controversies. He edited two publications in which he articulated his revolutionary views.

One was the English-language *American Israelite*, which is still published in Cincinnati today. He also edited *Die Deborah*, which he wrote in German. On their pages, he battled not only for changes in Jewish religious practice but also defended the Jewish people against bigotry and abuse.

In 1856, the governor of Ohio issued a Thanksgiving proclamation, which he addressed to the "Christian People" of Ohio. Wise became incensed and wrote to the governor. He reminded the governor that the people of Ohio are "neither Christian nor Jewish; they are a free and independent people."

In 1862, the Union general, Ulysses S. Grant, issued an order expelling all Jews from his department within twenty-four hours. Wise swiftly became Grant's formidable opponent. Wise also fought the attempt, during the Civil War, to bar Jewish and Catholic chaplains from serving in the Union army. In addition, Wise campaigned, with others, for our government to reject a proposed treaty with Switzerland, limiting the rights of American Jews living there.

Unfortunately, there was one issue on which he did not take a stand in his publications: slavery. Other prominent rabbis were lined up on either side of the issue. Rabbi Morris Raphall sanctioned slavery and found Biblical precedents for it, while Rabbi David Einhorn bitterly opposed it. Wise rode the fence.

He probably evaded this burning issue for the sake of expediency. Some have explained Wise's silence on slavery by the fact that many of the subscribers to the *Israelite* lived in the South. He feared that any condemnation of slavery would hurt his ultimate goal of establishing a united network of American Jewish congregations.

Wise's writings were not confined just to these two journals. His literary output was prolific. He wrote over ten books on Jewish history and theology, eight novels in English and three in German, and two plays.

Wise also produced a prayer book called *Minhag America*, meaning "the custom of America." Its contents were much more conservative than those of today's Reform prayer books. Wise hoped that *Minhag America* would become a uniform liturgy for all American Jews. However, the Orthodox criticized it for being too liberal, while some Reform Jews charged that it was too traditional. Nonetheless, Isaac Mayer Wise held steadfastly to the dream of fashioning a unified American Judaism that would combine both traditional and liberal elements.

In 1873, he founded the Union of American Hebrew Congregations. Note that he did not use the term Reform. He hoped to make it more inclusive. Then in 1875, to train rabbis for American congregations, he founded the Hebrew Union College in Cincinnati. He wanted this seminary to produce both Orthodox and Reform rabbis.

Wise became the first president of the college. His workload must have been staggering. He was simultaneously the rabbi of a large congregation, the full-time president of a burgeoning rabbinical seminary, and the editor of two publications.

Wise's dream for a pluralistic seminary was soon shattered. In 1883, it happened at a banquet celebrating the first ordination of the rabbis of the Hebrew Union College. When the first course of forbidden shrimp was brought to the tables, the more traditional rabbis who were present stormed out of the room.

Within a short time, they founded the Jewish Theological Seminary of America, which today is the fountainhead of American Conservative Judaism. By this time, Wise realized that unifying all of American Jewry religiously was impossible. He had to accept the reality of Jewish denominations. He then became an avowedly Reform spokesperson.

In 1885, he presided over a conference of rabbis in Pittsburgh, which produced the famous Pittsburgh Platform. This is the statement of eight planks, which clearly define Classical Reform Judaism. Among them is the view that Judaism is strictly a religion and not a nationality. Judaism is to be stripped of all ethnic features. Emphasis is to be on

Judaism, not Jewishness. Furthermore, Judaism is a rational faith. Nothing in Judaism can conflict with the discoveries of modern science.

Though Wise personally observed a modified form of the dietary laws, the platform calls for the abolition of all distinctive forms of Jewish diet and dress. The document is also militantly anti-Zionist. It does not favor the efforts to build a Jewish homeland, in what is today Israel.

Wise had lived with discrimination and prejudice in Bohemia and now tasted the boundless freedoms of the United States. Thus, Wise became a passionate American patriot. He firmly believed that it is in America that the new Judaism could be best lived. He was convinced that God had ordained America as the arena to fulfill the ideals of our ancient Jewish prophets and sages.

To realize this dream, America's Jews must be God's "priest people," a light to the other nations, bringing the ethical message of our Bible to all human beings on earth. The platform also stresses social justice. It insists that the task of the Jew is to correct all societal ills, like poverty and discrimination.

Wise's founding of the Union of American Hebrew Congregations, the Hebrew Union College, and the Central Conference of American Rabbis represented massive personal achievements. Even the Orthodox and Conservative movements within a short time copied this three-fold organizational scheme of a congregational body, a seminary, and a rabbinical organization. Wise continued to work full-time until his last days.

On Shabbat morning, March 24, 1900, Wise preached his final sermon at the Plum Street Temple. He was already nearly eighty-one years old. Early that afternoon, he was meeting with one of his classes when he was felled by a sudden stroke. He lost his power of speech and writing and soon slipped into a coma, from which he never recovered.

His funeral was one of the largest in Cincinnati. Surviving Wise were a wife and eleven children. He had fathered fourteen children, ten from his first wife who had died, and four from his second wife. Three of his children had predeceased him.

Wise's enduring legacy was not only his brilliant organizational scheme but also his philosophy of American Judaism. Reform Judaism now stresses more ritual observance and is pro-Zionist. Yet Wise's concepts, formulated over a century ago, still form the basis of Reform ideology today, as is evident in his definition of Judaism:

> a religion, without mysteries or miracles, rational and self-evident, eminently human, universal, liberal, and progressive, in perfect harmony with modern science, criticism, and philosophy, and in full sympathy with universal liberty, equality, justice, and charity.

About the Author

Rabbi Samuel M. Stahl became rabbi emeritus of Temple Beth-El in San Antonio, Texas, in 2002, after serving for twenty-six years as its senior rabbi. Previously, he was a chaplain in the United States Army and rabbi of Temple B'nai Israel (The Henry Cohen Memorial) in Galveston, Texas.

A native of Sharon, Pennsylvania, he was graduated from the University of Pittsburgh in 1961. He was ordained a rabbi at Hebrew Union College–Jewish Institute of Religion in Cincinnati in 1967. He also received earned and honorary doctorates from that seminary.

Rabbi Stahl has held numerous local and national leadership positions in the Jewish and general communities. Committed to enhancing Christian-Jewish relations, he is the first Jew ever to receive religious leadership awards from the Texas Conference of Churches and from the San Antonio Community of Churches.

For six years, he was editor of the *Journal of Reform Judaism*, the official quarterly publication of the Central Conference of American Rabbis. His articles have been published in *CCAR Journal, Conservative Judaism, Dor LeDor*, and *Church and State*. He is also the author of *Making the Timeless Timely: Thoughts and Reflections of a Contemporary Reform Rabbi*.

During the summer of 2003, he served as theologian-in-residence at Chautauqua Institution, in New York state, where he has also been a lecturer in its Department of Religion.

He and his wife, Lynn, have two daughters, Heather Katz and Alisa Stahl, and one grandchild, Austin Phillip Katz.